PENGUIN BOOKS

YOUR CHILD'S SENSORY WORLD

"Any parent interested in relating to and understanding his child's world (and his own as well) will find this a worthy book to own." — Herb Snitzer, Director, Lewis-Wadhams School, author of *Today Is for Children*

"For those of us in the educational trenches facing an indefatigable enemy — 'lack of basic skills' — it is both refreshing and reinforcing to find a comprehensive battle map of the true adversary. Long before the traditional decoy and ambush of reading, writing and arithmetic problems, parents and teachers must come to grips with the real basics — perception of a child's individual sensory patterns. When young people are finally trusted to pursue their own learning, as schools become open and aware, Ms. Liepmann's invaluable work will be both a foundation and a landmark for the sensitivity we all require." — Philip E. McCurdy, Headmaster, Beaver Country Day School, Chestnut Hill, Massachusetts

LISE LIEPMANN

Your Child's Sensory World

Illustrated by Matthys Lévy

Foreword by Lendon H. Smith, M.D.

Penguin Books Inc
Baltimore • Maryland

Penguin Books Inc
7110 Ambassador Road
Baltimore, Maryland 21207, U.S.A.

First published by The Dial Press, New York, 1973
Published by Penguin Books Inc, 1974

To Matthys, Monica, and Jennifer,
who created this book with me

Acknowledgments

There are many wonderful teachers and friends who made this book possible. My sincere thanks to all of them, and especially to Lee Strasberg, Fanned Tate, and Inge Bogner. I am indebted to Richard Dyer-Bennet, Paul Sheftel, and my father, Klaus Liepmann, for their help in the chapters on hearing, speaking, and touch as applied to music; to Etienne Decroux and Robert Carson for the chapter on movement; to Dr. Richard Kavner for invaluable assistance in the chapter on seeing. Re seeing, warm thanks also to my mother, Olly Liepmann, and to my husband, Matthys Lévy, who contributed as well to the chapter on taste, not to mention his drawing of the illustrations. Finally, I am grateful to all the children who worked with me in classes and from whom I learned so much, and to my own two "teachers" at home, Monica and Jennifer.

Foreword

Most of us had parents who were reasonably loving, competent, and accepting. Growing up was fun. They showed us things, took us places and made us laugh. Their parents did these things for them, so they couldn't help but do the same for us. It was part of the initiation into the society.

Many parents, however, are not able to provide more than board and room for their children because of depression, absence, boredom or lack of programming by their own parents. If your child drives you up the wall, Ms. Liepmann has a useful technique for making the episode a study of architectural uses of gravity.

Everything Ms. Liepmann tells us is true and she provides the reasons for it. Many of us are still hung up on the idea that if we are having fun, it must be bad because fun is equated with sex and that's the work of the devil.

Humans learn about themselves and the world better and faster if they are having fun. If a child does or makes something and his loved ones praise him, he feels good. We all need to feel accepted. Ms. Liepmann shows us how to find a child's strong points and then how to nourish them.

Learning waits on maturation. Learning is fun if a child is

exposed to the learning situation when his nervous system is able to cope with the concept.

I learned from the book because I was allowed to discover a few things about myself for myself.

Thank you, Ms. Liepmann, it is a fun book—not sexy—but fun.

Lendon H. Smith, M.D.
Associate Clinical Professor of Pediatrics
University of Oregon

Preface

This is a common-sense book for parents about sensory awareness in children. Your child's sensory world influences his whole way of life—learning, playing, and communicating. Actually, there are two "worlds": the external sensory world and the ways in which it affects your child, and his own sensory way of perceiving life—his individual sensory patterns.

"Understanding sensory patterns" is a fancy name for a very simple skill: an awareness of how a child is apt to respond in a situation. What does he like? What bothers him? Anyone who "has a way with kids" has this skill—parents, relatives, teachers, child therapists. It means listening more to the tone of a child's voice to catch his meaning than to the actual words. Or reaching out your hand because you feel that the child would like to be reassured by touch. Or moving away from a child who acts "crowded." It means observing a child to see how he is functioning.

I once saw a three-year-old sitting alone in a corner on the first day of a Head Start program. The teacher came over to talk to him, but he didn't answer. She thought perhaps he didn't understand English, and spoke a few words to him in Spanish. Still no response. Then she noticed that his eyes were focused on a toy airplane, high up on a shelf. She took it down and gave it to him. He took it without a word, knelt down on the floor, and began to play with it. He felt at home. This teacher was following through on the child's interest instead of trying to force him to relate to her verbally. In order to do this, she had to be sensitive to what the child was experiencing.

When your child is very young, he cannot talk at all, and even when he is older, he does not always express what he is thinking. If you understand your child's sensory patterns, you will be closer to your child.

This book will give you an understanding of your child's sensory pattern. Is he mostly a "hearer and speaker" who relates strongly to sound? Is he a "see-er" who experiments with line, form, space, and has an unusual sense of direction? Or is he a "mover" who works out individual body solutions to physical problems of speed, rhythm, effort?

Once you know your child's sensory pattern, you can increase his awareness in any sense (and your own as well) through sensory games. These games and exercises are based on my work in music, speech, voice, and dance of all kinds; my work in costume and set-design; a natural aptitude in taste and smell(!); and most of all, my extensive theater studies in improvisation and sensory awareness.

The games began almost by chance while teaching children theater games and creative drama in schools and community centers, and were then developed with my own children at home. Here's how it happened. I used to begin each class with some standard sensory acting exercises, such as "Pretend you're holding a glass of orange juice. Do you see the color? Do you feel the weight? The coolness? Do you taste the acid on your tongue?" Most of the children seemed to have trouble with this, so I decided to use real orange juice first and then stimulate their imagination to recall the sensations later. I was surprised to find that several quite normal children in the class did not really see or feel or taste very well, even with the real thing. I had always assumed that all children were sensitive in these areas until life-habits gradually dulled certain of their senses.

I began to devise sensory games for the children, games that would systematically exercise the components of each sense—*hearing games* for pitch, timbre, rhythm, and volume; *seeing games* for form, color, light, shade and spatial relations. The children enjoyed the games, and many of those who had had difficulties in responding improved rapidly. Their imagination and acting benefited, and often, according to their parents, their schoolwork benefited as well. Why? Probably because the children were approaching their studies in a new way. Reading aloud was approached as a way of hearing and speaking meaningful sounds—high pitched, low pitched, loud, louder, very soft, fast rhythm, slow rhythm, changing stress. Best of all, I saw the children become so stimulated and alive that they created constantly with sounds and words, with lines, forms and colors, with skilled hands and fingers, with expressive bodies.

You can play these same games with your own child. I have suggested the most suitable age for each game, ranging from three to twelve (see Guide to Sensory Games, page 305). These age-ranges do not take into account the individuality or temperament of your child. I hope parents will be guided by their own intuition in choosing a game, and by the level of their child's response in pursuing it. If a child is disinterested a game becomes a chore, and nothing is further from my intentions. I doubt that any child would want to play all the games listed for his age-range, and there is no reason why he should be pressured to do so. The games need little or no preparation or materials, require no special practice times, and are easy and fun. Besides, they should make life fuller and richer for both parent and child.

This book approaches the child's sensory world from three different angles: first, the child's point of view is discussed (Part I); then, the environment and its influences on the child's senses (Part II); third, there is a description of how parent and child can share sensory awareness through games (Part III). Since this organization of the material makes for a certain amount of repetition, the reader may want to skip around to the sections of particular interest to her or him. In a brief concluding section, I have sketched in some current trends relating to sensory awareness.

I have addressed the parent as "she" throughout the book, and because of current custom, many of my adult examples refer to mothers. My apologies to the fathers who will read this book, especially to those who currently spend as much or more time with their children as mothers. I must also mention my reluctance in referring to the child as "he." I know this is unjust and it provokes me, especially since I have two daughters, but until our language catches up with the status of today's women, I have no workable alternative.

L. L.

Contents

I Your Child's Sensory World

1 How Do Your Child's Senses Affect His Behavior?

Whether you are aware of it or not, your child, no matter what his age, has already formed many sensory habits. That is, his senses respond to the world around him in a characteristic way. For example, your nine-year-old daughter is afraid to go to school alone on the bus, although all her classmates are on their own. At home and at school she seems very independent. What's the problem? It may be seeing. She has normal vision, but has never formed a "map sense" of her school in relation to her home. You showed her how to recognize her bus stop, but she has no basic sense of direction. This makes her feel anxious and "lost" on the bus even though she's not. Visual difficulty may crop up again later when she studies geometry. There is no way to understand congruent triangles and supplementary angles if she does not "see" the forms when she looks.

Dr. Ray H. Barsch, Professor of Special Education at Southern Connecticut State College, says:

Everybody has a perceptual difficulty which dimishes his effectiveness to some extent. How many times have you heard someone say "I was never much good at figures"; "My handwriting has always been terrible"; "Don't ask me to draw anything"; or "I can't find my way out of a parking lot." These are examples of perceptual difficulties. Adults are very clever at concealing them. They shape their lives around them. *(From a talk at the Adams School, New York City, in 1968.)*

If your child is having trouble with mathematics or his handwriting at school and you can't understand why, you should check to see whether his sensory habits for these activities are good ones. He may be having trouble visualizing math concepts. His poor handwriting may indicate a bad touch pattern—perhaps he holds the pencil too tightly to write easily and well.

SENSORY HABITS AND YOUR CHILD'S POTENTIAL

When you understand your child's sensory habits, you will have a better understanding of your child. Suppose you and your son have a running argument about suitable winter clothing. You want him to wear a scarf and hat. He insists that he's warm enough without them. Once you know his overall touch pattern, you may discover that he's right. Everyone has an individual response to heat and cold. What feels cold to you may be comfortable to him. Once you have established this, you will have eliminated a source of friction between you. Furthermore, you will be telling him, "I respect the way you function. It's different from my way, but I respect it." This is the root of real sensitivity. And out of this kind of experience he can learn to develop the same respect for you and for everyone else he knows.

When you understand your child's sensory habits, you can help him develop necessary skills. For instance, your eight-year-old daughter is upset by her small, illegible handwriting. You notice that her hands and fingers are very stiff and cramped when she writes, although her hands are flexible and controlled when she plays the piano. You can help her change her "touch habit" when she writes so that her hand-writing looks better. And she will be more relaxed when she works, which will improve her concentration and probably her grades.

When you understand your child's sensory habits, you can help him to find himself—to find out what he likes and what he doesn't like and how to balance the two. Suppose you discover that your six-year-old son is especially sensitive to sounds, is physically skillful, but is not very visual. He may love to learn how to play a musical instrument because it involves his best senses—hearing and moving (kinesthetic sense). Music lessons will compensate for the effort he needs to make at school, where he probably sits a lot instead of moving about as freely as he would like. At school he is also using his eyes continuously as he learns to recognize printed words, to work with groups of objects and form number concepts, and to form accurate letters and numbers with a pencil. Music will be a constructive home activity that is easy for him and fun. This satisfying occupation can prevent the desire for destructive "fun" like drugs. A teen-ager I know is crazy about ballet. I asked her what she thought about using drugs. She said, "Well, I don't know about the other kids, but wouldn't I be stupid to spend four dance classes a week building up my body, and then mess around with it the rest of the time?"

Whether you call these activities fun or hobbies or creative work or exploring your child's talents doesn't matter. You are helping him to find his potential in life through your awareness of his sensory pattern.

HOW TO FIND YOUR CHILD'S SENSORY PATTERN

By the time your child is three, you will be acquainted with many of his sensory habits. Three-year-old Janet loves to go barefoot on the sheepskin rug and can't wait until she's old enough to have a coat like Mommy's—with a furry collar. But she refuses to wear the beautiful sweater her aunt knit for her. She loves to eat—everything except cheese. She seems to enjoy drawing animals and is very skillful in managing her crayons. She is also good at handling her tricycle and can stop on a dime without falling off. She is friendly and talkative but often doesn't listen to you, and is bored by music.

If you want to describe Janet's sensory pattern, you could say that she is sensitive to touch and especially likes the texture of fur, but not of wool. She is interested in her visual world and has enough manual dexterity to draw it. She has good motor ability, but her ears don't react strongly to sounds and music. She gets the most out of her sense of taste and likes to eat. Possibly she dislikes cheese because of the smell. Lots of children hate cheese and milk because of the smell, not the taste.

This is a common-sense approach to sensory awareness. Of course there are many possible interpretations of a child's behavior, and most parents lean more to the physical and psychological than to the sensory. But it is not difficult to find the source of Janet's likes and dislikes. Does she want the furry collar because it is an adult status-symbol rather than for the fur itself? Well, how does she react to your other grown-up clothes, such as your brocade evening wrap? And what about the fur of the sheepskin rug? Does she hate her aunt and not the wool of the sweater? You can check her with other wool clothing. What about the hearing—is it a physical problem? Unlikely, if she's a good talker, but not hard to discover through testing. Is she not listening to you in particular because she's going through a stage where she doesn't want to hear you? You can see how she listens to others. In short, your child is a physical, intellectual, emotional, and sensory being. To understand his behavior, you will need to know his sensory patterns as well as his other patterns. If you don't, you may misinterpret what he does. It would be too bad if Janet's mother scolded Janet for being unkind to her aunt when the real problem is Janet's sensitivity to wool. And it is really not difficult for a parent to become aware of sensory patterns as he observes and listens to his child.

You may wonder what you should do once you've become aware of your child's senses. This is up to you, but just knowing about your child's sensory pattern will change your approach. If your daughter is like Janet and you want to plan a treat, you'll take her to the zoo instead of to a children's concert. You'll be aware of the texture when you buy her clothes and furnishings. That special birthday present might be an imitation-fur rug for her bedroom. And her hearing— should you try to do something about it? Again, this is up to you and depends on your schedule and your relationship to your daughter. It may be worth your while in the long run to spend a little time on it now. A friend of mine once nagged at her child for several weeks to improve the spacing of her math homework: "I can't read it . . . it's messy . . . it's too small. How can you see what you're doing?" My friend was not aware that the child did not know how to change the layout of the homework paper. One day we all played a twenty-minute seeing game together, which solved the problem for most of the year, with only a few minor lapses.

If you decide that this is not the right time to try to correct a difficulty, remember that everyone has at least one sense that is less developed than the others. And Janet, for instance, is getting a lot out of her other senses—touching, moving, seeing, tasting, smelling. If she seems to be ignoring you when you speak, you may find it easier to be patient if you know this is a sensory habit and not a personal reaction to you.

It would be nice if there were certain "symptoms" a parent could spot that would indicate a particular pattern: "Does your child like to weave? Then he's a toucher—he has a good tactile sense." Unfortunately it is not as simple as this. The child may like to weave because it reminds him of his grandmother who liked to weave. But if he likes to weave, is skillful at drawing, and loves to feel fur and mud and fine sand, you can assume that your child has a fine sense of touch. If he doesn't like to work with his hands at all, touch must be one of his less developed senses.

The next chapter gives some guidelines on how to look at your child from a sensory point of view. Most children share similar experiences at home, at school, on excursions and vacations. The difference between one child and another is in his response to these experiences. Once you know some typical sensory responses of a child who is a hearer, a see-er, or a mover, you will be able to spot your child's individual sensory pattern—his best sense, his least developed sense, and those in between. Your child won't be exactly like the example because no two children are alike, and your child may have some unusual sensory conditioning at home, such as a musical family, which increases his hearing ability, or a cramped apartment, which inhibits his movement (more about this later). But in general, you will be able to recognize which of the sensory examples sounds most like your child.

2 Is Your Child a Hearer, Vocalizer, Speaker?

A very young "hearing" child is often soothed to sleep by music or singing. His nighttime ritual includes a bedtime story repeated night after night. He hears the sounds as if they were a melody. He may make his own sounds by humming or chanting in bed for hours at a time.

A young hearer and vocalizer will experiment with his lips, tongue, teeth, throat, and breath to make sounds. He may decide to wail like a fire engine instead of talking, or to chirrup like a frog. He may imitate and exaggerate the sounds of television characters, animals, people he has heard. He will make sounds and noises as he moves in various rhythms—high and low pitches, loud and soft sounds, hums, chants, melodies, rhymes often full of puns, jokes, and imaginative figures of speech, like this observation by the three-year-old child of a physician, quoted by Kornei Chukovsky in *From Two to Five*:

THE STUPID CAT

The cat sees a pit
And swallows it.
Off to the hospital with her.

Your Child's Sensory World

All this racket may be irritating to parents, but often it is not intended to annoy anyone. Your child is exercising his speaking mechanism and making patterns in sounds.

A child of four or five who likes to hear listens to the sounds of speech. He chants in rhythm as he hops or skips: "Good-bye-yi-yi. O why me-yi?" Most adults would call this a nonsense verse, but a speech or singing teacher would recognize the variety of vowel sounds and consonants. This child is forming and hearing speech sounds, not using language as a means of expressing ideas or a source of information. Watch him break into a run as he vocalizes and speeds up the rhythm or tempo. He gets louder and softer on various sounds—hisses, clicks, hums, chants, wails. He changes the pitch to form melodies. He roars and screeches for fun. It really is fun for some children to make a loud noise with their voice. (Luckily, some adults are like this too, or we would have no opera singers.)

A hearer and vocalizer will enjoy learning to read. If you ask him to name words that rhyme with "cat," he can reel off dozens: bat, mat, sat, pat, rat, vat. He may not know what "vat" means, but he enjoys saying and hearing the pattern of rhymed vowel sounds. Once he has said a new word, he will probably want to learn the meaning, so he adds quickly to his vocabulary. He'll love the sound and feel of consonants as he moves his lips to form *b*'s and *p*'s. If you ask him to say "Peter Piper picked a peck of pickled peppers," he'll like the sensation. He'll also get pleasure out of moving his tongue in his throat, against the roof of his mouth, against his teeth, to say *c*'s, *g*'s, *d*'s, *t*'s, *j*'s, and *s*'s.

ACTIVITIES THAT SHOW YOUR GROWING CHILD'S HEARING AWARENESS

READING. As soon as he learns to associate visual patterns with the vocal patterns he feels and hears, he will be able to read. Later, when he reads aloud, he'll do well because he can hear and feel the rhythm and melody of the sentence structure. He'll intuitively stress the important words and drop his voice at the end of a sentence. In fact he may be able to do this even when he doesn't fully understand the meaning.

As your hearing child grows older and more experienced, he will learn to express aloud longer phrases in sentence groups and paragraphs. In the second and third grades at school, when he learns about parts of speech and synonyms and homonyms, he will connect the way the words sound with their function and meaning. In the fourth and fifth grades, if he studies poetry and outstanding literature, he will recognize the writer's ability to express thought and emotion in beautiful or unusually expressive words. Even though he no longer says the words as he reads, the fact that he is alive to verbal sounds gives the hearing child a special feeling for language all his life.

Incidentally, a beginning reader who is not fond of using his voice usually hates to read aloud, which may affect his schoolwork. Six-year-old Jane is an above-average reader, but her teacher doesn't know it. When she calls on Jane to read aloud, Jane gets so nervous that her throat tightens until hardly any sound comes out and it hurts to speak, but there is no other way that the teacher can check her reading ability at this stage.

ENGLISH, POETRY, AND DRAMA. An older child who likes to hear will do well in English class at school because he'll have a feel for the sound of words in essays and novels, the rhythm of poetry and drama. He'll be able to express himself grammatically in written composition because good sentence structure has a flow to it. Also, vocal-verbal children stand out in class discussion, debates, and oral reports. A verbal child knows that the same words can have different meanings, depending on who says them and why. Such perception of human nature helps the hearing child analyze character in novels and plays.

HISTORY. If your child is a top student in history, the chances are that he is using an ability for language and verbal communication. Much of history describes how important figures of the past realized successes or failures through negotiation, intrigue, plots, organization of political and military allies, diplomacy, and treaties. These events all involve communication, most of it verbal. For example, a verbal child would be fascinated by the trial of Galileo, which involves the power of language under extreme circumstances: a scientist who escapes death by publicly denying the scientific facts he had himself proved. A child who can empathize with Galileo and imagine how the scientist felt as he muttered, "and yet it moves," after the trial will be motivated to explore relevant historical facts about the Catholic Church, religious traditions, and the scientific method. For such a child, history becomes a vivid experience.

FOREIGN LANGUAGES. Your hearing-speaking child will have a feel for foreign languages. Modern language schools such as Berlitz stress hearing and speaking and repeated sounds. One Berlitz advertisement shows a picture of a very young child with the caption "If she can speak perfect Icelandic, why can't you?" The text explains that the child is as yet unable to read but can hear and speak. Sound and speech help the hearing child to memorize unfamiliar words, syntax, and idioms rapidly.

MUSICAL ABILITY. What about musical ability? Most hearing children have it. Your hearing child listens intently to music on the radio or phonograph. Even at a very young age he may be able to sing melodies with accuracy—perhaps even after one hearing. He'll like to make sounds with pots and pans, drums, harmonicas, paper and comb, running a pencil along the posts of a banister. He's not just letting off steam, he's trying out different types of sounds, pitches, rhythms, accents.

When your hearing child gets older, you may discover that he has perfect pitch—that is, the ability to repeat the note of the scale on which a melody begins. This auditory memory corresponds to a photographic memory of letters and words on a page. For example, if four-year-old Sam sings "Mary had a little lamb" at home on three different occasions, he'll always begin the song on the same note. He may also recognize rhythmic patterns and musical forms and point out that "Mary had a little lamb" has the same beat as "London Bridge is falling down" (LONG, short, LONG, LONG, LONG, LONG, LONG), or he may observe that a melody "plays over and over," as in a round, or rondo.

An older child who takes music lessons will be working alternately and simultaneously with his sense of touch, movement, and hearing. He uses his sense of touch and movement to find the right note on the piano or stringed instrument. Or if it is a woodwind or brass instrument, he will be struggling with fingering plus breath, which is also a physical action. The sound may be terrible, even if he is at an advanced stage, whenever he is practicing *how to move* in order to get the sounds he wants. Of course, it is his ear that tells him whether his hands or breath are right or wrong. When your child is concentrating on hearing, he will be more aware of the quality of the sound than of what he is doing to make the sound. Even a beginner can play simple groups of notes and listen sensitively in order to improve the quality of what he hears. This indicates a musical child.

POSSIBLE PROBLEMS FOR A HEARING-SPEAKING CHILD

Noises that do not bother you at all may pain your child's ears as they do the sensitive ears of a dog. Your child can't help his response, so don't blame him for it. Be aware of indoor noises like those of the vacuum cleaner, the food blender, a knife sharpener; outdoor racket like pneumatic hammers, a steam shovel, piercing sirens, screeching subway wheels. "Happy times" that may hurt your child ears are the circus (loud bangs from firecrackers), children's movies (a raucous, poorly focused sound track), or the high decibel level at a children's party.

At school your hearing child will have trouble working in a noisy classroom or with a teacher who has a really poor speaking voice. The sound of the voice may affect him the way squeaking chalk does, and lower his grades no matter how much he enjoys the work. An exceptionally noisy lunchroom can deprive a child of all appetite if he is sensitive to sounds. This is an involuntary physical response—the stomach and intestines tighten. Even the music period at school may upset your child if the teacher tries to get the class to "sing out" and the tone becomes ugly. And a musical child who has the ability to repeat a melody or rhythm after one hearing will be bored to death if the class spends twenty minutes learning a song.

Most teachers use an abundance of charts, maps, diagrams, illustrations on the blackboard, mimeographed papers to study at home, plus the visual math aids like Cuisenaire rods and "geo" blocks. If this visual material is not getting through to your child because he is a hearer, you can't blame the teacher for being confused. She is teaching with her eyes and your child learns best through his ears. A related point: If your child is a terrible speller, make sure he is *looking* at the words as well as hearing and speaking them. How could anyone arrive at the spelling of "island" or "captain" through his ears?

CREATIVE OPPORTUNITIES FOR A HEARING-SPEAKING CHILD

Music. Music lessons are among the activities that will make the most of your child's apitudes. If your child has manual dexterity in addition to his hearing-speaking-vocalizing ability, he will do well on any instrument, but you should try to find the best available teacher for his favorite-sounding instrument, such as the clarinet, oboe, or drums. Your child may not necessarily grow up to be a musician, but with excellent instruction he will "learn to learn" music. He can apply this skill, discipline, sense of form, and expressiveness to other areas of his life—an experience that will give him pleasure and self-confidence.

A musical child who is not so skillful with his hands can play the trumpet, French horn, or trombone, which require breath control more than finger dexterity; or the xylophone and drums, which need coordination and rhythm. Other fields in which such a child will find satisfaction are musical composition, singing both classical and "pop" songs, and choral work in a glee club or church choir.

The Spoken Word. "Speaking" children enjoy experiencing drama and hearing spoken poetry, as well as writing poetry and prose; these are all activities that involve a feel for the melody and rhythm of words. They also enjoy plays with puppets and marionettes.

Crafts. Some crafts that require good hearing are piano-tuning and building any type of musical instrument—from recorders to drums to stringed instruments.

Science. Scientific experiments with radio and tape can include work with the voice and sound effects or with the more technical aspects of sound—engineering, control of recording levels, splicing tapes, and mixing sounds. Your child might also like to learn something about the science of sound—physics and how the ear functions, the Doppler effect, hearing in animals, how echoes work, sonar, and hearing in bats, or the study of acoustics in structures.

3 Does Your Child See Form, Color, Design, and Spatial Relationships?

A very young visual child may fall asleep at night by watching lights out the window: stars, lit-up houses, airplanes, the moving headlights of cars. He may like to make shadow pictures against the bedroom walls with his hands. He watches the figures change shape or move at different speeds. All these experiences are pleasantly hypnotic.

At night a seeing child likes to examine picture books alone or with you. He may point out forms, colors, designs that attract his eye rather than illustrate the story. He is intrigued by the shape of letters and the design of the type on the page, even if he can't read.

When the seeing child plays with toys, games, crafts, and art supplies he likes to find new ways to use his eyes. Three-year-old Jason is crazy about his set of blocks. He tries out what makes sense, what will balance, and what makes an interesting design: "Look at the big parking garage. See, the cars drive in here, or the elevator takes them on the roof. The roof has an extra part for fun and besides, people can stand underneath it when it's raining." Each time Jason takes out the blocks he discovers a new visual arrangement.

Other activities that combine eye-hand coordination are puzzles and lotto games, a pegboard with wooden pegs, felt games, color-forms, interlocking mosaics, pop-beads. Your seeing child practices ways to combine all kinds of forms and shapes to please his eye—flat, round, and random, of uniform or varying colors. When he arranges model cars and trains into patterns, or sets up a doll house or play dishes, he is training his awareness of shape and size. What makes a house look real? Where do the plate, the glass, the fork belong?

ACTIVITIES THAT SHOW YOUR GROWING CHILD'S SEEING AWARENESS

ART WORK. Art work such as drawing with crayons or chalks, painting, making collages, cutting paper designs, working with clay, finger painting, all use various visual and tactile combinations. Collages map your child's textural favorites in hand and eye. A drawing shows an awareness of shape and size: a man's body, a house, a tree or sun—outlined on a square white surface. A painting adds the element of color and a paintbrush provides new ways for your seeing child to make his own particular mark.

According to art educator Jane Cooper Bland, it is the process of doing, not the final product, that is most important to the child who likes to paint, so he may be extremely visual and gifted in art even though his pictures end up as a series of experiments one on top of the other. Here is Sally, who brushes red squares, then green rectangles. Pretty soon the whole paper turns brown. That's enough for today. To an adult it looks like a smeary mess, but Sally has learned about squares, rectangles, red, green, maybe even how to mix brown. If Mommy expected an art work, she'll be disappointed unless she has a movie camera and can photograph the creative process in sequence like a flower unfolding before it dries up and falls to the ground.

When a child has a friend over to play, there will be a lot of interaction that has little to do with his sensory habits. Suppose your child and her friend love to play house and often serve clay "spaghetti and meatballs." This does not necessarily mean that either child enjoys the tactile or visual qualities of the clay. They may just want some pretend food and the clay is handy. But if you see your daughter experiment with the clay and make designs or animal shapes out of balls, ovals, "ropes," or wind the "spaghetti" round and round into a cylinder and smooth it out with her fingers, she is clearly using her eyes in a purposeful way.

CLEANING HOUSE. Your seeing child can be a big help to you in the house if he feels inclined. For example, what makes a good duster? The ability to pass the dust cloth over all the dimensions of a piece of furniture; for instance, over, under, and in between the supporting rungs of a chair. A young see-er will be more adept at putting away his toys because he can recognize spatial relationships—what goes where and how. Even if all his toys go into a large box, there are two ways to fit them in: one so the cover can close and the other so it can't—just as in packing a suitcase.

An older child with good eye-hand coordination will have no trouble arranging his possessions neatly if he wants to. Even if his drawers and closet are a mess, he is likely to have some favorite collection of model cars, dolls of all nations, stones, shells, or matchbook covers, which shows his aptitude at spatial organization. On the other hand, a child who lacks this visual skill may be messy because he needs practice at seeing. (You can help him with a game—see pages 269–270.)

INTERIOR DECORATING. Every child likes to decorate his room with posters of people he admires, pictures of horses or dogs, or other decorative objects. Look at the walls and shelves of your child's room. Is there a sense of layout in the décor? Did he carefully place the poster midway between the edge of the doorframe and his bed? Does he seem to favor a particular color or hue? Has he taped up some "original" paintings of deep blue, bright orange, pastel browns, and pinks? Look at the shapes in the pictures. Does one form predominate? Circle, square, rectangle? What about the objects? Are there lots of round, smooth curves, or glass knick-knacks with sharp, clean edges? Is the glass placed so that the light will shine through it? Are there favorite marbles on a shelf or intricate models of cars, trucks, or boats? If your child seems to get special pleasure out of color, texture, shape, light, and overall design, he is not just displaying what is important to him, he is also using his eyes in a sensitive manner. He is a visual child.

Often your seeing child will have excellent ideas about decorating his room with color-coordinated bedspread, curtains, throw-pillows, or an ingenious solution to a storage problem via a "custom-designed" cupboard. Why not let him try out a plan or two? The project need not be expensive —fabric remnants, sanded and painted orange crates, and a construction out of pine boards can be highly effective. By letting your child arrange his own special environment you will be encouraging him in something he is good at, which is wonderful for his morale.

CLOTHES. When your seeing child is old enough to help you select his clothes, you may be amazed at his taste and judgment. This child's "seeing" sensitivity helps him find clothes of a flattering fit and shape—how the shirt hangs, the placement of the shoulder seams and neckline, how the skirt drapes. The boy or girl who always looks like a fashion plate has an intuitive ability to select clothing in colors that complement his complexion and personality. He can match his skin tone to the most flattering shades; usually, beige, olive, and dark skins go with orange, lime, rust, turquoise, and cerise, while light skin-tones look better with black, blue, clear reds, and greens. If the garment does not meet your child's standards and you buy it anyway, it will probably just hang there in his closet. Even when your seeing child dresses like the gang, he is liable to look a little better than the others.

SENSE OF DIRECTION AND VISUAL AWARE-NESS. When you take your young seeing child out on errands and excursions, you will notice his sense of direction. He has a visual ability to orient his path in relation to space—a kind of "map sense." He is also especially observant of landmarks. Incidentally, this directional awareness is another seeing aptitude that can be developed by a game or exercise.

Your seeing child will spot more than landmarks. At the supermarket he will find your favorite brand of soap powder, even if you have just walked right past it. He will comment on the television camera you never noticed, the one installed high up in the store to prevent shoplifting. An older seeing child may describe a new friend's appearance or home so accurately that you could draw a picture of it. If he happens to observe a car accident, he makes an outstanding witness, because his eye will have recorded the lane in which each car was driving and the relative speeds, color, appearance, and make of the cars, the name of the street or intersection, the merchandise of some of the shops on the street, the time of day as measured by the degree of light and shade.

READING. How does this kind of child do at school? A seeing child who becomes interested in learning how to read will feel at home with the shapes and sizes of the letters. He will be less likely to mistake a *b* for a *p* or to reverse a word—"tap" for "pat"—because they look so different to him, as different as a triangle from a square. If his ear is good enough so that he can relate the shape to a certain sound, he is all set.

A seeing child may function in reverse to the hearing child: The former sees "Peter Piper picked a peck," recognizes the shape of the repeated letter, and then connects what he sees with the spoken word-sound. The hearer listens to and feels the spoken sound, then relates the repeated sound-pattern to a repeated visual pattern. In each case, however, the result is reading. Incidentally, some pediatricians and optometrists feel that many six-year-olds lack the visual maturity to discriminate letter-forms accurately. This has nothing to do with intelligence, but rather with the child's physiological development at that particular stage.

A visual first-grader will see the similarities between most small letters and their capitals. *B* is like *b* except for an extra semicircle. *C* is a giant *c*, and so on. For the same reason, this child should have no trouble learning to read script. *ℓ* is similar in design to b except for an extra line, loop, and the slant. The same is true of *d* and d, *ℓ* and l, and others. Many seeing children become excellent spellers because they can visualize the words in their minds.

WRITING. Neat handwriting of letters or numerals requires eye-hand coordination. Spacing letter shapes or number shapes attractively on the page is a visual skill similar to those operating in graphics and typesetting. When we look at our children's homework, most of us are so concerned with accuracy that we seldom notice the layout. Next time, see if the paper has a nice design regardless of right or wrong answers. If so, here is another indication of your child's visual ability. A less visual child may not even be aware of the design that letters and numbers can make on a page. If he learns to look at the whole page as if it were a picture, the overall spacing and individual letter and number forms will improve as well, and your child may discover some careless mistakes. For instance, your eight-year-old son will suddenly notice that he has written *mother* instead of *mother* or ₂ instead of *2* . Before, his papers were so messy he was unable to see the difference, although he understood the work.

MATHEMATICS. A seeing child is already well prepared when he begins to study math because, as Lancelot Hogben says in his book *Mathematics for the Million,* mathematics is the language of size. So if your seeing child has always worked with shapes and forms at home and at nursery school, he will already understand size, proportion, and balance. The work at school with Cuisenaire rods and other proportional forms will merely confirm something he has already sensed. Suppose your child noticed at the age of five the graded packages of soap at the supermarket and compared the weight and relative size by eye and hand. He will understand what is involved when he weighs three pebbles, then six pebbles, on a scale at school. If he learns a new fact —that one pebble can weigh more than a handful of paper scraps—he has a visual basis for this knowledge. The next time he goes food-shopping he may compare the relative

weight of soap powder with a can of tunafish. Even if he can't
read numbers, these mathematical facts become part of his
experience because he is a see-er.

Jean Piaget describes such an experience:

> This example . . . was first suggested to me by a mathematician
> friend who quoted it as the point of departure of his interest in
> mathematics. When he was a small child he was counting peb-
> bles one day; he lined them up in a row and counted them from
> left to right and got to ten. Then, just for fun, he counted them
> from right to left to see what he would get, and was astonished
> that he got ten again. He put the pebbles in a circle and counted
> them and once again there were ten. He went around the circle
> the other way and got ten again. And no matter how he put the
> pebbles, when he counted them they came to ten. He discov-
> ered here what is known in mathematics as commutativity; that
> is, the sum is independent of the order. But how did he discover
> this? Was commutativity a property of the pebbles? It is true
> that the pebbles, as it were, let it be done to themselves; he
> could not have done the same thing with drops of water. So in
> this sense there was a physical aspect to his knowledge. But the
> order was not in the pebbles; it was he, the subject, who put the
> pebbles in a line and then in a circle. Moreover, the sum was not
> in the pebbles themselves; it was he who united the pebbles.
> The knowledge that this future mathematician discovered that
> day was drawn, then, not from the physical properties of the
> pebbles, but from the actions that he carried out on them.
> *(From "Genetic Epistemology,"* Columbia Forum, *Vol. XII, No. 3:
> Fall, 1969.)*

Your seeing child will like to measure dimensions. If
Matthew, at five, notices that the cracker he's eating looks
like a tiny kitchen floor (that is, both surfaces are square), he
will have no trouble learning that a number of little squares

will fit into one big square. Later, he will learn how to measure squares and rectangles with inches, feet, and yards, both around the edges (perimeter) and all over (square measurement of area).

Matthew may also have noticed relative volumes—familiar containers and how much they hold. He sees milk in glasses of different sizes at the dinner table. How much milk does each glass hold? At school, when he learns to measure volume, he'll remember the milk glasses at home, and how his eyes used to trick him with the tall, thin glasses and the short, fat glasses.

Most visual children will have little trouble in thinking of numbers abstractly. It is not hard for them to imagine that the symbol "3" can represent "***" or "888". These are just different types of visual operations. Even in more complex mathematics, the seeing child has an advantage. He no longer "sees" the quantities, just as an advanced reader does not "hear" the words. But a child who has never related to word-sounds will have trouble with Shakespeare, and a child who has never "seen" relationships will not do well in algebra.

Incidentally, a less visual child can find many ways not to "see" during a math class. He may be listening to the sounds the Cuisenaire rods make as they click and glide on the plastic table-top, or feeling the different-shaped "geo" blocks with his fingers. If he learns to add and subtract by counting on his fingers, he will be able to feel the different quantities on his skin, but if he does not learn to see them as well, he is translating math into his touch sense instead of the other way around: "8 + 2" is a relationship, not a pressure of two fingers.

A child can also "hear" math without seeing it. If Christine learns addition by the sound of the numbers, she can become very speedy. She will say "2 + 3 are 5, 2 + 4 are 6" almost as if it were an advertising jingle, but if she never gets around to "seeing" the quantities, she is not learning math, she is using her hearing and speaking sense. When she grows older and starts to study algebra, she can make up charming stories about John struggling valiantly upstream in his canoe, sweating in the sun, while George glides easily downstream with the current, his hands behind his head. But she will never visualize the force of the current nor the energy of the paddle stroke. The *x*'s and *y*'s will have no meaning for her.

And what about geometry, since Chris has never learned to look at size and shape? One child I know memorized all the theorems by rote, but was in trouble whenever a problem varied from the textbook. Instead of seeing that "the square on the hypotenuse is the sum of the square of the opposite two sides," she learned the first letter of each important word and put them into a rhythm:

     s h s,   (square, hypotenuse, sum,
     s ot s.   square opposite-two sides.)

This child was inventing a code, not studying geometry.

SCIENCE. A child who does well in any science sees well. He must use his eyes to understand how organisms and plants function in biology, and botany. A good physics student needs to visualize how forces interact—weights balancing on a rod, the energy and resistance of a rolling wheel. The same is true of elementary chemistry, geology, and astronomy, but on differing scales. Chemistry is concerned with very small quantities—atoms and molecules. Physics and biology are life-sized. Geology is the examination of large movements of land and sea over a vast period of time. And astronomy stretches our eyes to the limits of time and space.

The child who loves to see can extend his vision with magnifying glass, binoculars, microscope, and telescope. He can examine photographs: the bird's-eye view of land and sea from an airplane, of earth and moon and sky from a rocket ship, and even views of Venus and Mars from outer space.

SOCIAL STUDIES. Social studies involves many sensory factors, but if your child does especially well in geography, earth studies, and anthropology he is probably using his visual aptitude. Aside from map study, which is clearly visual, your seeing child may be looking at dress and how it is affected by climate and social customs. Perhaps he'll sketch what people wear and why—both clothing and ornaments; how people live and work, which is related to what is plentiful and what is scarce in the area. He can find out what materials are used for shelter; what is the design and function of public buildings for recreation, study, ceremonies; what characterizes the monuments and art works. If he moves back and takes a longer perspective, he will see the physical characteristics on top of the land (topography), underneath the earth (geology), and above the countryside (meteorology). This should lead him to an understanding of population pressures and the balance of national power, past and present: why nations have always fought over valuable land containing fertile soil, fresh water, natural harbors and natural resources such as oil, coal, aluminum, iron ore, and precious stones.

POSSIBLE PROBLEMS FOR A SEEING CHILD

Sometimes a seeing child is so busy looking that he does not communicate much, which makes a parent feel left out of his child's experiences. But if you ask him to tell you what he sees, you will be amazed at his observation and logic. Here is what one four-year-old saw from his living-room window: "I'm watching those men put in that big new pipe. First they broke up the street to get the old one out and now they're taking it out to make room for the new one. And I like to watch the sun move around the corner to shine on that little tree. It comes earlier every day."

You may be able to draw out an older child by playing a "what did you see" game at the dinner table. Here's what one visual eleven-year-old answered. "Coming home from school on the bus I was thinking, How fast is the bus moving? Is this one a good driver? Not very—he brakes too quickly. What's the weather like? Cloudy. Can't tell how soon the sun will set. I see the construction at that school is coming along. There's a group of kids going on a trip. Funny, I thought it was a boys' school. Oh yeah, I guess some of the boys have long hair—ha ha."

A seeing child may be unusually disturbed by a cluttered person, someone who is overdressed or whose grooming is at loose ends. He will be uncomfortable in a room with visual irregularity such as poor color combinations, poor lighting, or imperfectly designed or manufactured objects. He probably won't learn to verbalize what's bothering him until he's older. An architect I know wanted to move out of his roomy apartment and his wife couldn't understand why. One day he explained to her that it was an old building, none of the walls were plumb, and he sat there every night staring at those crooked walls—it drove him crazy.

At school, your seeing child may be troubled by the lighting. Fluorescent light is inexpensive and gives adequate illumination, but most current fixtures create a spooky effect that changes skin color, brings out hollows, and emphasizes blood vessels, all of which, to a child with acute seeing would come across like going to school in a nightmare. Other classrooms are not planned well in relation to sunlight. If sunlight falls across a face or desk, a child instinctively turns his head to avoid the glare. The seeing child will be distressed at the distortion this causes in his handwriting. The same thing happens if your child is too big or too small for his desk or table. The effort to make written work visually attractive creates a strain on your child's back, neck, eyes, and hand. If he is at a bad angle from the writing surface, all the forms look distorted: an "o" turns into an "⟳" because the figure becomes foreshortened. If your child's class is very large, the constant movement in the room makes a restless visual background for your seeing child—for him the experience is rather like trying to read in a moving car.

A more serious problem occurs in achievement tests, where your child may fail to recognize ambiguous drawing not because of his cultural conditioning but because of his visual acuity. For example a visually sensitive child would be hard put to recognize "beauty" in this sketch from a reading workbook on vowel sounds (*Checkups for Skill Book 3*, Copyright 1970, *New Readers Press*, publishing division of Laubach Literacy, Inc., Box 131, Syracuse, N.Y. 13210):

b___ ___ ___ty

Nabokov, in his novel *Pnin,* describes an artistic child whose mental capacities scored from moron to genius, depending on the visual content of the examination.

Some "happy times" that may backfire because of your child's keen eyes are trips to art galleries or museums. If your child is too small to see properly, the works of art will appear to him to be as distorted as a carnival mirror. You may try to bend down to your child's level and feel that this isn't so, but your eye remembers the painting's actual appearance in the normal position. If you don't want to carry your child around at a higher eye level, wait until he grows taller before exposing him to such experiences.

Your young seeing child may destroy the fantasy of a children's movie by noticing: "That's not a really a monster. I can see the strings." Or, "How come Super-Hero flies through the air and his hair never moves?" One solution: a good puppet show, where there is no pretence of realism, and the visual effects are usually charming.

CREATIVE OPPORTUNITIES FOR A SEEING CHILD

These resources and activities will make the most of your seeing child's aptitudes.

Art, Crafts, Toys. Art supplies such as poster paints, pastels, Japanese craypas, (like pastels, but they don't smudge,) charcoal, clay, collage material: glue, plus scraps of paper and fabric, or other items such as beads, wire, string, shells, acorns, pebbles, straws, toothpicks, paper clips, pipe cleaners. Many of these will also make three-dimensional mobiles or constructions. Model kits of cars, boats, airplanes. Construction toys such as Tinker Toys, Erector sets, building blocks, interlocking blocks. Puzzles and visual memory games with painted pictures. A camera. Tools and building supplies like lumber, nails, hammer, saw, screwdriver. Sewing materials and patterns for dolls' clothes and interior decorating for doll houses and rooms of the house. Puppets and puppet theaters. Craft supplies for jewelry, leather, weaving. A game that combines visual awareness with intellect is chess.

Science. Science books and kits on optics, the physics of light and vision. Reading about how animals, reptiles, simple organisms, see and react to light. For instance, certain species of fish supplement poor eyes with electric "radar," which also helps them find their way through muddy streams. Observing geometric forms in nature: honeycombs, snail shells, enlarged photos of crystals such as snowflakes. Nature study such as collections of shells, plants, ferns, butterflies, insects. Work in mathematics and physics. Optical instruments like a magnifying glass, binoculars, microscope, telescope. A prism. A kaleidoscope. A kit of small geometrical shapes. Scrapbooks. Photography. Bikes, old radios, doorbells, clocks to tinker with and to repair.

Visual Experiences for Parent and Child to Share. Characteristics of people's homes, of public places such as the library, train station, supermarket. Environments in miniature: scale models of historical scenes, ways of life, stage settings, model train and car set-ups.

Large outdoor views from tall buildings, airplanes, or high up on a hill or mountain. Large flat views at the seashore. The night sky in city or country. A planetarium with an artificial night sky.

Museums of painting, sculpture, mobiles, artifacts. Artificial environments, life-sized or enlarged, such as at a museum of natural history. Exhibits illustrating natural phenomena by mock-ups, magnified pictures, and scale models.

Exhibits or books on architecture. What form predominates in Romanesque, Gothic, Baroque, Japanese, Greek Orthodox?

If your child is verbal as well as visual, he can write or describe objects, people (both form and face); scenes, events, animals, paintings, statues, buildings, and structures such as bridges. Even if he does not express his enjoyment to you, he will be happy in any place that rewards his eyes.

4 Is Your Child a Toucher?

Your child's touch awareness covers his degree of skin response to external experiences such as heat, cold, humidity, air, water, texture, and pressure; how well he uses his hands; and his ability to communicate with others by touch. Your child may be a toucher and not be responsive in all these areas, but you will recognize his sensitivity in many situations involving touch.

Your baby's favorite blanket, teddy bear, or other stuffed animal was once a pleasing touch experience for him—and may still be, even if it is now worn and ragged. Some tactile children like to stroke their hair at night, or a soft sheet, or their blanket. If you give them another blanket because theirs is in the laundry, they may have trouble getting to sleep. One mother replaced a worn quilt on her four-year-old's bed and it took her son a whole week to get used to it.

ACTIVITIES THAT SHOW YOUR GROWING CHILD'S TOUCH AWARENESS

TEMPERATURE AND TEXTURE. If your child has a naturally warm body temperature, he will have trouble falling asleep when he has too many covers or when the room is too warm. Long-haired children may complain that their hair feels too hot, or they may throw off all their covers and strip naked. This is infuriating to some parents, but the child is usually just trying to tell you that his overall body temperature is too warm for sleep. You can have him put on his pajamas and open the window wider, or let him sleep under a sheet and cover him up later. Other children need a lot of blankets and sometimes even socks on their feet to be comfortable. If your child is sensitive to cold, his feet may feel cold to him, even though the room seems warm to you.

A young tactile child will have very definite preferences of temperature and texture in food. Some like very hot soup and very cold ice cream. They may like the feel of raw carrots and celery sticks in hand and mouth. They may hate the bland texture of some hot cereals, puddings, or Jell-O (you can try adding raisins or nuts). A happy "touch" experience for an older child is eating corn on the cob.

With an older touching child, who is more mobile, the more of his environment he contacts the more reactions he has, both positive and negative. His skin will react to the overall temperature and humidity of your home; to drafts or air currents from the window or the air conditioner; to the texture of your furnishings and your floor coverings. Some children have very tactile feet. They love to take off their shoes to feel the furry rug or the smooth tile. You can tell your five-year-old to put on his slippers until you're hoarse, but it won't do any good if he is this kind of child.

Your touching child reacts to texture in other people. For instance, a kiss from an unshaven father is really painful, especially if Daddy is wearing a rough tweed jacket. A well-meaning bear hug may exert enough pressure on your child's sensitive skin to cause him irritation instead of pleasure and warmth.

If your child is a toucher, he finds shopping for clothes and shoes quite an ordeal. If he is really allergic to wool you'll see the rash, but if it is a less severe reaction, you may just think he's being fussy. (Try him on orlon sweaters.) Other hazards: rough denim that chafes the skin, or stretch fabrics that pull uncomfortably when your child moves or don't let in enough air so that the skin can't "breathe." Shoes are even trickier. If your eight-year-old daughter takes fifteen minutes on each pair to decide whether or not they feel right, let her be. Otherwise, they will just sit in her closet.

When you dress your young toucher to go outdoors in winter, be aware that his adaptation to cold is different from yours. If you are out together and the wind is cutting through you but he doesn't mention it, or he looks forward to walks regardless of the temperature, he is better adapted to cold than you. That extra sweater or scarf or hat will just make him feel bulky and uncomfortably warm. Or perhaps your husband seldom wears a topcoat in winter. He takes your daughter out sledding without her hat, and she comes home crying with the cold. In her book *Freezing Point,* Lucy Kavalier holds that men don't feel cold quite as soon as women do, but in either case, there is no "right" way to feel —response to temperatures is an individual difference, like brown or blue eyes.

FINE TOUCH ACTIVITIES. Your toucher has manual dexterity—the ability to use his hands delicately, flexibly, accurately, and with timing (the control to apply manual pressure when necessary). When he is very young, your toucher will be able to color in his coloring book carefully, inside the lines; this is a repetitious touch activitity much like knitting. Your child will like to string beads, sew wool neatly through prepunched cards, weave loop pot-holders.

Outdoors he'll feel the sand in the sandbox and shape it into tunnels and castles. He'll make roads, domes, and pies out of dirt and mud, play sailboat in a brook, puddle, or gutter (provided the water doesn't feel too cold to him). In winter he creates snow statues, snowmen, and igloos. He collects and hoards seeds and pods, sticks, leaves, flowers, bits of glass and stone, or live specimens like worms and frogs. Even if you hate frogs, you should admire the tactile skill it takes to catch one—they're so quick and slippery. Your toucher may also like the feel of snakes, hamsters, gerbils, and your pet cat.

An older tactile child will create many treasures with his natural aptitude for knitting, crocheting, weaving on looms, macramé lanyards, leather work, jewelry-making, embroidery, and sewing. A favorite game might be pick-up sticks or jackstraws. A different type of child with fine-touch ability will construct model airplanes or anatomic human models, mount stone and shell collections attractively, carve out of wood and soap, tinker with dismantled clocks, bikes, radios, do some elementary carpentry, set up a model train or car track. Of course these are seeing activities as well, but touch is the more important sense, as you will realize if you examine the work of blind craftsmen.

SCHOOLWORK. At school your toucher will do well in written work. He'll love to make neat rows of lines, loops, and circles or half circles to form letters and numbers. Your child will have a flexible, steady grip on the pen or pencil. If the touch is too loose, the figures become sloppy. If it's too tight they become cramped, just like the stitches in knitting. A page of neat numerals, like a row of even stitches, shows you that your child is handy.

Lab work also requires manual dexterity for measuring chemicals accurately, handling hot glassware, arranging physics experiments in light refraction, dissecting frogs in biology.

GROOMING AND TABLE MANNERS. At home your toucher will start to display his manual skill early. He will feed himself efficiently with spoon and fork, button and unbutton his shirt and sweater, tie his shoelaces, brush and comb his hair, and wash himself. By the way, preferred temperature for bath water is another overall touch sensation that varies from child to child, so be sure to observe the bath temperature at which your child is most comfortable.

Later on, your toucher will do a good job at brushing his teeth, shampooing and styling his hair, manicuring his nails, applying makeup or shaving. It may seem odd to you that good grooming requires manual dexterity, but stop and think about the tactile skill of a good hairdresser, barber, manicurist, or makeup artist.

Incidentally, if you have discovered that your child concentrates more on his other senses than his sense of touch, he will be slow in learning these activities and may need a little extra time and some pointers and games to help him develop in these areas. Lots of children six through ten are very careless about cleaning nails and brushing hair and teeth. Make sure your child knows how to do it right if he wants to. You may have to guide Phyllis's hand on the brush so that she really starts at the scalp and pulls the brush through her hair, or show Dan again how to hold the toothbrush and move it to massage the gums and teeth. With an older child, try to find out if your daughter is really massaging her scalp when she shampoos in the shower and is letting the water flow through her hair when she rinses. A boy may be too embarrassed to discuss this, but if he complains about dandruff or grubby nails, you can make sure he knows what to do about them and how. He can learn to enjoy the process as well as the result. You might mention to your children that many encounter groups use massaging the scalp or soaping the body as a means of feeling alive. It really is a pleasant feeling.

HOUSEHOLD CHORES. If your child is a toucher, he can help you with many household chores. A four-year-old can clear the table and put the knives, forks, and spoons into the proper container. He can even help you to prepare food if you teach him how. He will chop cucumbers and carrots, although he'll work slowly and the pieces will be chunky. He can take the tops off strawberries. He can gently stir sauces, knead dough, and shape hamburger into patties.

An older toucher can clean patterned silverware, hem a skirt neatly, wash hand-laundry efficiently, smooth out a bed with hospital corners, and iron. He can attempt some more elaborate meals on his own, with sauces, grilled meat and fish, baked desserts. He can tackle a project like rearranging the dish or glass cupboard or sorting the nails at the workbench. He can use simple tools—hammer, screwdriver, plane, pliers—with skill. You may feel that some of these activities are more suitable to boys and some to girls. That is up to you. But the aptitude is identical in touchers of either sex.

One last point—be sure to compliment your child if he excels in household chores. His aptitude should be appreciated so that he feels proud of it. The eleven-year-old daughter of my neighbor was such a speedy, accurate ironer that her mother came to take her work for granted, although a regular dayworker was employed for cleaning.

COMMUNICATION BY TOUCH. If your child communicates by touch, you're a lucky parent. Most babies like to be cuddled, but a toucher receives and expresses love physically all through his school years and beyond. He will have a repertory of direct touch communication—a simple placing of the hand to attract attention or give comfort, a tight grip to express fear, and best of all, a gentle caress or warm hug to show affection.

POSSIBLE PROBLEMS FOR A CHILD WHO IS A TOUCHER

Your tactile child may be disturbed by environmental problems he cannot control. At school, physical crowding plus steam heat in winter make hot stuffy classrooms. An open window causes a draft for those sitting nearby. In warm weather, many classrooms get adequate ventilation only from wide-open windows and doors, which often raises the noise level intolerably.

Your child may be assigned to a desk or table that is too small for him and presses against his skin. Like the seeing child, he'll be distressed by the messy result poor posture has on his written work.

If your whole family communicates easily by touch and your child's teacher doesn't, the two may not get along. Your child will think his teacher doesn't like him, and the teacher won't know *what* is going on. Or sometimes the teacher has a way of touching that is sharp and angular so that your child shies away, like a dog or horse.

The same goes for other adults who communicate negatively to your child by touch. What about kind Aunt Edith, whose clammy spaghetti handshake gives your child the chills, or the boisterous kid next door who slaps your Eddie on the back in a friendly way and can't understand why Eddie bursts into tears (it hurts him).

Happy times for a toucher seldom happen in a supermarket or a library. Just imagination if you were five years old and entered a huge room full of many-colored objects just crying to be arranged into neat piles or unusual shapes, and someone told you, "No, dear, don't touch the books," or "Put that back, we don't need any cereal today." A sculpture gallery is even worse; it focuses on all the tactile pleasure the artist created with smooth flowing curves and interesting angles, and the museum guard insists that this is off limits for your toucher.

CREATIVE OPPORTUNITIES FOR A CHILD WHO IS A TOUCHER

These resources and activities will make the most of your tactile child's aptitudes.

Theater.   Acting and mime classes are wonderful for the child intrigued with communication by touch. You can increase the older child's awareness of speech and touch communication by going with him to films and live theater, and by watching dramatic shows of good quality on television.

Art.   Art classes, especially those offering work in sculpture, mobiles, collage.

Crafts.   Classes in crafts: weaving, ceramics, knitting, sewing, jewelry-making, leather tooling, mosaics, model planes and cars, woodworking, carpentry.

Music.   Music lessons, especially in playing keyboard and stringed instruments which require more complex manual dexterity than the woodwinds, brasses, or percussion instruments.

Science and Technical Skills.   Science projects: collecting and mounting shells, ferns, butterflies, insects. A dissecting kit with specimens. Experiments in physics and chemistry.

Work with electrical appliances, clocks, machinery, gadgets.

Take your child to a laboratory or workroom to observe trades and professions that require exceptional manual dexterity. He would enjoy observing architectural or mechanical draftsmen, a surgeon, laboratory technician, research biologist, botanist, engineers (including civil, electrical, mechanical), and machinists and mechanics of all types, from those who work on cars to those who manufacture electric lightbulbs. Also, master chefs, cooks, bakers. And don't forget your family dentist.

Performers.   Another master "manipulator" your touching child will delight in is a good magician or card trick artist. A magic set would be a good game for your child.

At Home.   You can help your toucher create a beautiful environment in his bedroom with fake fur floor-covering, stuffed animals, velvetlike pillows, a smooth, silky bedspread, a "nesting" chair, and a few mellow wood objects.

Trips.   Two unusual trips to take with your child: a school for the deaf which teaches sign language (one sign-language expert who is also a brilliant performing actor with the National Theater of the Deaf, has the reputation of having "golden hands"). If your child is interested in this type of communication, he might want to look up the sign language of the deaf in the library: *World Book Encyclopedia*, or C. O. Peare's *The Helen Keller Story*, or the dance hand-signs of India in a book such as *The Gesture Language of the Hindu Dance* by La Meri.

Another trip might be to a workroom or factory that employs blind craftsmen and artisans.

A vacation might be the best trip of all for your tactile child. You might try to accomodate his preference so that he'll find softer, more humid air, or a dryer, crisper atmosphere; warm caressing water to swim in or icy water that makes him tingle. There might be earth, grass, sand for hands and bare feet; warm sun and wind for the body; shells, pebbles, plants, seaweed to feel and collect. Or for the cold adapted child, bracing wind, soft curving snow to touch and shape, hot sun, and a wind so biting that he feels alive all over.

5 Is Your Child a Mover?

A child who is a mover—that is, who has exceptional kinesthetic perception—would live outdoors if he could. City or country, there are so many wonderful opportunities to run, balance, jump, swing, climb, slide, and even fall. Yes, a physical child instinctively knows how to fall—to give as he hits a surface and to take the impact with the largest possible part of his body. A less physical child of any age may do the opposite out of fear. If you are a nervous parent, you might take a look at your child and make sure he knows how to fall —to bend so that he won't break, or ask a teacher of physical education or of modern dance to show your child how to take the impact of a fall most safely.

A mover will be especially good at maneuvering his tricycle or bike—stopping, starting, and turning. He'll learn early how to pump on a swing, how to climb up a slide backward, how to bump on a seesaw without falling off. If you watch him hanging from play equipment or a tree branch or leaping from one rock to another, you'll notice that he moves energetically and adapts his body quickly to physical change. This behavior shows the kind of aptitude required by athletes, acrobats, and dancers. If your child is less physical than his best friend and it bothers him, or if he keeps hurting himself, you may be able to point out to him what the moving child does instinctively: control of weight, balance, timing (see "Movement Games"). If you feel that your child can't handle any comments from you at this stage, you might suggest some outdoor touch activities such as creating sand castles or mud pies (they're dirty, but safe) or else a nature walk during which your child can collect acorns, leaves, pebbles, insects, and other objects of interest.

ACTIVITIES THAT SHOW YOUR CHILD AS A MOVER

ACROBATICS—INDOORS AND OUTDOORS. If your child is a mover, he'll want to act the same way indoors as he does outdoors. He hops, jumps, skips, gallops, bounces on the bed, balances on a chair, rolls over and over on the carpet, turns somersaults, sees how high he can kick, or suddenly bursts into a soft-shoe, a wild jig, a flowing adagio. This physical activity means more to your mobile boy or girl than you may realize. Once my daughter, aged three, taught herself to climb up on a stainless-steel garbage pail. This achievement crowned a long period of trial and error: left hand on cover of pail, right knee on cover, both knees on cover; right hand on window sill, both hands on window sill, stand up slowly. Hooray! For my child, this experience was a personal triumph against physical odds, like scaling Mount Everest, but to me, it only represented a ruined garbage pail. When I replaced it and told her not to climb up on the new one, she was heartbroken. I finally understood what her climbing meant to her and gave her some giant blocks on which to practice.

A very physical child may like to catapult clothes off walls and ceiling, jump over furniture as if it were a hurdle, or tunnel under the couch on his stomach. He may play with a toy car for a minute and then zoom it across the room into the wall, not to be naughty but because he likes the physical sensation. If it's a car big enough to sit on, he may bump himself into walls and furniture. The jarring feeling is like the experience of driving a bumper car at a carnival, or being tackled at football. The fact that it marks up your walls and scratches your chairs is irrelevant to your child. Unless he's really angry over something, he is not deliberately destroying your home, he's practicing movements of different speed and force, working with his sense of balance and physical rhythm, learning how to control his arms, legs, and torso so that they will do what he wants them to. You might want to create a modified indoor gym with a rope ladder, extension bar, punching bag, or air-filled toy. Show your acrobat that he or she can practice balance, strength, agility, and timing without upsetting you. But do tell your child what your home means to you. You will improve his sensitivity to others as well as protect the appearance of your house. Besides, he's going to have to learn how to be civilized indoors sooner or later, and learning how to control physical energy is as important for him as being able to let it loose.

Incidentally, laryngologist Paul Moses mentions an interesting relationship between speech and young motoric children. He says such children learn to speak more rapidly and with greater ease than visual children, because children who are physical can translate heard sounds more quickly into the oral movements that become speech.

HEAVY HOUSEHOLD CHORES. If your young mover is willing, you might be able to channel some of that physical exuberance into heavy household chores like scrubbing the floor or woodwork (especially dirty fingermarks), beating out pillows, sanding furniture, or polishing wood. If you show him the purpose of the job and he is serious about helping, it will teach him to control the way he moves. Otherwise he will spill water all over the place, drop the pillows, and make valleys in the unfinished furniture. Of course if he doesn't really want to try, forget the whole idea before you lose your temper.

An older child can run the vacuum cleaner across a thick carpet that needs energetic treatment, wash or wax a floor, rake leaves in the garden, mow the lawn, clip the hedge. Incidentally, if you send your mover on an errand, he will rarely get lost. He will have a kinesthetic sense of himself moving through space which orients him. It seems hard to separate this aptitude from seeing (map sense), but blind people are familiar with it.

APPEARANCE. Take a critical look at your moving child's appearance. You'll probably think, "Why is he [or she] always such a mess?" He may not be a messy child at all, but if he is always on the move, his hair and clothes will show it. You wouldn't expect someone to look neat and well-groomed at the end of a race, and mobile children love to race the wind and move freely through their day's activities whenever they can.

Suppose your child wants to be neat but always looks like the tail end of "crack the whip" because he is so active. He can keep his bouncy vitality and still look great if his clothes and hair match his movements. Clothing that doesn't fit snugly but does hang well lets your active son or daughter move freely. This means well-cut shirts with long tails that will stay tucked in, or overblouses cut and hemmed to be worn loose; pants or dresses with elastic or well-fitted waistbands, or loose, well-cut shifts for girls.

As for hair, you and your child have to make a decision. An active child with long hair will always look messy (unless it is tightly braided.) Many children prefer a "casual" appearance, but if your child really wants to look neat, you might point out that he can't have it both ways. The friends he admires who look good with long flowing hair have a different movement pattern from his.

On the positive side, the body of a moving child is often strong, well-coordinated, and well-proportioned. His body is well-aligned and balanced and the movement is controlled. And a good body means that your child eats the right amount of food in relation to the energy he uses, so that his appetite is in proportion to his activities.

You may not consider body condition and food intake a sensory aptitude, but the relationship between the two involves a balance of sensory habits that most of us lack. Your child's good posture means that the weight and counterweight of the organs and limbs are evenly balanced against the pull of gravity. This also means he must move well. If he did not, his alignment would change. Just as a poorly adjusted car pulls to one side, eventually straining and wearing out the tires on that side, the strain of poor alignment in a person distorts the posture. Your well-balanced child's food intake is like the fuel of the car: it is being properly burned with a minimum of residue (or accumulated fat).

Incidentally, if your child is dissatisfied with his shape and wants to try various exercises or changes of diet, you can take the opportunity to explain about the body, movement, and food. Since it takes a lot of effort to change moving and eating habits, your child may not be willing, but at least he or she should know the principles involved. That way, your child knows that an attractive body is not some kind of gift from above, but that it requires work, and that anyone can improve his appearance if he really wants to, through posture, movement, and eating habits.

CHOICE OF SCHOOL. What about school for a mover? Fewer schools today restrict physical movement and force the children to "sit quietly at your desks" for long periods of time. Your mover would probably flourish in an "open corridor" or "child-centered learning" set-up in which he can move wherever his interest takes him.

READING. A very young physical child can get a feel for reading from the singing games many schools play. His voice says, "Here we go LOOP de LOO," as his body goes "Run-run-run SKIP run SKIP." He learns to relate the body accents and the verbal stresses, first in a spoken form and then in a written form like a hearing child.

Many infants who are movers amaze their parents by their ability to imitate movement. If mother stands over the crib and sings and gestures "clap clap nod the head, clap clap nod the head, ROLL YOUR HEAD AROUND," the baby can copy what he sees and hears with his body and hands in perfect rhythm.

An older child will imitate characteristic movements of animals and people: "I can crawl like a monkey." Or, "Watch me waddle like fat Miss Roberts." If "fat Miss Roberts" happens to be his second-grade teacher, your child's gift for pantomime can get him into trouble.

MATHEMATICS. Many schools now teach beginning mathematics through physical movement. When the teacher has the children "act out" the relationships with heavy objects, your mover will feel the movement pattern with his whole body. For example, Stuart puts eight apples into a basket and gives it to the teacher. The teacher hands it back and says, "Put in two more." Stuart does so and feels that the weight of the ten apples as he lifts and moves them is greater than when he performed the same movements with only eight apples. Ten is more than eight.

WRITING AND MUSIC PRACTICE. The act of sitting and writing is hard for an active child, but if he starts out with a balanced body position, he can learn to use part of his energy to keep his body still and the rest to move his arm and hand easily (see Hand-Eye Coordination Close Up, page 177).

The same approach works for your mover during music practice at home. Just be sure that he has a good body position. The music teacher has probably shown him how to sit or stand, but he may have forgotten. He should be able to touch the floor from the piano stool or chair. If he can't, put a book under his feet. Even if he kicks it aside, give it a try. If he's standing, make sure that the music stand is at the right height in relation to his body and eyes.

SPORTS. If your child has always been active outdoors and in, he should have the stamina, agility, and coordination to excel in physical education at school. If he doesn't, it might be because he dislikes competitive sports. Try him on swimming, skating, acrobatics, tumbling. Or sometimes, your moving child needs practice in visual coordination. Sports like baseball, basketball, volleyball, in fact, any game with a ball, need body-eye teamwork.

Incidentally, if your child is not physical, he may have an awful time in gym class through no fault of his own. There is nothing worse when you are eight than being chosen last for a team because you run so slowly, or being laughed at when you can't throw a ball well. Although school is supposed to be a place to learn, few gym instructors bother to tell the nonphysical child, "Ed, you'd run faster if you held your tummy in. You're wasting energy because your body's crooked, and it slows you down." Or, "Alice, you're throwing from your elbow instead of swinging your whole arm and body." A sympathetic physical education teacher once told me, "Most instructors are so athletic themselves that they don't relate to these problems." Whatever the reason, the child who needs the most help and practice in games and sports is usually given the least.

If this sounds like your child, you can take the mystery and threat out of his poor performance by explaining that sports involves physical coordination, timing, balance, and agility. Then, compare this physical aptitude to your child's best sense. For instance, if Alice can't throw but is very musical and plays the piano well, show her that she has an ear for rhythm and melodic line, just as her athletic sister has a body for timing and physical movement through space. If Alice is interested, play some movement games with her. (See the Guide to Sensory Games, on page 306).

POSSIBLE PROBLEMS FOR A CHILD WHO IS A MOVER

Your moving child feels uncomfortable whenever he cannot use his body freely. This means that he is likely to be irritable among crowds in a department store or supermarket, on the subway, or even on happy excursions such as a social visit to adults he really likes, a good movie that is too long to sit through, a camping trip with too many rainy days. Any long car-ride is a real misery for a physical child. It's not that he is impatient, it's just that his body feels so odd and "achy."

This kind of child is likely to run into some problems at school, such as an uncomfortable desk, table, or chair, and restricted movement (even a school that favors free movement for the pupils cannot permit them to bump into one another or into the equipment). More serious school problems will face the mover who has not learned to be still and look. His mobility will interfere with his learning, because what you look at changes appearance as you move. That is why people at an art gallery look, then move back, stop, and look again for a different view. If you move past the pictures at a fast clip, you cannot really see them. When the first-grade teacher draws on the board A α a and asks your child what he notices about them, he must stop still and look (unless he already knows the answer). If his eyes are jiggling up and down and from side to side because he's moving, the visual input is too confusing for him to understand.

If a child is not seeing and there is no other learning problem, his parents can often help him by means of seeing games. Once he learns to see better, he will be more interested in the work and able to concentrate on it. Besides, learning to see well is important for living as well as for learning.

Your moving child may have a problem in communication if he would rather move than speak. At an early age, such a child would rather push, hit, bite, or kick when he gets angry than scream or call someone a "stinky pig." He may not understand why his physical way of reacting is worse than the verbal way.

An older mover may prefer to act out a situation with his body rather than describe it with words. Here is how one twelve-year-old described his day: "I was trying to get off the bus, and this big fat lady was in the way, so I went like this [squeezes to one side] and then like this [squeezes to the other side.] Finally I said, 'Excuse me, can I get past?' And she said [pulling himself up and sticking out his stomach], 'What's the matter with you, young man, there's plenty of room.'" This whole incident could be mimed with no dialogue at all, and many movers love action television, films, and books because they empathize with the movement. They laugh at comedies of physical situation, such as the Keystone Cop or Charlie Chaplin variety. The verbal child, on the other hand, loves puns and plays on words, and finds situation movies with minimal dialogue a big bore. Sometimes, though, your mover will have trouble communicating what he feels, because certain emotions or subtle situations really cry out for words.

Your mover will instinctively pick up "body language" from others. Perhaps he dislikes an adult who crowds him physically, or a child whose body appears arrogant or servile. One mobile child described his teacher like this: "That clumsy woman keeps dropping her papers and she can't work the windowshades. How am I supposed to pay attention to what she says?" To a nonphysical person, this criticism may seem absurd, but such behavior is truly distracting to a moving child.

The parents of a mover will have a problem because of the wear and tear on clothing and shoes. He may need new heels every three weeks and wear through elbows and knees constantly. This is so much extra trouble and expense for you that it's tempting to say: "Don't tell me you made another hole in your jacket. Your brother's had his for a whole year." But this isn't really anything your child can control, because he can't change the way he moves.

CREATIVE OPPORTUNITIES FOR A CHILD
WHO IS A MOVER

These activities will make the most of your child's aptitudes.

Movement. Classes in dance, mime, acrobatics, tumbling, gymnastics. Sports activities of all kinds.

Music. Music study in the Dalcroze or Orff technique, or lessons on such instruments as the xylophone or drums, which demand rhythm and body coordination.

Crafts. Creative work activities for your mover are sculpting, weaving (especially large objects like rugs and wall-hangings), candle-making and soap-making, leather work for clothing and furniture.

At Home. Heavy work activities such as gardening, building houses and stone walls, reparing heavy machinery; indoor chores such as scrubbing, waxing, cleaning; redecorating, carpentry and painting, kneading homemade bread.

A good project for an older mover is designing and helping to build a room environment for maximum movement. For example, a platform bed at the top of a ladder, bookcases, giant storage boxes to walk or crawl into. For further ideas of this type, check out a small kitchen in a modern apartment. The space restrictions require the cook to be an athlete, since only one-third of the equipment is at a normal level. The other two-thirds require climbing or stooping.

Animals. Work and training with large animals: horses, large dogs, even cows.

Social Activities. Social activities centered around sports: swimming, bowling, ping-pong, tennis, skating, skiing.

Active physical fun at a carnival: bumper cars, roller coaster, "snap the whip."

Movement Observation. Here are some activities for the child who is gifted in observing movement:

Cartooning, line-drawing, sculpture of the human body in "frozen motion." A trip to a museum exhibit of Greek and Roman statues of athletes.

Study of choreography and movement plans in sports like football; outstanding techniques in sports like tennis or in ballet, and dance concerts of other styles.

The scientific study of movement and its application to various fields, such as psychotherapy and kinesics (body language).

Architecture and a study of layouts and floor plans in housing and public buildings.

Studies of spatial patterns: automobile traffic, boats in harbors and on navigation lanes, airport patterns of landing, takeoff, and holding.

Movement patterns of animals, insects, birds and fish from mating to migration.

6 Is Your Child Sensitive to Smell and Taste?

Your child may have a very high level of sensitivity in smell and taste. Some scientists call them the "orphan" senses because, unfortunately, we know so little about them. The best a parent can do is to be alert to the possibility that his child is a smeller or a taster and that this affects his behavior in many ways. Here are some true examples of behavior on the part of such children:

The mother of a three-year-old found "magic tape" stuck all over her daughter's pillow. The little girl was crazy about the smell of it. This same child threw away a new set of plastic blocks because she missed the "wood" smell, and would not look through her beautiful volume of fairy tales because of the pungent odor of the printer's ink.

The father of an eleven-year-old became furious with his son, who absolutely refused to rake up the fallen leaves in the yard. Later, the boy explained that a neighbor was burning his leaves at the time, and the smell made him nauseated.

Here is the most dramatic story of all. The daughter of a friend of mine was given an audiometer test in the first grade and registered below normal. The concerned parents had her retested by a specialist, who assured them that her hearing was excellent. Later the little girl happened to mention that she couldn't hear during the school test because of the smell. It seems that the earphones had a strong disinfectant odor that so distracted her that she couldn't perform properly.

And here is a story about an exceptional taster. A neighbor of mine took her eight-year-old daughter out to dinner at a fine French restaurant.

> Veronica (*politely to the waiter*): Will the beef be rare?
> Waiter: Yes, Mademoiselle.
> Veronica: And are there herbs?
> Waiter: Yes, Mademoiselle.
> Veronica: And is the sauce brown?
> Waiter: Yes, Mademoiselle, brown sauce with herbs and mushrooms.

A child like this, who is already something of a gourmet, can learn a lot about people through a study of food cultivation through the ages, including eating customs, national and staple foods, religious food restrictions, and the effect on food of famines and wars.

And if your child is intrigued by odors, he can trace the manner in which smells, both fragrant and unpleasant, have a close historical connection to a way of life. How did various cultures handle sanitation, from the intricate Roman sewers to the present crisis over raw sewage? What was the effect of indoor plumbing on building design? What are the cultural differences in relation to body odors? For instance, an Arab might recognize you by your individual body odor as well as by your face. Even if this strikes your child as funny, if he has a good sense of smell he might be interested.

For more details on this, and for suggested activities relating to smell and taste, see Chapters 15 and 16. You will also find more ways to track down your child's level of smell and taste in Chapter 8, How Does Your Home Affect Your Child's Senses?

How Sensory
Patterns Develop

7 How Does Society Affect Your Child's Senses?

How did your child develop his overall sensory pattern? Why does he use his eyes acutely, for example, but show less sensitivity in hearing? Is there something you as a parent can do to keep your child totally aware in all of his senses?

We have no factual answers yet to these questions. Scientists know that the brain continuously registers an enormous number of sensory impressions, but electrophysiologists have shown that there are many more stimuli than the brain uses. Which brings us to another question: Why does the brain select certain sensory data and ignore others? When we know this, we will not only know how sensory patterns are formed, we will be on the way to understanding how the brain works, how children learn, how memory functions, and many other complex and marvelous things.

Therapists currently use various types of sensory games to help impaired children: those who are retarded, handicapped, brain-damaged, or emotionally or neurologically disturbed. These specialists use an empirical approach to get through to the child in any way possible—verbal and auditory, visual, physical, tactile, or by taste (food as a reward). Encounter groups, "T" groups, and sensitivity sessions of the Esalen type have a similar objective with adults:

to reach the individual and make him open up to greater awareness.

A third approach is that of the behavioral psychologists, educators, and some experimental optometrists who are evaluating how children learn. This approach includes questions such as: What visual patterns and sequences does a child retain, and why? How can an auditory (hearing) child become more visual? Should a child learn by rote? Should a child experience learning situations through his senses?

Most current information on sensory patterns is still too specialized to be useful to the average parent, but there are some general areas of agreement that are important for all of us to know:

1. *Sensory patterns do exist.* Every baby has an individual response to his surroundings, based on factors such as his needs, likes, and interests, as opposed to his dislikes and fears.

2. *A normal baby is sensitive to all stimuli in his environment.*

3. *An enriched sensory environment helps your baby's development.* You can't change the sensory pattern your baby brings into the world, but you may be able to do something about the way in which your child's environment conditions his senses.

INFLUENCES ON YOUR GROWING CHILD

IN INFANCY. Most infants and babies have a marvelous sensory environment. Parents manage to surround the baby with rattles and records, furry and squishy toy animals, mobiles, bright colors, and tempting foods and liquids. Parents also know it is important to hold a baby and to respond to him so that the baby is using his eyes, ears, voice, and body as well as his senses of touch, taste, and smell.

This approach to the baby is a change from the past, when children were considered unformed adults. Toys were designed to improve the morality and intellect of the child; any sensory appeal to the child's eye or touch was regarded as distracting or even sinful. Times changed, and recently, studies of institutionalized babies showed that a deprived sensory environment affected the baby's health, intelligence, and general well-being. When the baby was surrounded by sounds, light, shapes, color, and cuddling, he improved rapidly. There are now any number of baby toys on the market which are attractive but also instructive—in the baby's terms, not in terms of what an adult thinks a baby should be learning. The average contemporary parent is truly solicitous of his baby's sensory environment.

IN THE PRESCHOOL CHILD. What about the sensory environment of the preschool child? Sensory deprivation at four and five affects learning ability in first grade and after. Head Start classes were started as the result of these findings. Researchers also discovered that a child's ability to communicate, respond, and create often suffers in an insensitive environment. Most parents of a preschool child know the importance of sensory games or creative play. Whether at home, nursery school, day care center, or kindergarten, the three-to-five-year-old will probably paint, model clay, build up and tear down block structures, sing, speak in various voices, act in dress-up clothes, play simple musical instruments, and make discoveries in taste and smell. If work starts in reading or mathematics during these years, it is of the reading readiness or beginning number concept variety. Few parents or preschool teachers would try to force a child of this age to concentrate beyond his interest span. The sensory needs of most preschool children are well provided for in their daily environment.

IN THE PRIMARY-SCHOOL CHILD. Most primary-school children have a problem sensory environment. With a few exceptions, schools suffer from overcrowding and lack of money, two conditions that hurt our children's senses and their learning ability. Few public schools were designed to minimize noise level and many schools, both private and public, have inadequate lighting or fail to take into account negative lighting factors such as direct sunlight on a desk or writing surface. Many schools have standardized furniture, so that un-standard-sized children are uncomfortable as they work. Overcrowding in classroom and lunchroom requires regimentation ("Keep in LINE"), and school lunches lack taste, as do all mass-prepared meals. An indirect but important result of all this stress is the tension of many teachers, which is reflected by their harsh-sounding voices and nervous movement patterns.

Some recently built schools (in Columbus, Ohio, for instance) have solved many of these problems with sound-proofing, carpeting, creative lighting, and learning centers that feature free-flowing movement. Other schools have reorganized within the restrictions of their older buildings by an ingenious use of classroom and corridor. These innovations solve sensory problems for some children but create new ones for others. Free movement, talking, and several simultaneous activities in adjacent areas can distract some children. But the thinking behind the new schools certainly represents an increased awareness of the sensory conditions under which our children learn.

Sometimes a primary-school child has a more subtle sensory problem—a parent who believes that sensory awareness and learning don't mix. The parent's argument goes like this: "Sensory awareness and creative play are fine through kindergarten, but starting with first grade, a child must learn to work." This implies that a child's senses are valuable in preparing him for formal schooling, but that the child can't really begin to use his brain unless he first learns to turn off his senses.

Perhaps we're still brainwashed by our Puritan background, which told us that sensory experiences are basically emotional and sexual, that emotions are illogical, sex is pleasurable, and work is not because it is "the curse of Adam." Therefore a child must learn to "stop playing" and "start working" as soon as possible. You may recall that this theory once applied even to babies. As a matter of fact, science has disproved these notions for children of all ages; we know now that the emotions, the brain, and the senses are interrelated. If a child suppresses one part of himself, it affects his ability in every other area. This doesn't mean that a child can live without self-control and discipline. He needs to learn what kind of effort to make, what is most effective and appropriate for a given situation. For example, learning mathematics is an intellectual experience based on visual (sensory) information about size and shape. If your child spends math period drawing a cartoon of the teacher, he is using his visual sense, but not to learn mathematics. He is making the wrong sensory effort. The Puritans made the wrong sensory effort also, with their sense-sex taboo, the reasoning of which was "Since sex is always sensory, and sex should be restrained, learn to restrain all sensory experiences." How ridiculous, when we think of such nonsexual sensory experiences as brushing our teeth, whistling a tune, or adding up a column of figures!

Today we know that learning can be as much fun for a child as playing. So can work activities like washing oneself, cleaning up a room, setting a table. It all depends on the child's attitude. And this in turn depends on you as a parent and on what you believe about learning. Here is one way to check yourself. Do you picture the brain as a type of thinking machine or computer that operates *after* the senses have fed in information, to give you an answer? Most scientists and psychologists hold that there must be a *continuous* give and take between the sensory information ("input") and the brain. The medium is the message, and what you perceive is based on what you know and vice versa.

Here is an example of a change in perception through experience, as described by Jean Piaget, the famous Swiss scholar and child psychologist who has written many volumes on how children learn to reason. At six months, Piaget's son Laurent holds in his hand a small box as he lies on the sofa. When he drops it, his eyes search for it on the sofa. Earlier, at three months, Laurent would have simply continued passive viewing of the place in the air where the object vanished. At a later age, Laurent would be able to retrieve the box even if it had fallen out of sight under the sofa. Piaget concludes that for the young infant, the box is gone when it leaves his field of vision. For the older infant, the box exists and can be relocated in a new position in space. For the toddler, the box can be recovered even if it has totally vanished from view. The older child sees the box differently from the infant, or, as Piaget stated, children evolve the ability to reason through conclusions drawn from sensory information.

Another pioneer in sensory learning was Maria Montessori who said in 1912, "The education of the senses should be begun methodically in infancy, and should continue during the entire period of instruction which is to prepare the individual for life in society." The Montessori type of teaching materials that are currently used in many schools include blocks, beads, and rods for mathematics, and tactile letters for reading.

The most recent innovation in American education is the informal classroom, based on the British infant school system:

> The school sets out deliberately to devise the right environment for children, to allow them to be themselves and to develop in the way and at the pace appropriate to them . . . It lays special stress on individual discovery, on first-hand experience and on opportunities for creative work. It insists that knowledge does not fall into neatly separate compartments and that work and play are not opposite but complementary. A child brought up in such an atmosphere has some hope of becoming a balanced and mature adult. (*From the Plowden Report, "Children and Their Primary Schools," published in England in 1967 under the auspices of the Central Advisory Council for Education.*)

Primary-school children in "open classrooms" are encouraged to experiment with reading and speaking, writing and listening, observing, measuring and weighing, moving, touching, drawing, painting, and when appropriate, tasting and smelling. That is, they are learning through all their senses.

Other methods of learning may also be exciting and effective for your child, as long as you don't give him the idea that he must think and work instead of feel and sense. Sometimes a parent gives a child this idea without intending to by using school as a substitute for discipline or self-control at home. For example, if your son is going through a jealous stage where he is determined to marry his mother and nothing else in his life seems to matter, or your daughter dawdles so much getting dressed in the morning that she often misses the school bus, it is tempting to deal with such situations by saying something like "Your main job right now is going to school." Although this is a true statement, it really has nothing to do with your child's emotional difficulties or scheduling problems. If you handle your child logically, you won't make school (and learning) the scapegoat. And you will help your child keep his spirit and love of life during the primary-school years.

IN THE OLDER CHILD AND ADOLESCENT. The older your child gets, the more he is exposed to the "American way of life," much of which, unfortunately, violates our senses. If he lives in the city he is crowded on street, bus, and subway. There is no joy of movement. He is surrounded by high-decibel noises that hurt his ears. The high air-pollution level makes his nose uncomfortable. Visual beauty is expensive, so out of doors we have too few plazas, fountains, or flowers; and indoors, many homes and apartments suffer from poor design. Refrigerated and frozen foods as well as chemical preservatives decrease many good taste sensations. And our hurried pace robs our senses further. Rudolf Laban, the well-known German choreographer and analyst of movement patterns said, "Too much speed makes nervous, irritable people." Nervous, irritable people lose out on sensory pleasures because they are unresponsive. Have you ever watched an expert wine-taster as he looks at the color of the wine, sniffs the bouquet, tastes the wine slowly, stops, waits, sips again? It is not often that any of us takes this much time to savor an experience.

Some children rebel against our contemporary way of life because a deprived sensory environment is making them miserable. The wrong approach to learning makes education seem dull, and working for success is meaningless if the environment stays the same. These are the teen-agers who try to "get back to their senses" by going to the country, working with their hands, growing their own food, baking bread, playing the guitar and flute, writing poetry, painting, swimming, hiking. These pursuits give them the sensory pleasures of moving, touching, hearing, speaking, seeing, tasting, and smelling that they miss elsewhere. A teen-aged girl who left home for a commune in the summer of 1970 said, "I really felt stagnant back in Michigan. I didn't know what I wanted. I felt sensually deprived." Some parents dismiss this way of life by criticizing the promiscuous sex and drug experimentation that sometimes coincide with it. But let us not lose sight of the underlying philosophy, which says that living fully is beautiful.

Living fully is also healthier, a fact that is of major concern to environmental scientists today. As they begin to solve problems ranging from overpopulation to ecology, all our senses will benefit. We will enjoy cleaner air, clearer water, purer food, a lower noise level, and the conservation of parks and natural resources. Their research will also produce better design in schools, public buildings, and homes; better utilization of space and natural light; improved artificial illumination; and perhaps more outdoor sculptures, plazas, fountains, and flowers in urban settings. This overall

improvement in our sensory world will provide natural pleasures to replace those artificially induced; the person who
placed a real-estate advertisement which boasted "Lovely
home, LSD view of Long Island" had something like this in
mind.

HOW TO IMPROVE YOUR CHILD'S
SENSORY SURROUNDINGS

There are many ways you can help improve your child's
sensory surroundings. Any work that corrects desensitizing
conditions such as air and noise pollution or overpopulation
will help your child and many others. So will work to improve conditions at your child's school, either on your own
or through a parents' association. Some schools welcome
assistance in classroom or lunchroom, and the more responsive adults there are, the better for the children's learning
potential and overall sensory awareness. You might also
check on any technical problems in the school having to do
with the use of space, lighting, or noise absorption. Often a
great deal can be done to improve seating arrangements and
light fixtures, and noise level can be lowered through inexpensive carpeting and acoustic tile.

If you are about to choose a school for your child, take his
sensory pattern into account as you visit the school. Be
aware of the overall design, freedom or restriction in movement, noise level, the visual layout of classrooms, the lunchroom procedure. If your child is sensitive to noise, for instance, the sounds of an active free-moving classroom may
be too much for him. He may need a more structured teaching situation for auditory, not disciplinary reasons. If your
daughter is a mover, notice how much the children are per-

mitted to move around. Is there a good physical education program for girls? If not, you will want to supply an active after-school activity such as dance, sports, or a heavy work project, to balance things out. (See page 53 for suggested activities).

But sensory responsiveness, like charity, begins at home. The best way to improve your child's sensory awareness is to discover the sensory makeup of your home.

8 How Does Your Home Affect Your Child's Senses?

Since environment is so important to your child's sensory awareness, you'll probably be curious about the sensory makeup of your home. You may also be apprehensive about your child's sensory weaknesses and tell yourself something like "It's all my fault; I know my child is insensitive to sound because I yell all the time." This isn't so. Your child's patterns come from inside as well as outside, and they might be the same even if you had never raised your voice.

In the second place, a normal child is so impressionable that he can easily change his responses. For instance, if Jeffrey is not "hearing" because of a sensory habit, you can change the habit by making him more aware of sounds. With a little more effort you can even change your own pattern. You can learn to make a less harsh sound, one that is lower in volume, when you yell. This won't help a bad temper, but it will improve the sound climate of your home. You don't need special instruction or classes. Since you use all your senses every day, you can alter a pattern by focusing on different aspects of yourself or your surroundings.

For instance, if you were to classify each sound you heard today during a fifteen-minute period on a scale of one to ten (softest to loudest), your awareness of volume would be greatly increased.

When it comes to your own sensory awareness, your child can often help you. He is a "newer" person, so all his sensory reactions are sharper and fresher than yours, except for those senses that you practice and use in your occupation or hobby. Even if you have a physical problem, such as near-sightedness or a trick knee, you can still learn to use your senses as fully as possible.

The same of course goes for a child with eye or ear trouble, difficulty in coordination, fallen arches, or a weak spine. After you've checked out the problem with a doctor, try to encourage your child to exercise the affected sense as intelligently as possible. If you are not sure how to do this, your pediatrician can advise you. Then, make it an exercise game and not an exercise chore. Some children end up much better than average through such practice.

Here is how you and your child can help each other. On a walk in the country with your son, he comments on a bird call. You listen, but you can't really hear the melody. It blends in with all sorts of other sounds. You are disturbed because you can't share this experience with your child. You decide to try a general hearing game with your child while you are both waiting in the dentist's office. He says, "Mommy, what's that bell ringing?" You answer, "You mean the phone next door?" "No, it's a slow, deep bell." "Oh, yes. That must be the church clock on the corner. I never noticed it before." Your child's hearing sensitivity has helped you become more aware of a sound. This should make your child feel proud of himself, and it is fun for both of you besides. In the same way you can work on your sense of seeing, touch, movement, taste, smell—first alone, and then with your child.

Now that you (hopefully) have a positive attitude toward yourself and your child's sensory environment at home, you can read ahead to discover what he hears, sees, touches, tastes, and smells.

HIS HEARING AND SPEECH

Is your home filled with a great many unavoidable sounds? Perhaps you live near a building-construction site, an airport, a super-highway, or above a noisy street. There are loud noises in the country too—jet planes, power saws, motorized lawn-mowers, bulldozers, and barking dogs. And a small space full of children is always loud.

Noise desensitizes everybody's hearing and manner of speaking. To cut down noise, you can use sound absorbers such as carpets and draperies, or, if you can afford it, use air conditioning and climate-control and close your windows to external sounds. (Although the air-conditioner makes a humming sound it is less hard on most nervous systems than varied irregular noises. In fact, acousticians call such a cover-up sound "acoustic perfume.")

Try not to use the dishwasher, clothes washer, and vacuum cleaner in a steady sequence throughout the day. Arrange some quiet time with no machine or voice sounds (especially if your child is practicing his music). Schedule television, phonograph, and radio so that the sound is not continuous. This gives ears a rest and increases hearing sensitivity. Try to lower the vocal level at home. If one person talks less loudly, others tend to follow. If the noise level is too high, you have to yell to be understood, and everybody gets louder and louder. (This often happens at cocktail parties, although everybody assumes it is only the effect of the alcohol.)

If you have a baby at home, watch how he relates to external sounds such as your singing or the click of the refrigerator door. These sounds are important to your infant because they mean warmth and food. If he hears another lady singing, or a different mechanical noise, his response will not be the same. And if he continuously hears unpleasant sounds, such as loud volume or high pitch, he will begin to block them out. This is how hearing patterns begin.

Your baby also hears and makes "internal" sounds with his voice, his tongue, his lips, and his throat. These sounds feel good to his vocal organs and sound good to his ear. And sometimes, as with "ma" or "da," they can even conjure up a parent.

By the time your child is two, he has a tremendous hearing vocabulary, both external and internal. There are sounds he likes and likes to make, sounds that frighten him, sounds that make him angry, and sounds he makes when he's angry. All this is the shape of his hearing profile, which, as he grows older, will become clearer and more defined.

How does your child react to other voices in your home? Does he imitate anybody? What does his voice sound like? His speech mirrors his hearing and vice versa. His hearing is affected by all sounds, including the sound of his own voice. If this sound is ugly, his ears become less sensitive every time he opens his mouth.

What about the sound of your own voice? Babies and children, just like animals, respond primarily to the sounds of vocal expression. You train your dog to "stay" by using the same tone of voice each time. If you say "Stay" with the same inflection you use for "Come here," the dog will come to you because the tone of your voice affects him more than the actual word. And if you punish him for disobeying the literal meaning of your words, he will be hurt and confused because he was responding honestly to the tone of your voice. An adult can hurt and confuse a child in the same way. Have you ever played this version of the "Emperor's New Clothes" with your child? You both look at the Emperor, you both know that he's naked, and yet your words admire his nonexistent robes. For example, you tell your daughter in words, "Isn't it nice that Great-Aunt Mary is coming for dinner?" but your tone says "How on earth am I going to stand that boring old biddy all evening?" You may think you are teaching your child good manners, but you are really teaching her three bad habits. First, to lie: To say one thing and mean another. Second, you are conditioning her not to hear. If you keep it up, she will soon learn to react to the actual words, rather than to the emotional color of the sounds. In the process, she will lose sensitivity in hearing. Third, you are giving your child a very negative idea about speech. By not saying what you really mean, you are indicating that talking is something you do for others, but not for yourself. She may very well decide, "It's not much fun to talk if you can't say what you feel. I'd rather not bother." And so she learns to keep her thoughts and feelings to herself rather than to share them with others. If she concludes that words never express thoughts and feelings, she may hate reading all her life.

You may be wondering how to get around a social dilemma and remain both honest and polite. It is not difficult. For example, in the above situation, you might have said in a matter-of-fact tone, "Great-Aunt Mary is coming for dinner." The chances are that your child will let it go. If she puts you on the spot by asking, "Why? You don't like her, do you?" state another fact and an opinion, such as, "Well, she talks a lot, but she's lonely and needs to visit us once in a while." This is teaching civilized behavior. If you need to let off steam about Aunt Mary, tell your husband or your friend, not your child.

Speaking should be fun. If you speak in an honest manner to your child, he will learn that speaking is fun because it gives him a chance to express himself. He will learn to blend what he says and how he says it—the words and the sound —in an effective way. This is terribly important. Success in life depends a great deal on our ability to express ourselves well vocally. It is the way we win friends and influence people.

So encourage your child to increase his vocabulary, but don't teach him to ignore the range of vocal sounds. That way he will like to listen to all types of speech. He will want to mirror the sounds with his own voice, in words and in wails and growls, with panting, gurgles, clicks and lisps, with roars and coos.

A friend of mine took his three-year-old son to a boat show. While the father was examining a houseboat, he heard a familiar fire-engine wail. He thought, "There goes Robert with that infernal noise again." But when he reached the sound, he found a second "fire-engine." Another little boy was communicating with Robert by means of *Woo-woo-woo*.

It may be easier for you to put up with these vocal experiments if you remember that your child is training his hearing, exercising his organ of speech, and practicing sound as a means of communication.

Your Child's Sensory World

HIS VISUAL, SPATIAL, AND TACTILE SENSES

What are the design characteristics of your home? Are the rooms big or small? Lots of windows, or do you wish there were more natural light? How is your home furnished? Do you have a great deal of furniture or is open space part of the design? What is the form created by your furniture? For example, French eighteenth-century antiques create a curved shape in space, whereas contemporary furniture has smooth planes. Neither one is wrong or right, but what does your child see, move through and around, and touch every day? These elements in his environment influence the shape of his visual, movement, and touch patterns.

Some other influential factors are the color scheme of the walls and furnishings, your choice of decorative objects and paintings, your use of texture in furniture, floor-coverings, and furnishings—wood, tile, plastics, wool, silk, synthetics. What is the average "climate" of your home? Do you feel stifled or comfortable at 70 degrees Fahrenheit?

Your child is also affected by the movement and touch patterns of other members of the family as well as by the texture, color, shape, and style of everyone's clothing, including his own.

VISUAL ENVIRONMENT. Even if your child is not visual, he is an experienced see-er because about 80 per cent of our information about the world comes to us through our eyes. Your child will have an individual response to what he sees, based on his interests, likes, and dislikes. He will communicate this to you verbally or in action—by imitating what attracts him, or by painting, drawing, and creating it, by moving toward or around or under it, by holding it, by running away, by throwing it, or by destroying it.

How your child communicates depends on his age and temperament, and of course there are more elements to express than just the visual. But here are a few guidelines to help you track down your child's seeing response at home.

A baby or young child will reach for, explore, and try to become part of what looks good to him. This may be a special toy, a "nest" or "trail" of furniture in the living room, a shiny mirrored surface or silver jewelry that makes light dance. He will also be attracted to light playing on water, shining through glass objects, or forming rainbows with prismatic surfaces. Your baby may be attracted by a brightly colored object such as his sister's gold sweater or a spot of sun on a red carpet. If your home were empty of bright color, your child would miss out on these visual experiences.

Your child responds actively to form. At one stage my young daughter fell in love with our coffee table, a free-form slab of English walnut. She spent long periods of time examining the whorls and grain of the wood, tracing the shape with her eye and fingers, and walking around the random shape. If our table had been of a different shape and texture, she would have had a different visual (and movement and touch) experience.

An older child will often paint or create what interests or distresses him about his surroundings. An art-teacher friend tells me that many ghetto children have a dark, dreary palette of colors—black, grays, washed-out greens, dirty pinks. One eight-year-old boy who lived in a small tenement apartment with his large family reacted against these cramped quarters by constructing a layout with flexible partitions; he also drew many "dream" floor-plans of apartments with enormous room dimensions.

Your child may hate a certain picture in a storybook and scribble over it or rip it up. I can still remember doing this at the age of four to the picture of the dying king of the first *Babar* book. He had turned green from eating a poisonous mushroom. I was frightened by the picture, and to this day I still cannot stand that shade of pastel green. This experience became part of my seeing pattern.

Your child may want to change a room by using fresh paint or paper or fabrics. Even if you have to scold him for having ruined the wall, try to figure out if he had a specific visual effect in mind (don't push it, though—he may have just felt like scribbling and pasting). Sometimes a child gets very ambitious plans about how he wants his own room to look. It may be worthwhile for you to discuss possible compromises with him and follow through on them.

An older child is usually rather direct about the appearance of his home and family and what pleases or displeases him. It is easy to get yourself all bogged down in trying to figure out his psychological motivations, or else to become so irritated that you walk away from the topic. But when your pre-teen-aged daughter announces to you that you really ought to change your hair style, take an objective look in the mirror and try to figure out what's behind the comment. Shape of your face? Line of the hair? It may give you a clue to how she's seeing, unless she was just being pointlessly critical. (If you decide she was right, of course you don't have to tell her unless you want to.)

In another very common situation, ask yourself: does your son really hate the color of his rug or bedspread? Maybe he does. You can check by getting his reaction to another object of similar color. If he dislikes that also, he probably does want a change of room color. His objections to this color may be a new pattern, or perhaps one he is more aware of now that he is older and spending time studying in his room. Speaking of growing up, have you ever stopped to think that your child sees you and your home differently as he grows taller because his eyes move to a higher level?

PHYSICAL RESPONSE TO MOVEMENT PAT-TERNS. Does your home actually affect the way in which your child moves? Yes, your child develops movement patterns through repeated exposure at home, just as he acquires speech and seeing habits. In *The Efficiency of Human Movement* Dr. Marion R. Broer says, "As a child grows, he develops a habit of aligning his body segments in a certain way. He finds a characteristic pattern of movement which is usually influenced by the models he observes and the importance of those models to him." A child may imitate a parent's way of moving even when their body types are completely different. I once knew a family where both sons unconsciously copied their father's pot-bellied posture, even though the boys themselves were not overweight. If you take a close look at your child you may be able to discover whom he admires and favors physically. Does he walk like someone else in your family? How does he hold his head? Swing his arms? In what rhythm does he tend to move his legs? Where does he sit to get comfortable—a chair with his legs slung over the arm? Sprawled out on a couch with his neck resting on the back? Does anyone else in the family relax in the same way?

Would you consider your family mobile or sedentary? What about sports? Do you play baseball or tennis? Do you ski? Swim regularly in the summertime? All of these will affect your child's movement pattern; so will the way you and others feel about the human body. Is someone at home very concerned with physical fitness? Body health? Diet? Overweight? Is there anyone who should be concerned but isn't? Are there any strong positive postural characterisitcs such as military bearing, relaxed coordination, or negative ones like sloping shoulders, curved spine, pelvis thrust forward? Unfortunately, posture has a qualitative dimension, unlike home furnishings. No particular period of furniture or color scheme is preferable for your child, but someone with good posture sets a better example than someone whose physical balance is out of line. Since few of us are perfectly balanced, it is reassuring to remember that your child has many models from which to choose; besides, posture isn't everything. I know a wonderful professor of classical languages who has a poor body but a penetrating mind. He says, "I know I'd be healthier if I exercised every day, but I'd rather read." No one can deny that he has a great deal to offer his children and grandchildren.

If your family is not active physically, you may have trouble with your pre-teen-aged child because of the current mystique of physical movement and fitness-promoting activities. Your child may become fascinated by the outdoor life: hiking, farming, and building stone walls and simple wood structures. He may press you to initiate activities like baking bread, weaving baskets and rugs, making candles, working with leather. Many young people attach a philosophical meaning beyond the physical to this type of work. In the words of Lao Tse:

> The wheelwright, the carpenter, the butcher, the swimmer, achieve their skill not by accumulating facts concerning their art, nor by energetic use either of muscles or outward senses, but through utilizing the fundamental kinship which, under-

neath apparent distinctions and diversities, unites their own primal stuff to the primal stuff of the medium in which they work.

Even if your child is extremely critical of you and the machines you make use of, there is no reason for you to change your physical pattern; you can communicate to your child the fact that while this type of activity is not your cup of tea, you understand intellectually how he feels about it. Once your child realizes that you are not against his way of life, he can stop expending so much energy in trying to convert you. You can always tell him that you would be delighted to eat home-made bread so long as he is willing to bake it.

LAYOUT. Your child's movement is also affected by your own preferences in interior decorating. That is, your arrangement of rooms and furniture forms the traffic pattern of your home, through which your child moves every day.

Is yours a physically fast or slow child? An energetic bouncy girl or boy will cover a lot of ground (literally), whereas a careful, slow child is more limited spatially. Of course each child will vary—sometimes he races around, sometimes he sits and plays (or works) in one place. But each child has a movement average. If you have a very active child, remember that he needs to spend time in a relatively free space. Many families move out of the city for this reason, but there are other possiblities. Perhaps you can set up at least part of one room with some active play equipment At one point, I had a dining room with a hanging ladder, an extension bar, and a large air-filled clown punching-bag. The table and chairs could be folded up against one wall. The room lacked elegance for dinner parties, but it had a certain surrealistic charm. If you are unwilling to have such equipment in your dining room, you might make your child's bedroom an environment with built-in furniture on several levels and a bed on a platform, so that your child can be active vertically, if not horizontally. You can also change the arrangement of his room frequently. If you think back to the last time your family moved to a new apartment or house, you will remember the fatigue you experienced, which is caused not just from the unpacking, but from your adjustment to a new spatial pattern. If your child is very active, he will like the extra steps he takes as he works this out in his rearranged room. But for both your sakes, you might want to discover some sit-down activities for him: books on subjects that interest him, or occupations that involve working with his hands in some way—art, crafts, or science projects. He needs to learn to enjoy quiet times as well, or he will have a hard time adjusting to today's way of life.

Perhaps your child has the opposite quality. For example, your daughter needs enclosed space to feel comfortable, but you prefer an interior of free-flowing space. You can make a nest for her even if she shares a room. Put pillows in a corner, make a window seat, or set up a screen or partition to give her an enclosure. But you should also find some direct means to encourage her to move around. If she hates sports and outdoor activities, perhaps you can get her a dog who will need to be exercised. Or she might like to redecorate her room with paint and some supervised carpentry. You can also rearrange her things so that she needs to move to get to them: books on different levels, or for a young child, a toy box large enough to crawl into.

Some parents forget that an older (and therefore larger) child has changed movement patterns. You should be sure to readjust your home if your child no longer "fits" where he did before: the furniture in his room, his chair or place at the dinner table—perhaps the traffic pattern in the living room if he is the oldest child. A wide-ranging five-year-old will upset furniture and objects in a living area that contains clusters of tables and chairs. You need to arrange a family room to suit the movement pattern of an older child, just as you did when he started to crawl.

ROOM TEMPERATURE AND HUMIDITY. What is the average temperature at home? Do you feel comfortable at 70 degrees or do you like an overall temperature that is cool enough to keep you awake? Is your home very hot in summer? Does the heat bother you? Everybody's skin reacts to the air temperature and humidity, but no two responses are the same.

It is natural to assume that your child feels hot or cold when you do, but this may not be so. Of course he can adapt himself, but the next time you're cold and turn up the heat, or feel stifled and throw open the window, or turn on the air conditioner, take a minute to notice your child's reaction. For instance, does your daughter really wilt in summer heat and complain a lot? You can tell her you can't change the weather, but a little sympathy is in order even if you're not affected yourself. By the same token, you can ask her to be considerate of you if you're under the weather and she isn't. Perhaps your child is a polar bear. He wants windows open, uses only a light blanket at night in winter, and seldom catches cold. Don't tell him he's wrong, even if it makes you shiver to go into his room. What feels wrong to you feels right to his body.

Your child's skin also responds to humidity in the air. If his skin is drier than yours and your home is very dry in winter, it may make his skin itchy and his disposition cranky.

He's unlikely to tell you about it because the cause of the condition is not obvious to him, but if you have ever taken a winter holiday in a warm climate (or a steam bath, for that matter), you will have some understanding of his situation. Remember how nice the change in humidity can feel on your skin; you can almost sense the pores opening up.

AIR CURRENTS AND WATER TEMPERATURE. Air currents (draft or wind) and water are two other elements that affect your child's skin. Some of us like the feel of air blowing on us, some of us don't. Your child's body may be particularly sensitive to drafts in one area, such as the back of his neck or his arms. If his place at the dinner table is near a fan or an air conditioner, he'll be uncomfortable even if you're sitting next to him and are not bothered at all.

Every child has a different response to water temperature. Your eight-year-old daughter may like a bath so hot that the feeling of it on your hand makes you gasp. Incidentally, when you take your child swimming, remember his individual response and don't tell him, "The water's not cold" if he says it's freezing. You are each right in your own way.

CLOTHING. When your child is young, you'll select clothing for him that is attractive and appropriate to the weather. But here again, you may forget that your child responds to weather differently from the way you do. Warm, bulky clothing feels terrible to the skin of a child whose natural body temperature is high, and clothing that is too lightweight makes the skin of a cold-sensitive child contract —sometimes into goose pimples.

Children also vary in their response to the texture of clothing. An extreme skin reaction to wool or nylon shows up as a rash, but a less severe irritation may just make your child feel uncomfortable. You might keep this in mind if he consistently refuses to wear a new garment. Also, check the texture of his favorites: soft denim? orlon? banlon?

Now think of your child's clothing and shoes in relation to fit. A tight pair of pants will chafe his skin and narrow shoes will leave a pressure mark. But there are less extreme pulls and pinches that might also affect your child if he is sensitive to touch. For instance, is your daughter's closet full of unworn shoes that you urged her to buy? At the shoe store, does she spend long minutes smoothing every wrinkle out of her socks, easing her foot into the shoe, walking in it, adjusting the straps or laces, only to inform you that it doesn't feel right? Do you get so impatient that you pick a pair for her, take it home, only to find that she hardly wears it? Or does your child just refuse to put on his new jacket because he says it feels tight even after you've checked the shoulders and arms and find nothing wrong? Before you lose your temper, remember that when it comes to his skin, only your child knows how he feels. Some children are literally more thin-skinned than others—like the fairy-tale princess who felt a pea through twenty mattresses. This kind of child will complain a great deal because his skin bruises, chafes and blisters when it comes into contact with an unfriendly surface. Though "thin skin" can ruin a professional boxer's career, it often gives a beautiful translucent glow to a child's appearance. So it is not really such a disadvantage so long as you're aware of it.

Sometimes a child has the opposite problem: his skin is so insensitive that he does not complain when he should (at least not right away). You may notice a pressure point on his feet or a chafe mark on his body, but you'll have to track down what caused it.

HOME FURNISHINGS. How does your child's skin respond to your home furnishings? Does he like to run his hand over the polished-wood coffee table or feel the corners and curves of an ash tray or knick-knack? Does he have a favorite chair or place on the floor? What is the feel of the fabric or carpet? Smooth, velvetlike nap? Rough nubble weave? Is it warm from the radiator or the sun? How about the touch-sensation underfoot? Do you have springy carpets or cool tile? Does your child like to go barefoot indoors?

Your child's room should contain some touch sensations that please him—underfoot and everywhere else: these can be supplied by the rug, bed, bedspread, chair, desk, and smaller things like soft throw-pillows, stuffed animals, or smooth glass objects. A friend of mine once took her four-year-old daughter Susie shopping for her new quilt. Susie, a very tactile child, made her selection by running her forefinger back and forth along the top of the fabric, a little ritual she carried on every night before falling asleep. A quilt that didn't feel right to Susie would have upset her entire sleep routine. No matter what age your child is, you can relate to his touch pattern when you furnish his room. Whether he says so or not, he's sure to appreciate it.

MANUAL DEXTERITY. Is there a handy man or woman at home? Someone who knows how to fix clocks and appliances? How about skill in other fields which involve fine touch ability, such as music, art, crafts, sewing, cooking, hobbies such as shell collecting? There is usually at least one person in a family who is good with his hands in such activities as applying makeup, shaving, writing by hand, typewriting, chopping up onions and parsley. A young child will try to imitate these touch patterns just as he copies movement patterns, and his own way of using his hands depends on his model, his aptitude, and your attitude.

No child is as handy as an adult, but if you encourage your child's efforts regardless of his skill, he will gain confidence and keep trying. If you put down his attempts or fail to show him what to do when he can't manage, or just take over the job yourself, he will begin to think of himself as clumsy and he won't enjoy using his hands. This is a real disadvantage in life, even if he learns to joke about it when he grows up: "I can't even boil water," or "I'm all thumbs with a screwdriver."

A multitude of important activities, from dressing and eating to writing and figuring at school, all need some degree of manual dexterity. Children vary in the ability to use their hands, and there are other reasons why a child may be having trouble. For example, your daughter might be in the dawdle stage, when she hates to get dressed in the morning. Or she may be expressing the opinion that she hates school. She may have a problem with food, so she bangs around with her knife and fork instead of trying to eat. Your child may not like his teacher, so his written work is messy, his arithmetic illegible. There may be a visual difficulty, which affects eye-hand coordination. Or there may be a serious functional or organic disorder, such as brain damage or mental retardation. But most frequently, your child will have acquired a touch habit that is not very efficient and can be easily improved.

Almost every child needs a simple bit of instruction now and then. Once my daughter had a new eight-year-old friend over for dinner. Elaine was a darling, and obviously on her best behavior. But she sawed away at her veal cutlet without being able to cut the meat. I noticed that she was dangling her knife from a bent wrist, and applying no pressure. When I showed her how to make her knife slice into the meat, she had no further trouble.

For some reason, parents tend to stop teaching such things when children get to be three or four years old. Some children have enough ability to figure out how to work almost everything. This ability is often connected with mechanical aptitude. They can fix zippers, clocks, electrical gadgets. And it is good to let your child explore an object alone, before you make any comment. But an average child may need help in learning how to hold a needle or a jackknife. Not just a quick "Don't hurt yourself" but concrete pointers such as "Sit easy, and hold the knife and the wood slightly away from you," or "Press the knife hard only as you scrape the wood; don't clutch the wood and knife so tightly," or "If you try to shell the peas that quickly, they'll fall on the floor. Start off slowly and soon you'll get the hang of it and catch up to me." This is not interfering, but teaching your child how to succeed at a task. And nothing is worse for his ego than a series of botched-up jobs, even though he may have "done it all himself."

Some parents hinder their children in acquiring tactile ability without meaning to. If your four-year-old daughter has graduated to the family dinner table, she needs a cushion or book to raise her up so that her hands can function well when she eats. She also needs a support for her feet, so they don't dangle in the air. It's as if you were to sit on a high stool, let your feet hang loosely, hold your arms up and out at chest level, and try to set your watch accurately. So when your child sits down to practice the piano, write, or eat, make sure that his overall position is the right one to accomplish the job.

COMMUNICATION BY TOUCH. Does your family communicate mostly by words or do you also use your sense of touch? Most parents try to give their babies a certain amount of cuddling, but what about other touch communication? Do you enjoy expressing affection by holding your child on your lap or hugging him when he wakes up in the morning? Do you comfort your child when he's hurt or sad by putting your arm around him? Do you like protecting your child by holding his hand or arm when you cross a busy street? How do you react when your child brushes against you by accident? Kisses you good-bye in the morning? Leans against you for warmth or comfort? If your child doesn't do these things very often, you may not have encouraged him to communicate by touch. This is too bad, but it's never too late to start.

If you decide to practice more communication by touch, remember that timing is important. A warm hug will not mean affection to your child if he is racing outdoors to play with a friend. It will just mean an obstacle to be pushed aside. It's up to the parent to be aware of the circumstances. But a misunderstanding is nobody's fault. If your child is in a hurry and you don't know it, and reach out to him, explain how you feel so he can become more aware of others. Something like, "I guess you're in a hurry, but if you don't tell me and just brush me aside, it hurts my feelings."

Here's another touch situation where a parent can help— when your child is communicating something by touch but is not aware of it himself. For example, your son may handle everything and everybody too roughly. He grabs your arm playfully. You yell, "Ouch!" and he says reproachfully, "That didn't hurt." What he means is "I'm not mad at you, so I know I didn't hurt you." Point out to him that this isn't so. After all, it's *your* skin, and if he wants to touch your arm playfully, he must adjust the pressure of his hand so that it is pleasant for you, not painful. Just remind him to keep his sense of touch flexible. When he grows up, his wife and children will appreciate this training in touch awareness.

Be observant of your child's other touch communications. They should vary depending on the circumstances. For instance, when your daughter comes home from school, touches your arm, and says, "Hey, Ma, guess what? I'm on the basketball team," her touch should be more firm than when she reaches out to you and says, "Mom, can you see if I've got something in my eye?" A free tactile pattern is expressive of many emotions, just like the tonal variations in a speaking voice. If your child's touch is always soft or always firm, it's like a voice that is a monotone. It means that something is out of balance and if this pattern continues for a long time you should check with a doctor.

Sometimes children go through stages where they are embarrassed about touch as communication. You can handle this in any one of a number of ways, depending on your own touch pattern. Psychiatrists advise parents against behavior that could be misinterpreted by a child who is going through a psychosexual stage. But there are many physical ways to indicate warmth, affection, and reassurance without being at all ambiguous. It all depends on how you do it. An arm around the shoulder and even a kiss on the cheek can be loving and in no way seductive. In fact, if you're naturally outgoing, and your child is having difficulties, it can make things worse for him if you suddenly stop any physical contact. He might think that he really doesn't deserve your affection any more. Of course, he may not feel like responding to you, but that doesn't mean you shouldn't reach out to him if it seems appropriate.

Some children are very ingenious about finding adaptations to difficult touch situations. They may get very ticklish all of a sudden. It is not an open hostility, but it certainly prevents anyone from being affectionate physically. Other children seem to be ticklish all the time, even though they're full of love.

Here's how one little girl of five used touch to express feelings she could not verbalize. She was angry at her mother because of a new baby brother, and needed comfort, but didn't want to admit it. Periodically she'd say, "Mommy, here comes the kitty" and climb into her mother's lap, snuggle up, and "purr." Mother was supposed to stroke her hair gently. It worked very well for both of them.

If your child is a rough toucher and is trying to become more gentle, he needs a chance to let loose occasionally with someone who doesn't mind—perhaps his father, a friend or even a punching bag. Perhaps there is a chance for him to groom a horse, or rough-house with a large dog.

Most children know how to tease by touch. A big sister keeps stroking her little sister's arm over and over, like a machine. The little one yells, "Cut it out!" The big one says very innocently, "What did *I* do?" You need to let her know that touch can be as telling as words.

HIS TASTE SENSITIVITY

Your child's sense of taste is probably more affected by family habits than his other senses. This is because taste sensitivity depends on how and what you eat—two factors that your child can't always control. For instance, taste buds don't work well if you gulp your food in a big rush, so if everyone in the family always hurries through mealtimes it's hard for your child to become a taster. If everyone eats much more than he needs (which also decreases taste sensations), your child probably will too. In the sad event that there is often not enough food, hunger will drown out taste. If food is a real problem to someone in the family who is very heavy or very thin or seriously ill, your child may not really want to enjoy eating and tasting.

You yourself can unintentionally distract your child from the pleasure of tasting by too much emphasis on posture and manners, and also by too little—so that he feels like a slob and doesn't know what to do about it. A parent who serves a child a too-large portion and then asks him to clean his plate is also killing taste.

Your young child cannot prepare his own meals, so his sense of taste is at the mercy of the cook and the family food budget. A monotonous diet, poor quality, and poor preparation of food will not encourage a child to explore his sense of taste. If your family has average eating habits, however, your child will have leeway for increasing his awareness of taste.

Does your child enjoy his sense of taste? Many mothers are so eager for their child to be a good eater that they lose sight of what eating is all about. Everyone has to eat to stay alive, so nature through our sense of taste made eating fun. A good eater is really someone who enjoys tasting, and conversely, if your child doesn't really taste, he can't really get much pleasure out of eating. Furthermore, eating that is not pleasurable is not good for his digestive juices or his teeth. Worst of all, it puts him out of step with himself because the way in which he relates to food and drink affects the way he feels about himself, and vice versa. So many family and communal activities revolve around food—parties and business gatherings, christenings, confirmations and bar mitzvahs, weddings, wakes—that a nontasting eater really has a problem. If your child enjoys tasting he will be in a pleasant frame of mind, which will help him socially.

Does your child have a pattern in taste? Yes, definitely. The ability to taste can be coarsened or heightened just as your hearing can be deadened or made more acute. Some of us are born with more taste sensitivity than others. Psychologist Conrad Mueller compares this with color awareness and color blindness. Everyone's taste abilities vary throughout the day and are affected by individual hormones and blood-sugar function. Eating habits will also affect your taste pattern. For example if you've been on a diet and have avoided sweets for a few weeks, a candy bar will taste too sweet to you at first. You will also become aware of the sweet taste in hidden places, such as apples or oranges, which was drowned out in your previous way of eating.

A long-range change in taste patterns occurs through the growing up process. Children have more sweet taste buds than adults, so an ice cream sundae may taste great at five and much too sweet at forty-five. For all these reasons, a parent should remember that what he tastes is different from what his child tastes.

Does your child rush through meals? If your child often gulps his food without much chewing, he is decreasing his taste sensations. He may be doing this because he always feels in a hurry or because the food is soft and goes down easily (like much commercially produced white bread). But chewing is what releases the taste. When his teeth cut open the food, a chemical reaction occurs in the mouth which gives him a sensation of sweet, sour, salty, and bitter, or a combination of these tastes. Chewing food also releases the odor, which adds to your child's eating pleasure. Other sensory experiences that make eating fun are the appearance of the food, its feel or texture, its temperature, and the sound made by chewing crisp food like lettuce or carrots. When your child races through a meal, he robs himself of all these pleasures (in addition to the bad things he is doing to his digestion and to his teeth). To keep your child from hurrying, help him become aware of what he is missing. This will get better results than the familiar "don't gulp your food." You can ask him to find where in his mouth the taste is most pronounced or to close his nose for a second and notice the difference in taste. (For more ideas, see the general tasting games on page 286.)

Does your child eat too much? If your child overeats, he is tasting less. Scientific tests show that the sensation of taste diminishes after the initial stimulus. In other words, the more you eat of one thing the less you taste it. Many of us are notorious overeaters, and we've only recently got over the idea that we should stuff our infants because a fat baby is a healthy baby. As a matter of fact, body types vary and many children are healthier when they are thin. Recent research in New York at Mount Sinai Hospital and Rockefeller University indicates that overfeeding in childhood produces excess fat cells that become a permanent part of the body. The fat child will probably become a fat adult whose metabolism will demand more food than is really good for him. He can never be a food taster.

Is your child adventuresome in taste? Does he enjoy many taste sensations? Variety is the spice of taste, according to food scientists. Certain tastes harmonize while others clash. Although what blends with what is not yet established scientifically, the French have long been empirical masters of the taste palate. A good French meal is a work of art from beginning to end, and the child of a gourmet gets taste training from an early age. He will be given samples of the appetizer, perhaps a delicately seasoned liver paté, followed by hot onion soup with grated cheese, and a sip or two of the accompanying dry white wine. Like his parents, he will nibble some crusty bread to clear his palate for the main course, which might be grilled steak with vegetables, each served with an individual sauce to complement the flavor. With this course he takes a few sips of a red wine, perhaps one that his father can recognize by year and vineyard from the taste alone. Next, a salad to clear the palate, followed by cheese and crackers, and for dessert, fresh fruit or sweet pastry. Sometimes a third wine is served with the cheese course— white, and sweeter than the other. The adults finish the meal with demitasse followed by a liqueur or brandy. Undoubtedly these pleasurable taste combinations will someday have an explanation based on a scientific relationship, just as modern medicine recognizes the healing properties of some medieval drugs.

Your child probably won't have such elaborate taste opportunities, but he can develop an appreciation of taste variations within your own particular menu, especially if you encourage him to sample new foods. However, your child can't taste what isn't there, and many of our food products lose taste through extended refrigeration or the addition of chemical preservatives that prevent food from going stale or bad but also affect taste, as well as nutritive value. Some manufactured food products cut corners in price, but also in taste: imitation milk, substitute whipped cream, processed cheese, non-dairy custards. One company advertised such products in a food-trade journal with the caption "Only Bossie knows for sure." I doubt it.

If you stop to look at and listen to television ads for children's cereals, you will notice that many more of them stress energy than good taste, but recent investigations of nutrition have raised questions about the actual food value. Perhaps the new trend toward natural foods will give us back both our nutrition and our taste.

GOOD SMELLS, BAD SMELLS, AND YOUR CHILD'S BEHAVIOR

Does your child hate the smell of milk? Many children do (the smell, not the taste). If you mask the smell with a little vanilla flavoring and some sweetening, your child may be happy to drink milk, even though the taste is much less changed than he thinks. As we eat and drink, the odor of food reaches our nose, first on the way to our mouth and then again from the interior of the mouth cavity.

Another characteristic smell at home is the burnt odor of slightly charred toast. Some young ones don't mind these odors; others are really hard put to keep from gagging. If your child is like this, don't blame him for being difficult. He really can't control his response to odor.

Your child could probably lead a full life with no sense of smell, but the lack would certainly decrease his pleasure. Just think how dull food tastes when your nose is stuffed up. And because smell is connected with vivid memory impressions, your child probably has some favorite experiences related to smells, like the pine odor of a Christmas tree, newly cut grass, or the aroma of a freshly opened can of coffee. His nose is also able to warn of such hazards as fire and tainted food.

Your child has his own pattern of using his nose—some of

us are very sensitive to smell, others less so. Scientists have no standardized test for smells because they're not sure how the nose works. For instance, they don't understand if there is a relationship between the chemical composition of vanilla and what your child experiences. They do know that some of us smell substances that others cannot, but how do you standardize a sniff? Where do you find an odor-free room for tests? Each odor mixes with the one before—for example, vanilla smells different in a kitchen where cookies are baking in the oven than it does in a kitchen where someone is slicing apples for a pie. And like taste, odors decrease in intensity after the first whiff and vary according to the temperature of the item that gives off the odor.

Luckily, you don't need to know how the nose works in order to be aware of your child's sense of smell. It doesn't really matter whether or not you can smell what he does because the odor won't evoke precisely the same response in you. But you can keep in mind the following:

1. He may be smelling odors that you can't.

2. Even if you are both aware of the same odor, your responses may be different, and his reaction is as valid as yours.

3. Memories of all kinds hinge on your child's sense of smell.

For instance, if your child says, "Ugh, I hate the smell of that paint," don't say, "It doesn't smell" just because you're not aware of it. Think how annoyed you'd be if an adult challenged you like this. Or if your child says the cigarette smoke in the car is making him sick, give him the benefit of the doubt. Don't assume, just because the smell doesn't bother you, that he's being fussy. Or if he says, "This room smells like rain," ask him what he means. What he smells may remind him of a walk in the country after a storm, and you'll end up sharing a happy memory. This receptive type of approach to your child's expression of his sensory perceptions will work for all of his sensory experiences at home, and should bring the two of you much closer together.

Games for Expanding Your Child's Sensory World and Your Own

9 How to Play Sensory Games with Your Child

You can easily increase your child's awareness and your own as well. In the following chapters, you will find a more detailed explanation of each sense, how you can find your own sensory pattern, plus games and exercises that you can practice with your child during the times you normally spend together. In this chapter, I have briefly mentioned a few basic points about approach, selection, and preparation for the parent.

You and your child will both be amazed at how quickly you can improve sensitivity simply by focusing on one of the senses that you ordinarily use in everyday living. Start with any sense that interests you and skip around. The order I chose seemed to be the clearest to me for describing the games, even though it differs from the order of senses in Part I. For example, in my opinion seeing is so complex that I have placed it farther along in Part III for better comprehension. But, of course, your sensory pattern may be different from mine.

Approach.   You and your child should enjoy these activities as if playing a game. The word "game" applies to the manner of playing, but not in a frivolous way. Although you're not playing to win, your goal is serious: to maintain or improve your child's sensory response.

Selection. At the back of the book is a guide that lists each game and its purpose (page 305). The general games are for every child and can be played almost anywhere. The specific games are designed as practice games to work out a difficulty: the fifth seeing game, for example, should improve the spacing of your child's written work; the third hearing game should help your child to focus on listening to rhythms.

Preparation for the Parent. If you have awareness of the sense involved in a game, you certainly need no preparation. That is, a musician is aware of hearing because he practices hearing every day. And probably, if you play an instrument, or especially enjoy music, or even just hate loud noise or ugly voices, you are sensitive to sound—hearing is one of your more developed senses.

But what about your other senses that may be less well-developed? Suppose you want to play a seeing game with your child but you have trouble parking a car or you often lose your way. You will need a little sensory practice yourself first. The introductory section of the chapter on visual awareness will help you by describing the characteristics of what you see: form, color, light and shade, spatial relationships. You will also learn how to discover your own pattern *within* a sense. You may have a very keen color sense but a poor sense of spatial relationships, which you need in order to park a car efficiently. As we get older, we develop such variations within our overall sensory pattern. Here is a simplified example of an adult overall sensory pattern. At the age of three, Roger was clearly a "seeing" child. He explored form, shape, color, and spatial relations. He was less sensitive to sounds and was bored by children's phonograph records. At ten, Roger did very well in mathematics and science (both involving his visual awareness) and also became interested in playing the drums (hearing rhythm and volume but not melody.) At thirty-three, Roger is employed as a structural engineer. He is using his aptitude in seeing, but he concentrates on form and spatial relations more than on the color. In fact, his office is decorated in black, white, and shades of gray. For entertainment, Roger prefers art films, but he owns some records of Latin dance music (rhythm), which he finds relaxing.

Roger's overall sensory pattern stresses the form and space areas of seeing, and the rhythm part of hearing. If he takes a walk with his three-year-old daughter, she may admire a melodic bird call which he does not really "hear." If he wants to share this experience with her, he will need to resensitize his awareness of pitch and melody. And if Roger wants to help his ten-year-old son in beginning French, he will need a basic awareness of hearing and speaking before he starts. He can achieve this by reading the beginning of Chapters 10 and 11 on hearing and speaking. If he wants to, he can test himself by playing a general hearing game with his daughter.

When it comes to seeing, Roger does not need practice (unless he wants to refresh his sensitivity to color). He can add his own knowledge to his children's sensory experience. If his daughter says, "That little man down the street would fit in my doll's house," he may answer, "No, he looks small because he's far away from your eye. But compare his size to that parked car next to him. I'll bet the man is a lot taller than I am." Roger is playing a variation of the seeing game described on pages 237–239. If he wants more ideas, he can glance through the other seeing games and the creative seeing activities for children.

Whether you are already fully aware of a particular sense or need some preparation first, sooner or later you should be able to play any of the following games with your child.

10 How to Increase Awareness of Sounds and Voices

Do you hear what your child hears? No two people respond to sounds in the same way, but if you are aware of what sounds make your child jump or cringe (loud voices? the electric knife-sharpener?) or give him special pleasure (rain on the roof?), then your hearing is sensitive. Your sensitivity to the sounds around you helps your child in many ways, and adds zest to your own life too.

If you want to improve your hearing awareness, the best way is to review what characterizes a sound and what types of sound affect you most strongly, either positively or negatively (your hearing pattern).

TYPES OF SOUND

How would you describe a sound? Imagine a glass shattering on your bathroom floor. You know that it is not a plate breaking because the sound is different. A glass and a plate hit a hard surface with characteristic noises which we recognize. One noise is not necessarily higher or lower, louder or softer than the other, but the sounds are different in quality. This difference is called *timbre*. Now imagine two instruments playing the same tone: a guitar and a piano, or an oboe and a clarinet. Can you tell them apart? You may not even be aware that the tone is the same, because the timbre or quality of each instument is so different.

Can you recognize your child's voice on the phone, no matter what mood he is in? Probably. He may be whispering, whining, matter-of-fact, or yelling, but the basic sound belongs to your child and only your child. In fact, some crime laboratories use voice prints as well as fingerprints because no two voices are exactly alike. A machine known as an oscillograph will make a visual image of these differences for purposes of identification; a skilled interpreter can recognize the basic timbre of a voice and also any attempt at disguising the voice, for instance by a kidnapper demanding ransom.

Close your eyes and try to identify objects by their timbre. You may hear a motor humming, a car moving, people talking, sounds like those of dogs, crickets, and birds. Now try to be aware of what the timbre tells you about the object. You hear the motor of a powerful car idling. How do you know it is not a jalopy? Because your ear can recognize that it has more cylinders and that they are better tuned. These facts register, even if you know very little about cars. Mechanical factors create a characteristic sound, or timbre, which tells us first what the object is and second how it works. And in the case of your child, the timbre of his voice reveals what mood he is in.

Pitch describes whether the sound you hear has a high, middle, or low tone. A police siren is high. So are screeching brakes and squeaky chalk. Queen Elizabeth and Jackie Onassis have high adult voices. So does Tiny Tim. And all of us have higher voices when we're young.

A foghorn has a low sound. So do a lion's roar and the motor of a truck climbing a hill. Most film actors who play cowboys have low voices, from the late Gary Cooper to John Wayne to James Arness. Carol Channing and Mae West have low female voices.

Some adults have lost sensitivity to pitch, but small children are extremely sensitive to it. They are like dogs—a very high sound can really cause pain. So if your daughter keeps whining when you take her on the subway for the first time, listen for the high-pitched sound of the scraping wheels before you tell her to stop fussing over nothing. Like adults, children prefer a rich speaking voice, male or female, to a squeaky, twangy voice that's like an electric guitar.

Volume and *Rhythm,* the other two elements of sound, bring to mind noises in nature, such as thunder claps or ocean waves, or a man-made example of volume and rhythm, rock music. The rhythmic beat of the music repeats over and over like a machine, and the volume is tremendous. We know scientifically that volume needs to be controlled, or it can injure hearing. A successful rock show in California was closed recently when a hearing expert testified that the cast would suffer permanent hearing damage over a period of months. Planes crashing through the sound barrier can smash windows, let alone our eardrums, and experiments with plants indicate that a steady diet of acid rock will kill them.

Although you can't protect yourself and your child from all loud noise, try to find some oasis of gentler sound now and then. Even in the city, you can tune in softer music at home, find quieter voices in places such as the library, and focus outdoors on the peaceful sound of water in a fountain or wind rustling the leaves of a tree. This keeps you sensitive to degrees of volume, and helps you hear better as well. It is also good for your whole system to be still now and then. That's why hospitals stress silence.

Rhythm surrounds us everywhere. Any pattern of sound is a rhythm and therefore all machines have rhythm because they perform actions over and over, which makes a sound pattern. Children love to hear a washing machine or a dishwasher because of the changing sound cycles. For the same reason, a clothes dryer or vacuum cleaner are not very interesting in terms of sound. Listen to rhythms yourself for a few hours. What pattern of sound do your shoes make on the sidewalk? How about an old man with a cane? A child running? Can you hear construction rhythms—pile driver, bulldozer, pneumatic hammer? Do you hear rhythms of people working, such as scraping paint off a wall, or sweeping a stoop, or collecting garbage cans? Provided you're not trying to sleep, the clanging of garbage cans sounds rather nice, but an adult may be turned off by the thought of the smelly garbage. If you can overcome this kind of hearing prejudice, you will be closer to your child's world of sound.

YOUR OWN HEARING PATTERN

What types of sound affect you the most? Once you can differentiate types of sound, you will be able to find out what sounds you like and what sounds make you jumpy and irritable. How about sounds with loud volume and high pitch, such as a baby's screaming? Some mothers cannot tolerate the sound above and beyond the anxiety caused by their child's screams. Dr. Spock advises such a mother to get out of the house at least twice a week, in order to give her ears and nerves a rest. There is no reason why you cannot do the same if your son keeps playing his favorite rock record. You can explain to him what the sound does to you, and arrange to be out of the room or out of the house when he plays the record. You might also mention his own sensitivity in a different hearing situation. "You know how you hate it when I leave a faucet dripping in the kitchen? The rhythm drives you crazy. Well, I feel the same way about the loud sound in your rock record." Notice that you're not insulting his record, because you're describing only one characteristic of the music which you happen not to enjoy. And if he is hurt, you can point out some melodic or rhythmic factor that doesn't bother you.

Once you are aware of your hearing pattern, you can help your whole family. Do you like music with a pretty tune, such as a folk ballad or perhaps an opera? You probably have a feel for melody, for various combinations of tonal pitch. Suppose your husband loves Latin music with a beat. Then he probably relates more strongly to rhythm. You may still argue about what records to buy, but at least you'll understand why—each of you has a different hearing pattern.

You will find that your sensitivity to sounds varies. For instance, some women are much more aware of loud volume when they are premenstrual than at other times. If you want to explain to someone how a sound affects you at such times, you might say that it's like hearing a loud noise when one has a hangover.

Be sure to take a look at your *own* sound—your speaking voice. Do you like to speak? Are you aware of it when you use speech as a weapon to hurt others, not just with biting, sarcastic words but with ugly abrasive sounds? How you feel affects the expression on your face and the sound you make with your voice. The sounds have a meaning separate from the words. Do you remember the voice of the stereotyped Nazi officer of 1940s films, or of Charlie Chaplin in *The Great Dictator*? Loud volume, rasping vocal timbre, high pitch, machine-gun rhythm. The message conveyed was: "I am stronger than you" *(loud volume),* "I hate you. I'm going to tell you to do something awful, and you'd better do it or else . . ." *(rasping timbre, high pitch).* "And if you don't understand what I want you to do, try harder" *(fast rhythm).* The words were German-sounding gibberish, but we all understood the meaning.

If possible, listen to your own voice on a tape recorder. Is it breathy? Does it have a nasal quality or timbre? How do you pronounce your words? Distinctly? explosively? sloppily? Don't forget that this sound is as present in your home as your furniture. If this idea upsets you, why not fix your voice? It doesn't have to be a major project. Just listen and experiment, listen and change. You can do it in five minutes if you concentrate.

You will observe that your baby or child is more affected by the tone of your voice than by the words, just like a dog. If your child goes to school, ask him what he thinks of his teacher's voice. On parents' visiting day, close your eyes and listen. It may be an ear-opener!

Keeping your ears open will provide information or a pleasurable experience that you may be missing. And a revitalized hearing and speaking awareness will help your relationship to your child and to everyone else.

HEARING GAMES

LISTEN TO THE WORLD
Any Age

This game is suitable for a child of any age and can be played anywhere. Besides being fun, it helps your child to become more aware of the world around him, and helps you to discover what your child likes to hear.

Pick a time when there is nothing else to do, perhaps when you are standing at a bus stop or waiting at the dentist's office. Both of you close your eyes and listen. After a minute, open your eyes and ask your child what he heard. He may answer, "An airplane, some cars, and a wooshy sound which was the wind blowing." You may think that last sound was traffic, but it doesn't really matter what it actually is. The main thing is to hear it and identify the *type* of sound. Traffic does sound like the wind blowing because both involve the interaction between air and an object. If your child is interested and you are knowledgeable, you can discuss this similarity with him, or you may want to check the scientific explanation in a book or with someone else. My daughter developed a real sense for physics through conversations like this with her father. It is a wonderful way to learn.

On the other hand, if your child is very imaginative, and says, "I hear a giant blowing out a candle," don't discourage him. He heard the same sound; he merely translated it into a new image, which shows intelligence, creativity, and a poetic feel for words.

In any case, don't spend too much effort on classifying the sounds by timbre, pitch, volume, or rhythm. Let the child tell you in his own way: "I hear a baby bird and it sounds nice. Soft and high and cuddly."

Incidentally, this is a good game for especially busy parents who sometimes have to spend what little time they have with their children in necessary chores: visits to doctors; going shopping for clothes or shoes; going to and from a music or dance class. A listening game can make such routine activities interesting and fun.

LISTEN TO A PLACE
Any Age

This game, like the previous one, is suitable for a child of any age, is fun, helps the child to become more aware of his surroundings, and helps you to discover what your child likes to hear. However, in this game the hearing process is more selective because your child listens to sounds in a particular place and relates them to one another and to the environment. During a trip to the zoo, listen to the bird cries: some shrill, some melodious, some raucous. See if your child can match the sound to the bird. It's not easy, especially with a parrot, who projects his "speech" like a ventriloquist. Some birds sound the way they look, others don't.

Visit the large felines—lions, tigers, panthers, cheetahs. You will hear two distinct sounds—a deep chesty roar and a high whiny snarl, but it's hard to match each sound with its owner unless you're looking right at the animal.

If you live on a farm or somewhere in the country, your child can play this game listening to any group of animals: a herd of cows, a flock of chickens, the neighborhood dogs, the birds nesting near your home. To follow up he might talk to a forest ranger or state conservation officer about animal and bird sounds. A veterinarian would be able to tell him about the variations in sounds when animals are sick.

Here are some other good "sound" places to visit together, where you can play this game. Go to a harbor and hear the water lapping against different objects: large, small, metallic, wood piers, boats, barrels. Can you and your child tell which is which with eyes closed? How does the rhythm change with the wake of a passing boat? Do you hear the wooden sound of boats rubbing against a pier? Are there any seagulls calling? How does their cry differ from a similar cry of a bird in an enclosed area? What happens to the volume of the sound as the bird flies toward you or away from you into the distance?

Go to a restaurant and listen to the clatter of preparing and serving food. Hear the type of "china" being used—heavy and sturdy, more delicate, perhaps plastic. If it is a lunch counter, listen to the sound of the food as it is being prepared. Is it sizzling on a grill, or whirring in a blender? What kinds of people eat there? What is the sound pattern of their conversation?

Find a place with an echo, and experiment with your voices. What happens to low tones or high, shrill tones? How does your natural speaking voice sound, or a whisper? There are many scientific applications here also, such as a study of bats and of sonar, and how echoes provide orientation. If you know someone who is blind, he might explain to your child how he interprets sounds and their source.

By now you probably realize that you can play this game almost anywhere, city or country, indoors or out. It is just a question of focusing your hearing and encouraging your child to do the same.

WHAT DOES THAT VOICE SOUND LIKE? (DETECTIVE GAME)
Ages: 5–12

This game explores what your child hears in other people's voices. Besides being fun, it helps your child to become more aware of speech sounds, and helps you to discover what your child hears in speech. Most children have an intuitive ability to characterize people by their speech: monster, mean lady, tired old man, vampire. With a little practice, you can help him to track down what he is hearing in the speech, just like Sherlock Holmes.

The next time your child makes a personal remark about how someone speaks, ask him what he means. For instance, suppose you and your child are riding on a bus and he blurts out "That man talks just like a monster." After you get off, and you've told him not to comment so loudly next time, ask him why the man sounded like a monster to him. Probably the timbre of the voice was hollow like a drum; the pitch was low, the volume loud and the rhythm slow. He may have heard breath mixed in with the tone, which can sound unearthly.

My own children at a roadside diner overheard a lady in the next booth who, according to them, talked "like a mouse." Translation: She spoke very rapidly in a high-pitched voice which spit out all the sharp consonants: *b,p,t,s.* A second apt comparison: "She sounds like a 33 1/3 r.p.m. record played at 78 r.p.m."

When you play this game, here are some things to listen for: How does the person breathe? Does he seem nervous because he takes short, gasping breaths? Does he sound tired or old because his breath runs out? How does the person use his lips, tongue, teeth, and throat to articulate the consonants? Does he enunciate clearly or does he sound sloppy? Does he speak with a dialect or accent? If so, which sounds are different? A Russian or Hungarian might say *d* instead of *th,* and roll his *r*'s. A Scotsman will also roll his *r*'s; so might the Midwesterner, but in a different way—he curls his tongue. The Frenchman might say *z* for *th;* the German *v* for *w.* If you know the appropriate foreign language, you could show your child what speech sounds in that language would be hard for us to say.

Notice the timbre of the voice. Is it raspy and throaty, like Jimmy Durante's, nasal like Bugs Bunny's "What's up, Doc?," or childlike and high like the voice of the cartoon character Rocky, the Flying Squirrel. Does the person speak too loudly, too softly, or does the volume vary so that the words are hard to understand? Is the rhythm appropriate? Some people race through their words as if to get it over with. Others talk so slowly that you forget where they started. Most people speed up when they're excited. Their voice will also rise in pitch, even if it was too high to start with.

DO WORDS ALWAYS MEAN WHAT THEY SAY? ("EMPEROR'S NEW CLOTHES" GAME)
Ages: 6–12

This game helps your child to become more aware of words and feelings, and it helps you to discover how vocal sounds affect your child. It is based on the story "The Emperor's New Clothes"; the idea is to find a situation where the words of the speaker do not express what he means. For instance, the next time you take your child shopping, see if you can find a saleslady who is a complainer. Her words say, "May I help you?" but her tone says, "It's too much for me. Well, I'll just do the best I can." Dr. Paul J. Moses, in his fascinating book *The Voice of Neurosis*, describes the sound of such a voice.

The complainer feels sorry for himself. . . . He is far down—in a depression. Vocally, he will express this in the range he uses. He will speak deep down, but he fights his depression. . . . The usual vocal pattern of complaining is a constantly up and down gliding pitch. . . . Complaining depresses the listener. . . . Like self-accusation . . . complaint beats on the breast of the complainer with its insistent rhythm, and at the same time, it wants to beat on the ear and conscience of the listener. It combines the request for help and accusation.

You may never go shopping again!

Here is another voice to look for—the man, perhaps at the post office, who says something like, "That package is out on the truck, you'll have to come back tomorrow," while his haughty tone expresses an emotion like, "If they had made me supervisor, this would never have happened." Your child may bring up the topic as one of my daughters once did, by asking, "Mommy, why is that man mad at us?"

Just for contrast, find a waitress or teacher or doctor whose friendly and interested voice says, as she goes about her work, "Yes, I really like people—there's always something going on." And here are two cases where our ears may trick us by our cultural conditioning; that is, by the American inflection to which we are accustomed. Listen to an American-speaking Italian, whose lively variations in pitch and fast rhythm make him sound very excited, even happy to our ears. Check to see how you think he really feels. Or in a Chinese restaurant, try to go behind the high sing-song of the sound for the meaning. Is the waiter really calm, or is he harassed or irritated?

Here, as in the previous speech game, your child may be quicker than you are at pinpointing personality types, but you will have greater experience in interpreting the reasons behind speech characteristics.

FOUR PRACTICE GAMES FOR HEARING

LISTEN TO RHYTHMS
Ages: 3–10

This game will help your child to practice hearing rhythmic patterns. This is important for reading, speaking, and for an understanding of the world around him.

First, collect some materials to use as percussion instruments. For a child from three to five, pots and pans are fine, or hollow boxes with pencils for drumsticks; also use rattles, a whistle, bells, and sand blocks (make them by gluing sandpaper on blocks of wood; your child rubs them together for an unusual sound). Older children like drums, both regular and bongos, gongs, maracas, finger cymbals, and castanets.

Now clap or beat a rhythm. Ask your child to repeat what you have just done. In case you don't know how to get started, sing part of a song in your head and beat that rhythm:

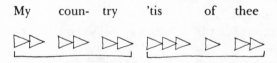

Now ask him to give you a rhythm for you to repeat. Keep the rhythms short and simple to start with. Later, you can make them more complicated by varying the accents and pauses, and increasing the length:

Oh   beau- ti- ful   for   spa- cious skies, for

am- ber waves of   grain

If you are uncomfortable about working with rhythms, ask your child to listen for rhythms around him: machines, such as the washing machine, or typewriter keys; people walking, or working in different rhythms. He can clap the rhythms he hears.

Follow up with records that contain interesting rhythms your child can hear and copy if he wants to. Some suggestions are:

"March of the Toys" (from *Babes in Toyland*), by Herbert
"Marche Militaire," by Schubert
"Toreador Song" (from *Carmen*), by Bizet
Nutcracker Suite, by Tchaikovsky
Bolero, by Ravel
Three-Cornered Hat, by deFalla (especially good if your child happens to have castanets at home)
Toccata for Percussion (3rd movement), by Chavez
Petrouchka, by Stravinsky
Dance music from Latin America, Puerto Rico, Haiti, Jamaica (calypso)
Abbey Road, by the Beatles
Jazz (Benny Goodman; Dixieland jazz artists such as Louis Armstrong and Jelly Roll Morton)

Even if you do not like some of this music, try not to impose your preference on your child; you want him to open up his hearing in any way he can. He will soon realize that he is surrounded by rhythms of all types.

LISTEN TO PITCH AND MELODY
Ages: 5–10

This game will help your child to become more aware of pitch and melody, which is important for reading, speaking, and understanding the world around him. It is a simple game unless you are unsure of your own pitch sense. If you've always been told that you have a "tin ear," ask a friend or your husband or wife, if they are more musical, to help you—and you can learn along with your child. Most musicians agree that almost no one is ever hopelessly tone-deaf.

Begin by asking your child to sing something—anything. It can be a nursery rhyme, a round, a hymn, a pop song. Tell him it doesn't matter if it sounds wrong. Listen for the tone that he repeats most frequently. Find this tone on an instrument. It doesn't have to be a piano—you can use a pitch pipe, a toy xylophone (preferably of wood; it sounds better than the metal ones), a recorder, harmonica, guitar, any instrument you can handle. Start on your child's "note" and have him sing it. Tell him that he's singing on pitch. Now play a few neighboring notes above and below, in a simple rhythm. Help him to sing them by showing him how little he has to change his voice to go from "his note" to the next note. Encourage him to compose a simple melody, using adjacent notes (no skips) and sing it for you. Now, sing it for him twice, once correctly and once making an obvious mistake. Ask him to guess which time was correct, first or second. He should be able to tell the difference. If he has trouble, stop for the day and try again the next day.

He may want to play the melody on the instrument rather than try to sing it, but this is much harder, because he has to coordinate his hand with what he hears. And you won't be able to tell whether a mistake comes from his ear or his hand. So encourage him to sing, even if he is reluctant. Tell him everyone can sing, and—if he doesn't feel he sings well —that he can learn to sing much better than he does now.

Once he is able to sing simple melodies, vary them. Put in a few skips, make the melody longer, use more complicated rhythms. At first, always start on the same note. When the child can find it easily, try starting on other notes. Remember to let him test you as well, because it's fun for him, it's good for his morale, and he has to listen hard to see if you make mistakes. Even ten minutes a day of this game should show results within a week.

As your child becomes more interested in melody, he might want to listen to phonograph records of music with interesting or beautiful melodic lines. Here are a few:

Indian music. Ravi Shankar, on the sitar. (Since this is "in" music, you might be able to persuade a rock enthusiast in your family to vary his loud rhythmic diet with these gentle melodies.)

Folk songs. Judy Collins, Joni Mitchell, Pete Seeger, Richard Dyer-Bennet, Theodore Bikel, Cynthia Gooding (especially her Italian folk songs).

Opera. Aida, by Verdi; *The Magic Flute,* by Mozart.

Choral music. The Coffee Cantata, by Bach.

Instrumental Music. Mozart, Flute Quartet in D major, K. 285 (2nd movement); Haydn, String Quartet ("The Lark"); Schubert, Piano Quintet ("The Trout"); Brahms's piano music (Intermezzi).

LISTEN TO THE QUALITY OF A SOUND
(TIMBRE)
Ages: 3–10

This game will help your child to become aware of the characteristic quality of a sound, known as the timbre, and it introduces him to the physics of sound.

Make a pile of unbreakable objects—a pencil, ball, book, a pillow—and cover them with a sheet. Ask your child to close his eyes as you drop them on the floor one by one. He should be able to identify them by the timbre of the sound they make when they hit the floor. Then try dropping groups of two objects that make a similar sound, such as a pencil and a ball-point pen; a small ball for jacks and a tennis ball; a dime and a safety pin. He'll probably be interested in why they sound alike. The pencil and pen have the same shape, but one is wood and one is plastic. The dime and the safety pin have different shapes, but they are both made of metal. Discuss these similarities and differences with him, and then have him test you. Now go to a different room and check the quality of sounds the objects make on a new floor surface, such as bathroom tile, vinyl, carpeting.

Suggest that the child create some sound effects, as if he were on a radio program. He can blow on a reed of grass, pour water into a glass, blow air across the top of a bottle. He might simulate the sounds of a creaking door, galloping horses, wind blowing; sounds made by a bird, dog, cat, rooster, donkey, cow; the sounds of various machines. If you have a tape recorder, he can record his sound effects and enjoy listening to the playback of his own creations. If possible, discuss with him what makes his sounds similar to the sounds he has imitated. The creaking door squeaks; his voice

Your Child's Sensory World

squeaks. The horses' hoofs are hollow as they hit a hard surface; he cups his hand and hits his thigh to make a similar sound. In this way, he will begin to get an idea of the physical properties of shape, resonance, and air that make up timbre. You don't have to be scientific yourself to talk about this. If you want to, you can simply limit yourself to a common-sense observation of what each of you hears and what you think makes it sound that way.

Now introduce him to the idea of timbre in music. How does the quality of the voice or instrument affect the composition? If you don't object, he can try this experiment. Let him take a recording that he knows and try it on the record player at various speeds: two minutes at 33 1/3 r.p.m., then at 45, then at 78. Ask him to describe the new quality with each change of speed. Encourage him to be imaginative, not to say "slow" but to describe in what manner the sound might be slow. Like an elephant? Like an enormous barrel of water? Like a huge trumpet? Show him pictures of the instruments of the orchestra. Discuss how the material and shape of the instrument affect the sound: wood gives mellowness to the strings; the double bass is the largest of the stringed instruments, so it has the lowest mellow sound. (If you're unsure of these facts, you'll find helpful books in your local library. A good one is Peter Smith's *First Book of the Orchestra*, published by Franklin Watts in 1963.)

Here are phonograph recordings that illustrate different instrumental timbres:

Peter and the Wolf, by Prokofieff
Young Person's Guide to the Orchestra, by Britten
Music for Stringed Instruments, Percussion, and Celesta, by Bartok (Listen to the last movement especially. A challenging musical experience for your child.)

If your child likes vocal sounds, point out that a singing or speaking voice has a distinctive timbre. He can listen to some of the recordings suggested in the previous section under folk songs and opera. Also:

Opera recordings of Joan Sutherland, Beverly Sills, Marilyn Horne, Jussi Bjoerling, and Alexander Kipnis

Aksel Schiøtz singing *Die Schöne Müllerin* by Schubert (a song cycle with a romantic story and superb melodies)

Rex Harrison in *My Fair Lady* and Zero Mostel in *Fiddler on the Roof* (These illustrate a different vocal technique—spoken sounds on musical pitches.)

Some speaking voices of exceptional tonal quality and diction are:

Siobhan McKenna, recorded reading "Piccoli" (a children's story, ages three and up)

Cyril Ritchard, recorded reading *Alice in Wonderland*

Franklin Delano Roosevelt, Fireside Chats (recorded)

Brock Peters on television, in films

LISTEN TO SOFTER SOUNDS
(VOLUME)
Ages: 5–10

This game is a variation of Find-the-Button that will encourage your child to become more aware of the volume of a sound—important for hearing sensitivity and speech. Take a clear glass and a spoon. Hide an object and ask your child to hunt for it. Instead of saying, "Colder" and "Warmer," hit the glass softly or more vigorously. He'll have to listen closely to the soft sounds, especially as he moves farther away and isn't sure which way to walk.

This is also a good party game to quiet things down. In fact, my father taught it to me and some very loud friends on my eighth birthday.

You'll find practice games for volume and your child's speaking voice in the next chapter.

11 How to Increase Awareness of Communicating through Speech

Before I describe the speaking games to play with your child, let me answer a few questions parents frequently ask me about their children's speech.

QUESTIONS AND ANSWERS ABOUT YOUR CHILD'S SPEECH

Should I correct my child's speech? Some parents are hesitant to correct their child's speech because they're afraid this will upset or inhibit the child. The mother of five-year-old Lisa was a perfect example. Lisa couldn't say *l*, so her name came out "Weesa," which made the other children laugh at her. One day I showed her how my tongue looked when I said *l*, had her look in the mirror, then asked her to say "lama." Within ten minutes she had learned how to say her name correctly, and was overjoyed. When her mother came to pick her up, I said, "We have a surprise for you," and her daughter proudly demonstrated what she had learned. To my amazement, the mother's face was a complete blank. As Lisa was putting on her coat I asked the mother quietly, "Did you ever try to help her say *l*?" "Oh, no," whispered her mother. "I thought it would upset her." This lady was really trying

127

to do what she thought was best for her child; she was not encouraging cute baby talk. But apparently, she had never considered how much more upset her daughter would be if the other children laughed at her than if her pronunciation were gently corrected.

Then there was the mother in my neighborhood who said, "It's such a relief having the kids away in camp. Their yelling around the house really gets me." I asked her if she ever told them to talk more softly. She looked surpised, then said, "No, I never did. I guess I thought it would inhibit them." As a matter of fact one of my daughters, then aged eight, had noticed the loud voices of these children. She once told me, "I really don't like to play with those kids. They talk so loud you can't hear yourself think."

Poor speech can hurt many areas of your child's life, but most of all it is a social disadvantage and reduces the effectiveness with which he communicates. Not only that, but speech improvement involves social attitudes; when a child learns to control volume and other speech characteristics, he is learning to become aware of the other person. You really owe it to him to try and help him out. Of course you would not want to nag at him until speaking becomes a chore, so be sure not to continue to correct him if he seems distressed about it. But a casual reminder about speech will not affect a normal child any more than some other remark, such as "Don't pick your nose in public." Most children are flexible and usually prefer to speak correctly and attractively because the sensation of good speech feels better to them and produces a better response in the people listening to them. Later, their ears may come to prefer a good sound as well.

What about speech therapists? Don't they correct children in school?
Speech therapists are specialists. In most cases, they deal

with severe difficulties like inability to read, stuttering and emotional factors that inhibit speech, and serious physical conditions like cleft palate or hearing loss. One nine-year-old boy I know spoke so indistinctly that I could barely understand him, even when I made a concentrated effort. I asked him if he had ever had any help with speech at school. He said, "Yeah, they sent me to the speech teacher, but she said it wasn't bad enough and sent me back."

How will I know if I should say something to my child about his speech? By listening. In most situations, you don't have to be a doctor to be aware of your child's state of health, and similarly you don't have to be a speech teacher to listen to his voice. Listen to the timbre, pitch, rhythm, and volume of your child's voice as well as to his breathing and his articulation of the words. If you are aware of sound, you will hear if your child has a consistently unpleasant vocal quality or timbre, if he frequently speaks too high in pitch or too low; you will be able to check his breathing pattern and his articulation, or if he frequently races his words together so that they are unclear.

One word of caution. According to my friend Lillian Freeman, who is a speech therapist, children are normally nonfluent until they are six or seven. That is, their words may get slurred, mixed up, or mispronounced in any of a variety of ways, including an occasional stutter. You might want to wait until your child is eight or older before you play speech games with him. But if you maintain the attitude that your child's speech belongs to him and that speaking should be pleasurable for your child, you needn't worry about a negative effect from these games at any stage of development. Just remember never to push the game to the point where it is no longer fun for your child.

Your Child's Sensory World

How did my child develop unclear speech? There are many causes. Your seven-year-old daughter may be imitating someone she knows or has heard—her best friend, a favorite television star, some member of the family. She may be doing this unconsciously or on purpose, and the sound may be completely wrong for her own personality and physical makeup. Every person's voice is different from every other's. Children sometimes imitate the wrong voice type for them, just as they may copy a clothing fad that looks dreadful on their particular body-type.

Sickness can cause bad speech habits. For example, a head cold or laryngitis might cause your son to adjust his voice so that speaking hurts as little as possible. Then he forgets to "turn" his voice back to normal when he is well again. A change in speech can result from any sickness that lasts a while—just listen to your own voice the next time you get the flu. We adults return to our normal speech easily after an illness because our habits are set, for better or for worse. But even three days of different speech can be a long time for a child—long enough to change his speech habits.

There are developmental changes that affect speech. Of course the most obvious is the changing pitch of an adolescent boy's voice, but a girl's voice also lowers in pitch at puberty although the interval is much less extreme. An earlier developmental change in both sexes is the loss of baby teeth. The whole mouth suddenly feels different. And throughout childhood, the throat and larynx grow along with the rest of the body, requiring constant readjustment in speech. Sometimes a child is not able to make the sound he wants to, so he settles for what he can get, even if it is not so effective. Nature does not always take care of us automatically. A cat cannot always climb down a tree.

But there is really no reason to worry about how your

child's speech developed as it did, since it's usually so easy to change it. Just think of speech as a learning process and yourself as a teacher. You are helping your child to speak more effectively just as you once taught him how to tie his shoes. With this attitude on your part, the appropriate speech games should be fun and useful to him.

SPEAKING GAMES

The first set of games described here, Speaking for Fun, will help your child enjoy the sensation of speaking. He cannot correct the way he speaks if he dislikes speaking in general, nor can he concentrate on the challenge of learning to communicate and to listen. Although a few children do not like to talk because of emotional difficulties and need a speech therapist, many children dislike speaking because they have stopped hearing and speaking for fun, as they did when they were babies. Speaking for Fun games should restore such a child's pleasure in speaking.

The three Sound Patterns games (see pages 140–144) will help a younger child who enjoys speaking to develop a sensory approach to reading the spoken word, through visual, touch, and movement patterns.

Each of the six Practice Games for Speech (see page 144) is intended to help remedy a specific speech difficulty: poor breath control, inappropriate speech rhythm, inexpressive vocal pitch, unpleasant vocal quality, inappropriate volume, inaccurate articulation. If you think your child would benefit from one or more of these games, have him pick some favorite speech sounds to say from the Speaking for Fun series.

Your Child's Sensory World

SPEAKING FOR FUN

RHYMES AND CHANTS
Ages: 3–5

Besides improving communication through speech, this game often helps beginning readers.

Most children like nursery rhymes and often make up their own nonsense rhymes as they move in different rhythms—hopping, jumping, and skipping. The results are not usually meaningful phrases, but the child is learning about words, word combinations, and the stress and pause of meaningful speech. You can encourage your child to experiment by making sounds yourself as you clap a rhythm:

1. Example:

   CLAP Clap CLAP Clap
   "BA   ba   BA   ba"

2. Different consonants, same rhythm:

   "DA da GA ma"

3. Different vowel sounds, same rhythm:

   CLAP clap CLAP clap
   "MA   may ME   moh"

4. Try a different rhythm:

   CLAP clap clap CLAP clap clap
   "BA   ba   ba   BA   ba   ba"

5. Change the consonant and vowel sound:

   CLAP clap clap CLAP clap clap
   "MOO moo moo MOO moo moo"

By now your child will probably be chanting along with you, perhaps as he moves in rhythm. The next step is to combine sounds into nonsense rhymes:

> "Mom-mee may moo,
> Da-dee may too"

With more practice, your child will learn to combine pleasing sounds into imaginative word pictures:

> "Ba-LOON, said the ba-BOON
> to the MOON, to the MOON."

The Russian poet Kornei Chukovsky marveled at the poetic gifts of young children, and collected many samples in his charming book *From Two to Five,* such as this one by a five-year-old girl:

> The radish is blooming
> The drum is booming.
> And I drink tea
> Excessively.

TONGUE TWISTERS AND VERBAL GAMES
Ages: 6–8

By the time your child is six, nonsense rhymes may seem babyish to him, but he'll enjoy tongue twisters and verbal games if you suggest them. Here are some examples. (More tongue twisters appear in the articulation game on pages 154–155.)

Tongue twisters:

> Tiny Tim went to tiptoe town
> To tiptoe town he went.

He couldn't talk and he couldn't turn
And he lived in a tucked-in tent.

Verbal ball-bouncing game:

A my name is A-lice
My husband's name is A-lec
We live in A-kron
And we sell apples.

B my name is Bet-ty . . .

Secret languages:

Pig-Latin. My name is Mary = I-may ame-nay is-ay ary-may.
Ithagy Language. My name is Mary = Mithagy nithagame ithagis
Mithaga-rithagy. (Syllable "ithag" is placed within each
spoken syllable.)

All of these games make your child aware of speech
sounds because the repeated vowels or consonants form a
hearing-speaking pattern. This is a fine way to learn reading,
as many first-grade teachers will tell you.

See if your child can make up more complicated speech
patterns, such as

Interior consonants in repetition:

"A*p*ples a*p*peared u*p*ward."
"Da*n*dy da*n*cers be*n*ding dow*n*ward."

Final consonants in repetition:

"Hit*s* and run*s*. Bat*s* and ball*s*."
"Begru*dge* the ju*dge*."

Repetition of vowel sounds:

> "R*aw* and t*aw*ny *aw*nings."
> "M*ee*ting l*ea*n Arm*e*nians."

You can play these games in many places—they may go over well on a long car trip, as an alternative to "ghost." They should help your child's vocabulary, spelling, understanding of poetry and well-written prose, as well as his own personal enjoyment of words and speech.

POETIC SOUNDS, GIBBERISH SPEECH, AND SPEECH STUDY FOR FOREIGN ACCENTS
Ages: 9-12

Poetic sounds. Poetic sounds will be familiar to any child who is (or was) a fan of the Beatles. Ask him to recite one of their classics, such as *Lucy In the Sky With Diamonds*, without music. He should listen to himself as he talks.

> Picture yourself in a boat on a river
> With tangerine trees and marmalade skies.
> Somebody calls you. You answer quite slowly.
> The girl with kaleidoscope eyes.

Encourage your child to experiment with other poetic sounds, such as poems by Lewis Carroll, Gertrude Stein, or e.e. cummings.

> 'Twas brillig, and the slithy toves
>   Did gyre and gimble in the wabe;
> All mimsy were the borogoves,
>   And the mome raths outgrabe.
>   —Lewis Carroll, *Through the Looking-Glass.*

"You may seek it with thimbles—and seek it with care;
  You may hunt it with forks and hope;
  You may threaten its life with a railway-share;
  You may charm it with smiles and soap—"
                    —Lewis Carroll, *The Hunting of the Snark.*

in Just-
spring   when the world is mud-
luscious the little
lame balloonman

whistles   far   and wee

and eddieandbill come
running from marbles and
piracies and it's
spring

when the world is puddle-wonderful

the queer
old balloonman whistles
far   and   wee

and bettyandisbel come dancing

from hop-scotch and jump-rope and

it's
spring
and
    the

        goat-footed

balloonMan   whistles
far
and
wee
                    —e.e. cummings, *Chansons Inocentes* I.

Don't press your child to give you the meaning of the verses; just let him relax and "swim" in the sounds he is speaking and hearing. If he comments on the visual pattern of the Cummings poem, show him the game on page 240, "Match the Letter Pattern with the Sound Pattern."

"Gibberish" speech. Talking together in "gibberish"— nonsense syllables in place of actual words, but with the original inflection—is an enjoyable way to increase your child's awareness of speech sounds. It is simplest to begin by using letters of the alphabet or numbers for the nonsense syllables. Then, proceed as if you are having a normal conversation with your child. For example,

"Hi! How are you?"

becomes

"Six! Four two three?"

He answers:

"Ten, sixty. Three-eight ninety?"(Translation: "Fine, thank you. What's for dinner?")

Or, if you're using letters of the alphabet, the "Fine, thank you, what's for dinner?" might be:

"A   M n.   Z   l   Q z?"

Once you both become comfortable with numbers and letters, you should then try to make up your own nonsense syllables:

"How are you?"

might become

"Ma lay loo?"

or

"There's a bird on our lawn."

might turn into

"Zud ne bink nee lee osh."

You will find out that in most cases, your inflection will have to remain the same, unless you change the meaning. Point out to your child: that the inflection usually carries the emotional meaning of the vocal sounds, and the speech syllables carry the actual content of what he is saying.

"Gibberish" speech with various meanings. Now practice repeating the same syllables with a different inflection to change the meaning.

Casual Statement:	"There's a bird on our lawn."
	"Zud ne bink nee lee osh."
Excited Observation:	"There's a BIRD on our LAWN!!!!!!!"
	"Zud ne BINK nee lee OSH!!!!!!!"

Ask your child to tell you the difference in vocal sounds between the two statements (both in English and in gibberish, since they should be almost identical). The difference between a casual statement and an excited observation will be expressed in most languages by louder volume, faster rhythm, more stress (accents) and usually, greater range of pitch (highs and lows). Excitement also causes the speaker to use a shorter breath.

"Gibberish" speech with the same meaning but different syllables. Make up examples with your child of different syllables to express the same meaning. (This game is a preparation for foreign language study.)

One nonsense-syllable for one actual syllable.

> "Hello! How are you?"
> "Ma dee! My lay loo?"

Any number of nonsense syllables for the number of actual syllables.

> "Hello! How are you?"
> "Des! Lackana aling?"

Foreign language syllables in place of the English syllables.

> (French) "Bonjour! Comment allez-vous?"
> (German) "Guten Tag! Wie geht es Ihnen?"
> (Italian) "Buon giorno! Come state?"

In each case, the meaning remains the same, the inflection is similar, but the syllables vary.

Speech study for foreign accents (when your child has begun to study a foreign language at school). If your child is studying a foreign language, he will need to listen to the sounds of the speech. This helps him remember vocabulary, phrases, and grammar, and in a deeper sense, it gives him a feel for the foreign country, since the characteristic speech sounds of a nation in some ways express a characteristic philosophy of life. These language qualities provide the differences in speech inflection even when the speaker is expressing the same meaning. Some languages are so different from ours that it is hard to trace any similarities in inflection. For example, the equivalent for *hello* in Japanese bears little vocal resemblance to the inflection of *hello* in English.

Your child can hear these language qualities long before he knows the language. He can practice them by speaking his own language "with a foreign accent," or rather, foreign inflection. This may make him laugh, but it is a wonderful exercise nonetheless. For instance, American English, with its typically casual language quality, might be inflected "How *are* ya?" In proper British English, this becomes "*How* ah yooo?" In precise French, "OW ah YOOO?" In emphatic German, "HOW AH YOOO?" And in mellifluous Italian, "OWahyooo?"

MATCH THE SOUND PATTERN

These games will help your child to develop a sensory approach to reading the spoken word. He will become aware that the sound patterns he speaks and hears can be parallel to visual patterns he sees on a page, touch pattern he feels with his hand, and movement patterns he makes with his body.

MATCH THE SOUND PATTERN WITH THE VISUAL PATTERN
Ages: 3–7

Space out a pattern of consonants, vowel sounds, or tongue twisters on a piece of 8 1/2-by-11-inch paper and speak the sounds with your child.

In the examples shown below, your child should be able to recognize that the sound and accent of his speech is parallel to the visual pattern on the page—repetition of large and small letters relates to the loud and soft sounds; the repeated vocal sound "oon" or "G" is repeated by the same symbol on the page.

PA pa PA pa

or

PA pa pa
PA pa pa

M**OON**   **G**reta
G**OON**   or   **G**arbo
L**OON**   **G**obbled
S**OON**   **G**or**G**onzola

Quartet

I.

W. A. Mozart.
1756-1791.
Köchel No. 465

—*Mozart, String Quartet in C Major, K. 465, 1st movement*

A more complex visual sound pattern is a musical score.
If your child is interested in music, show him this extract
from the score of a string quartet. Tell him it represents
visually the sounds of the four instruments. You can follow
up by letting him hear this section on a record so that he can
match the sound pattern with the visual pattern: high note,
high mark on the paper; many notes, many marks on the

Your Child's Sensory World

paper; sequence of similar melodic pattern in top three instruments; *p* means soft, *f* means loud.

MATCH THE SOUND PATTERN WITH THE TOUCH PATTERN (IMITATION BRAILLE)
Ages: 3–7

This game works even if your child has not yet learned to read. Take a piece of 8 1/2-by-11-inch paper and prick with a pin to form patterns of words, using the capital letters B, C, D, E, H, I, K, M, O, W, X. (See examples *a* and *b*.)

a.	*b.*	*c.*

8 1/2 × 11 paper with pinpricks 1/4" apart to form: BE HE WE	Paper turned over so pinpricks stand out, and upside down, so letters are in reading order (W becomes M).	Pinpricks connected by child to form words with repeated sound "E" vowel.

Now ask your child to feel the shapes with his eyes closed. After your child has felt the letters, ask him if his fingers traced any pattern more than once and point it out to him. In the example shown, for instance, the *E* is repeated with his finger and with his voice. If he knows how to read and has already recognized the words by touch, point out that the *E* sound is repeated by his voice and by the pattern on the page.

To finish, let him connect the dots of the letters with pencil, pen, or crayon (eyes open; see example *c*). Point out to him that he is writing letters, and that this is a different kind of touch pattern which forms a more complete picture of his speech sounds. (You might also mention the Braille touch alphabet used by the blind.)

MATCH THE SOUND PATTERN WITH THE MOVEMENT PATTERN
Ages: 3–7

Pick a simple rhythm and clap it together:

CLAP clap clap clap

or

CLAP clap CLAP clap

Ask the child to move to the rhythm in any way he wants, with hand, foot, head, whole body. Then ask him to speak sound patterns as he moves. He can count:

ONE two THREE four

or use alphabet letters:

A b C d

or syllables:

BUM   bum   BUM   bum
LA   lee   LA   lay

Point out to him that the rhythm and accent of his speech sounds is parallel to the rhythm and accent of his body. Tell him that his voice is a physical part of him, just as his hand or foot is, and that his voice likes to make sounds that are parallel to the rest of his body. He can check this by the following experiment:

Tell him to move in one rhythm and speak in another. For example, he marches

ONE   two   ONE   two   ONE   two

and tries to say at the same time

ONE   two   one   TWO   one   two

Very few children or adults can accomplish this feat without special training in music, dance, or Dalcroze technique.

If you have not already done so, you should now play with your child the seeing-sound pattern game on page 140. This will show him that his movement-speech patterns can be parallel to a seeing pattern on paper, and that his actions can be related to reading the written word.

SIX PRACTICE GAMES FOR SPEECH

SWIMMING GAME
(FOR BREATH CONTROL)
Ages: 5–12

A child who has a poor breathing pattern tires himself and his listener. At school, he may irritate the teacher; if he is a beginning reader, he may sound like a poor reader, even though his comprehension is excellent.

Panting breath. If your child pants like a puppy as he speaks (too many breaths in a phrase), this game will make him aware of a natural relationship between breath and speech. Ask him to sit in a chair and move his arms in a crawl-stroke as if he were swimming. If he doesn't know how, teach him: he breathes in deeply with his head turned to the side and arm up, and breathes out as he completes the stroke. He may want to pretend he is really in the water. After he has been "swimming" for a few minutes, tell him to speak on the exhaling breath. Count with him how many sounds he can say clearly on one breath as he "swims." Then have him speak the same number of sounds on one breath without moving. Point out to him that his breath may carry even more sounds this way, because he's not moving now, only speaking. If he goes back to panting later, you may want to repeat the exercise. Often, a matter-of-fact reminder such as "Don't forget to breathe with your words, not against them," will do the trick, because his body will remember the sensation of the exercise.

Running out of breath. If your child speaks like a radio that keeps fading out (too many phrases on one breath) the same game will give him the sensation of natural breathing and speech. After your child has been "swimming" for a while, tell him you are going to keep score of all the sounds you can hear easily. (Move about six feet away from him.) First, let him swim and speak a few minutes on the exhaling breath. Tell him his score, and mention that you couldn't hear the last few sounds very clearly. Suggest that he breathe more often, so that his breath can send out the sounds more vigorously. This should make him listen to the volume of his own voice so that as the sounds start to fade, he will take a new breath. At the same time, he'll be "swimming" faster and more energetically. Once he gets the hang of it, he can stop moving and concentrate on his speech sounds. Tell him that your ears will double-check his ears and his sense of how much breath he needs to talk clearly. At the moment he should breathe and doesn't, tell him matter-of-factly, "I can't hear you very well now." He'll soon learn to coordinate his breath, his speech, and his ears. He'll hear and feel which vocal sounds are too soft and what to do about it: take another breath. Once he experiences this sensation, he'll usually remember it with only an occasional reminder. Later on, he'll be interested to see that the proportion of breath to sound changes as the other person's ears move farther away.

FIND YOUR BEST SPEECH RHYTHM
Ages: 7–12

If your child has formed a habit of speaking so rapidly or unevenly that you cannot understand him, you can help him to find another rhythm of speech, which will be more expressive and less tiring to himself and others. First, tell him that everybody has a different rhythm of moving and speaking, and the two of you will play a game to find his own speech rhythm.

Begin a conversation with your child and ask him to copy your rhythm. Start by speaking slowly and steadily, like a machine: "To-day-in-the-news-the-as-tro-nauts-pre-pared-to-land-their-ship." Once your child can copy this rhythm, try some others: fast and even, fast and uneven, faster and faster, slow and jerky, slow and drawling.

Now tell him you're going to be his "tape recorder." Your voice will copy for him any rhythms he speaks. Encourage him to experiment with different rhythms as you did. Tell him to fix the "tape recorder" if you make a mistake. When you feel that he's hearing sensitively, ask him to speak normally and copy the sounds for him. At this point, he may want to change the way he speaks. If not, tell him you want him to hear without looking. Have him close his eyes and tell him an incident using his speech rhythm. He'll notice that the rhythm interferes in some way with the meaning: too fast, too slow, or uneven.

Now encourage him to experiment with different speech rhythms until he finds one that feels comfortable and expresses clearly to you what he wants to say. Tell him that this is his own rhythm—the one that's best for him and for the people he's talking to.

Incidentally, some children race their words because they are afraid of being interrupted before they can finish what they want to say. If your child is like this, and you are often too busy to listen to him, you can teach him to wait until you take a break. When you do stop, tell him it's his turn now: he can tell you whatever he wants, there's no rush, and you'll hear him out.

HOW HIGH CAN YOU SPEAK?
HOW LOW CAN YOU SPEAK?
(PITCH)
Ages: 3–12

If your child's voice is unnaturally high, the sound will be shrill and annoying. A second-grade teacher once confided to me, "Nancy's a sweet kid, but I hate to call on her. I can't stand that high, squeaky voice." A child has a higher voice than an adult, but the sound doesn't have to be strident. The other extreme is unnaturally low pitch. This makes your child's voice muffled and indistinct, which is also unpleasant to listen to.

If you tell a child to lower or raise his voice, he'll usually say he can't. A young child may not even know what you mean: raise it up to the sky? lower it down like a rug on the floor? make it softer? To show a child what high and low mean in terms of pitch, ask him to wail like a siren, or the wind, or a ghost, and show him which is high and which is low. Now he can relate the term to a physical sensation. Next, find approximately his highest and lowest note on a piano or another instrument. Tell him these two notes are his vocal range, and that his voice can make any note in between. Ask him to say some favorite speech sounds in his normal voice, and find his average speaking pitch on the instrument. (This may take you a few tries, but make it into a listening exercise for both of you until you find it.) Now, show your child how much lower or higher he can go than his average pitch by asking him to wail again. When you ask your child to speak again, he may have instinctively changed his pitch. If not, at least he'll know that he can when he wants to. The next time his speech sounds better to you, comment on it. He'll soon find that better-sounding speech feels better to him also, and he may be motivated to make the change permanently.

If your child is generally tense and has a high-pitched voice, the pitch can't come down until he learns to relax somewhat, because tight vocal cords make a higher sound, just like a tightly stretched rubber band. Before you ask him to speak, have him lie down on the floor on his back and pretend to fall asleep. This will release tension from his whole body, including his vocal cords. An older child may be self-conscious about this. If so, tell him it's like a yoga exercise for relaxation. (It is.) After the relaxation but without getting up, have your child speak and vary the pitch up and down as much as possible. If he's older, encourage him to speak on many pitches in "gibberish" (see page 137). He should now have some idea of his ability to control the pitch of his voice even when he's standing. After a while, he'll learn how it feels to relax his voice whenever he wants to.

RADIO GAME
(TIMBRE)
Ages: 6–12

Nasal Timbre. Nasal timbre (like Bugs Bunny) turns your child into a comedian even when he wants to be serious. And, like too-high pitch, it can make friends and teachers wince.

It's hard to hear your own timbre because the sound inside of you is different from what carries to other ears. So when it comes to vocal quality, many children need to be convinced that they really could sound better, and that it feels better too. To overcome this resistance, start with some vocal ear-training. Ask your child to listen to voices on the radio and tell you what kind of person is talking, and what he imagines that person looks like. Does the announcer sound like a big tall man? Does the lady giving recipes sound fat and dumpy?

For the next step, you need to own or borrow a tape recorder. Your child should record some "character" voices based on his radio experience: "Here is a short, nervous disc jockey . . ." or "Here is a sleepy lady . . ." He then continues by using his voice in any way he chooses to characterize the person. You should now record the voices of your child and some friends speaking together casually. Ask him to close his eyes and to listen to the tape very carefully. When he hears his own sound, ask what he would say about that voice if he had never heard it before? What kind of person would talk like that? This should motivate him for the next part of the exercise. If it doesn't, try it anyway, just for fun.

Here's how to help your child change the physical sensation when he speaks. Have him find some speech sounds without the letters *m*, *n*, or *ng* (the nasal consonants). He may want to use a tongue twister without these letters, such as "Peter Piper," or "She sells sea shells." Ask him to say it while holding his nose with thumb and forefinger. Then to repeat it without holding his nose. A nasal voice sounds "held" even when it isn't. As a matter of fact, it *is* held, but inside (by collapsing the back of the nasal pharynx). Show your child the difference in your own voice when you speak, first holding and then releasing the nose. Now record his voice again. Help him to experiment with various vocal timbres until he finds one that does not sound "held." Check it with the nose-holding experiment until the sound is clearly different. After a while, your child will probably prefer this speech because it's easier and feels better. In time, his ears will come to prefer it as well.

Throaty timbre. If your child speaks with a tight throat, the sound will be harsh and grating, and the strain may wear him out or even give him a sore throat. He may not know that speaking is not supposed to feel this way, so that perhaps in the first grade he begins to dislike talking and reading aloud.

Sometimes a child develops this type of speech because he wants to sound louder or more important. A girl is told, "Young ladies aren't supposed to yell," so she rebels and talks louder. A girl can learn to make a full loud sound without strain, but it takes practice, and our culture discourages this (except for lady opera singers). Some little boys, with naturally gentle musical voices, end up with a throaty sound because they try to sound tough and manly—our culture says that any other sound for a boy is feminine. You can help your child find his or her own speech sound, based on individual anatomy and temperament, regardless of sex.

Preparation.   Before you start working on speech with your child, you should practice on yourself. When your throat is relaxed, you will be able to feel the vibrations as you speak or sing low tones by placing your fingers lightly on your throat where your Adam's apple would be. If you tighten your throat, the quality of the vibrations will change. Actually, the tight throat deadens the richness of the vocal sound, causing the harsh tone that hurts both ears and speaker. A voice with a tight throat is like a hand bell that cannot ring out clearly when your finger is on the surface of the metal.

Continue to speak and sing low tones until you can feel the difference between a relaxed throat and a tight throat. If you now look in the mirror, you'll be able to see the muscles of the throat move downward as you change your vocal quality from throaty and tight to resonant and free.

Now you are ready to help your child. Begin by telling him you know of an easier way to talk. If he needs more convincing, start with the ear-training mentioned above under *nasal timbre.* When your child is ready to practice making different speech sounds, ask him to coo like a pigeon—high and gently. If he feels silly, tell him it's what some professional singers do to open their throat. He may need to relax on his back and then try it.

Once he can coo, tell him that his voice can feel the same way when he talks. Have him say, "Maw—Baw—Paw—" in a low voice like a foghorn. He should be able to feel the vibrations in his throat just as you did. Now have him speak normally and feel his throat tighten. Tell him that his throat can feel free, once he learns not to tense it. Since children naturally have a high speaking voice, he'll have to lower his tone below his normal range to get the sensation of the vibration. Then he'll have to practice speaking in his normal voice until he no longer feels the throat tighten when he speaks. Once he learns to feel it easily with his fingers, he can adjust it internally with his throat muscles. If you are working with your daughter and she wants to learn to yell without straining, this is the way for her to achieve it—by making loud sounds without tightening her throat.

LONG-DISTANCE TELEPHONE GAME
STOP! I CAN'T HEAR YOU!
(VOLUME)
Ages: 5–12

This game will make your child aware of speech sounds that are too soft or too loud, two extremes that make your child's voice uncomfortable for others to listen to, and affect his social relationships.

Tell your child you're going to show him how far his voice carries. Pick a topic for casual conversation—the day's events, an upcoming birthday party, weekend plans—and ask him to turn around and to walk slowly out of the room as he talks until you stop him. (If you tell him not to look at you but to pretend you are on the telephone, he will listen more intensely.) Stop him when you can no longer understand what he's saying. He'll be surprised—either because he got so far away or because he didn't. It is difficult to make your child speak more loudly without making him self-conscious. The best way is to encourage him to talk about topics that really excite him. Then, make him aware of his volume and try to get him to speak for fun in a pleasant full voice (see the games on pages 132–140). If he succeeds, the different sensation in his voice and ears may be enough to convince him to change his way of speaking.

If your child speaks too loudly, try some of the following: ask him to make an unusual sound—a high, clear tone, a low hoot, an animal noise such as a bark, coo, moo, or caw—and to repeat it at the same volume and in the same rhythm as he walks slowly out of the room. Stop him when you can no longer hear him. He will learn what sounds carry well even with minimum effort. He can then try to guess when his sound will stop reaching you. He walks away to a certain distance and speaks. If you cannot understand, he moves until you can repeat what he said back to him. If it's too loud, he should move farther away and try again. He'll soon get a graphic picture of the distance his voice carries, so that he can vary the volume as he wishes.

WHAT'S YOUR SCORE ON TONGUE TWISTERS? (ARTICULATION)
Ages: 6–12

Good articulation makes your child easier to understand and is also a tremendous social advantage. Your child's articulation depends on the action of his lips, tongue, teeth, throat, and roof of the mouth to form words. This is a physical process that your child can enjoy as much as his favorite sport. (If he's not athletic, tell him it's active but not exhausting.) If your child has good articulation, he will be easier to understand, and his good diction will prejudice people in his favor, as is described in Shaw's *Pygmalion* (*My Fair Lady*).

Tongue twisters are fun and useful for articulation. Your child can make up his own or use some of those suggested below. Help him to become aware of the movement of his lips, tongue, throat, and teeth. They should function easily, clearly, and without extra tension. He can check this by watching himself in the mirror when he speaks. If he is making faces as he enunciates words, there is too much tension. If the words sound unclear, there is not enough tension, or it is the wrong kind. He can relax his face by wiggling his mouth, dropping his jaw, yawning, wiggling his tongue, wrinkling his nose, furrowing his brow, even wiggling his ears if he can. Then he should start again.

You may want to keep score of mistakes as he speeds up the rhythm on each exercise. Also, try some yourself.

For the Lips: b's and p's; m's and n's; f's and v's.

Black babbling brooks break boldly through their bounds.

Peter piper picked a peck of pickled peppers.
A peck of pickled peppers Peter Piper picked.
If Peter Piper picked a peck of pickled peppers,
Where's the peck of pickled peppers Peter Piper picked?

Ma made macaroni Monday.

Nighty-night nods Ned.

Funny Felix found a frankfurter.

Vases of value.

For the Tongue and Throat: c's, k's, g's; for the Tongue, Throat, Lips. qu.

Cages of crawling cats are quiet.

Greta Garbo gobbled gorgonzola.

For the Tongue and Teeth: d's, t's, and th's.

A double dozen dirty dinner napkins.

Tiny Tim went to tiptoe town.
To tiptoe town he went.

He couldn't talk and he couldn't turn
And he lived in a tucked-in tent.

Through the thicket, Theodore.

For the Tongue and Roof of the Mouth: j's, l's, r's.

James and Jason jumped the juniper.

Lovely ladies looked at lilies.

Roto Rooter ran around a roller-skating rink.

For the Tongue, Roof of the Mouth, and Teeth: s's, z's, sh's.

Hans and Fritz are twins
And when their school begins
Hans moans and groans in the loudest tones
But Fritz just sits and grins.

Zippy zebra zoos.

She sells sea-shells
By the sea-shore.

Breath, with relaxed throat, tongue, teeth: h's (In this exercise, a lighted candle should flicker if you place it twelve inches from the mouth. If the candle makes you nervous, use an ostrich plume.)

Hannah helped the heaving halibut.

For the Lips: w's.

Walter waved the wand.

12 How to Increase Awareness of Touch

If you enjoy your own sense of touch, you will be able to show your child affection, comfort, and protection easily and wordlessly. You will have the pleasure of being able to use your hands skillfully in necessary and creative activities, and your child will be likely to learn manual dexterity from you. And if you have overall touch awareness, you will be able to relate to your child's preferences in temperature, textures, and anything else that touches his skin.

YOUR OWN SENSE OF TOUCH

The easiest way to increase your own touch awareness is to reacquaint yourself with all the touch sensations that you normally experience without noticing. You will become more sensitive to touch and you will also discover your particular touch pattern.

The best toucher in the world is an active two-year-old. He is aware of all substances—air, liquids, and solids. He pats and slaps his food and his bath water. He fingers and holds crackers and wooden blocks. He discovers that one crumbles and breaks into little pieces in his hand and on his tongue, and the other stays together, even if he bites it or throws it.

He experiments with different *textures.* He may run fine sand and rough dirt through his fingers; he puts them in his mouth, feels them with his tongue, spits them out. He will smooth out velvet and stroke fur. Sticky things like honey and dried fruit are fun for him—until it's time to have his hair combed.

A two-year-old becomes aware of *temperature* through warm or cool clothing on his body and warm or cool water and air on his exposed skin and scalp. He tests food temperature with fingers, lips, tongue, and throat. His hand feels too-hot objects such as a radiator, and too-cold objects, such as a frozen orange-juice can. Some temperatures are pleasant: cool metal, or a sun-warmed carpet. Like a cat, a child can show you the warm spots in every room.

When a child is learning about *size* and *weight,* he often looks like a clown. He may use too much or too little energy. He tries to grasp a brick until he bursts into tears of frustration, then laughs with pleasure at his strength when he can throw a balloon or an air-filled toy.

Shape and *spatial relationships* involve eye-hand coordination, and also touch. Your child learns to work a jigsaw puzzle by feeling a shape fit into an outline. He "sees" with fingers and eyes when he separates and arranges miniatures —cars, doll-house furniture, toy villages.

Experiments like these when you were little taught you what to expect: water flows away from a hand; chewing gum is for the mouth, not the hair; a balloon pops if you pinch it. You learned how to hold and manipulate objects so that they would do what you wanted them to. These are touch and movement patterns, and life would be chaotic indeed without them—we'd be at breakfast until dinnertime. But in order to resensitize your touch, you need to go back to the experimental approach of a child learning about his world through touch. One good way is to *touch without seeing.*

TOUCHING WITHOUT SEEING

First, pile up some fruits and vegetables on your kitchen table, sit down, close your eyes, and feel. Notice the textures —the rough dirt on a baking potato and a beet, the smooth hardness of an apple, the velvet softness of a peach. By closing your eyes, you break your customary tactile pattern; your touch becomes more refined as your fingers replace your eyes. Now check for weight and size. An onion is much lighter than a peach or a beet, but similar in form.

Collect some forks and spoons of various types, close your eyes, and touch them. Recognize the shape and size difference between forks and spoons, then between a salad fork, a dinner fork, and a serving fork; a teaspoon, a soup spoon, a serving spoon. Notice that all the metal implements feel much cooler than the vegetables and fruit, unless the food has just come out of the refrigerator.

A second touch experiment is to *touch with the "wrong" hand* (left if you are right-handed, and vice versa). Use the wrong hand to arrange a bunch of identically shaped spoons or forks in a compact formation, such as piled one on top of the other, or turned sideways. Place one next to the other, as close together as you can manage. You will get a new sense of their spatial relationship. Then try eating or writing with the wrong hand. Next, pick up an unbreakable object, such as a throw pillow, with the wrong hand and pass it very slowly to the other hand. Try to feel the texture and weight equally with either hand. Gradually loosen your hold until the object drops. Pick it up slowly with the "right" hand, using minimum effort. Now return it slowly to its place. It should feel quite different from the way it did before.

Compare this with your ordinary way of handling light objects. Do you grip them more than you need to? A tight hold gives you a strong inner feel of muscles working but reduces the outer sensation. Look at your hand when you grip tightly. Less of your skin is in contact with the object, and the blood circulation changes. You need to grip tightly in order to lift a heavy weight, but if you do it all the time, you lose tactile awareness and your fingers become stiff and inflexible.

Carrying out an activity with excessive speed has a similar effect unless you're a piano virtuoso like Vladimir Horowitz. Most of us lack the control to race through an activity and retain touch sensitivity. But if you have developed skill and flexibility in making music, in touch-typing, in cooking, carpentry, stamp collecting, sewing, and similar jobs and hobbies, you have *manual dexterity* and your touch is delicate and controlled.

If you lack this skill you can easily improve: (1) Become aware of the touch sensations you experience every day. (2) Learn not to rush through simple manual activities like writing by hand or chopping up carrots or onions. (3) Make a conscious effort to control physical tension in your hands (and in the rest of your body). Use only the amount of energy you need for the task. In other words, when you chop carrots, hold the hands just tightly enough so that you don't drop the knife and carrot. Then, apply pressure only when you need it, as you slice through the carrot, and not during the whole operation. You should be able to feel a change in sensation and efficiency almost immediately. You'll also find that you become less tired.

COMMUNICATING BY TOUCH

When you have retrained your tactile awareness, you will have a greater touch vocabulary for communication. You will be able to vary your touch, not only in relation to an object but to a person as well. For instance, when you handle a baby, a too-firm touch says, "You're in my way" or "I don't like you," even though you may be full of warmth and tenderness. What does your handshake say about you? Are you very tense, too limp, firm but friendly, hesitant and shy? Do you like to give your child a bear hug when he wakes up in the morning? Guide him gently but firmly across a busy street? Comfort him with a reassuring embrace or pat when he's hurt or sad?

Each of these touch communications should be different, depending on the person and the circumstances. Otherwise you will not be saying what you intend. If you guide your child across the street with a limp hand, you're saying "I guess this is the way, isn't it?" instead of "Come on, son, let's cross the street now."

Perhaps you feel that you are lacking in touch-communication and would like to do something about it. You will improve if you begin to notice when others reach out to you. You should then try to respond by touch whenever you can, and adjust your touch to the other person's reaction, just as you do when you speak. Most children are wonderful teachers of communication by touch. I once saw a lady sit down in the subway next to a little girl and her mother. The child was struggling to take off her sweater and chose to hand her pocketbook to the lady to hold. The mother seemed embarrassed, but the lady was delighted. She eventually handed back the pocketbook with a smile and a friendly pat. The little girl took the lady's hand in her own for a moment, looked up, and burst into a dazzling smile. It was a lovely, wordless conversation.

A conversation by touch depends a great deal on timing. The right manner of touching at the wrong time is meaningless, or even disturbing. Here's an unfortunate example.

Several years ago, my husband invited a business acquaintance to dinner. He brought along his wife and eighteen-month-old daughter, who was put down in a car-bed in my daughter's room. The little baby was terribly unhappy and kept up a steady wailing all through cocktails. The parents never budged from the living room. As we got up to go to the dinner table, the mother seemed very uneasy. I thought perhaps she was shy about going to the baby, so I told her we didn't mind waiting, or if she preferred, she could hold Sharon on her lap at the table for a while. "Oh, no," said the father. "We don't want to spoil her." By dessert, the baby had finally cried herself to sleep. At the end of the meal, the father got up, went to the bedroom, picked up the sleeping baby, and rocked her, whimpering, back and forth in his arms. "I just can't help picking her up sometimes," he said tenderly. "I just love her so much."

Poor timing like this communicates anything but love. However, if your child is older and misunderstands a loving gesture, you owe it to both of you to explain. Suppose your family is at the dinner table and your son can't get a word in because his sisters are chattering so loud and fast. You reach over to give him a comforting pat, but he shrugs you off. You can whisper, "Sorry. I was just trying to tell you that I know you're there." This approach helps your child's awareness of others, and often does wonders for your relationship.

UNDERSTANDING YOUR OVERALL TOUCH PATTERN—HOW DOES YOUR SKIN RESPOND

TO CLIMATE? Which do you hate more, a blistering hot day or a freezing cold day? What do you consider a comfortable room temperature—70 degrees F? Or do you get sleepy when the room temperature goes above 65 degrees? Do you have a dry skin that gets cracked and itchy in winter, or do you like cold, dry air and feel suffocated in summer humidity? Each of us has an individual response to heat and cold, humid and dry air, based on our body chemistry. Your skin acts as a personal thermometer that registers your reaction.

Air currents such as a draft or wind make some people feel free, even exhilarated, while others shiver miserably in the cold. Or your skin may respond selectively—a draft on one particular part of your body gives you a chill. This will affect your behavior and how you dress. For instance, I cannot stand cold air on my neck, so most of the winter I wear turtlenecks and scarves. A winter acquaintance met me one spring day when I had on a low scoop-necked blouse. She said in amazement, "What happened to you?" She thought I had been covering up in winter out of modesty, and that I had changed my whole personality in three months.

How does your skin react to water? Do you take a bath for relaxation? What temperature—very hot? lukewarm? When you go swimming, do you jump into cool or cold water because it's worth the first shock to be able to feel your limbs moving through the water?

These individual touch responses to climate are behind many family arguments about where to spend a vacation.

TO CLOTHES? Now take a look in your closet. Can you tell what texture of clothing your skin prefers? Banlon, wool, mohair, cotton, velour? How about the style and fit—do you like loose-fitting clothes or can they feel snug on your body? Do you hate a tight collar, or a waistband that won't let you breathe? Are your shoes flexible and comfortable, or can your feet tolerate a little discomfort for a stylish effect —platform or high heel? You can discover a lot about your overall touch pattern by noticing what you choose to place next to your skin.

TO FURNISHINGS? What is the feel of your living-room furniture? Is the fabric smooth, soft, textured, tweedy? What material is your coffee table made of—wood, plastic, glass? Do you like the spring of thick carpets underfoot? Bouncy tile? Parquet floor with area rugs? Check the other rooms in your home. What fabric is your bedspread? Do you have soft throw pillows? Where do you sit most of the time when you are in your room? What is the texture of the surface? Does anyone else in the family like to sit there? If you have a cat at home, you will notice how it favors certain places for naps, places that are usually warm, soft, and protected. Each of us also has a favorite kind of place, depending on our overall touch pattern.

It is natural to assume that everyone feels as you do—spouse, relatives, children, sometimes even strangers. Have you ever argued with your neighbor on a bus over an open window? "I feel a draft." "But it's so hot in here!" Both of you are right. Once you know your own overall touch pattern, you will realize that there is no absolute measure of heat and cold, drafts, humidity and dryness, smooth or rough textures, and you will be tolerant of responses that are different from your own.

TOUCH GAMES

Most of the following touch games are intended to develop *manual dexterity*—to help your child use his hands flexibly and skillfully in his daily activities. You can check his progress by reading the Manual Dexterity Observation Game for Parents on page 179. *Communication by touch* is almost impossible to describe in game form, but if both you and your child already enjoy nonverbal communication, you may want to try a more difficult "mime" communication (see page 184). As for *overall touch*—how your child's skin responds to texture, temperature, and air—it's involuntary and can't be practiced. Awareness of overall touch is really a communication situation between you and your child: you need to keep one another informed about how you "feel." The overall touch games on pages 186–187 should help you toward this type of dialogue.

SEVEN PRACTICE GAMES FOR
MANUAL DEXTERITY

YOUR FINGERS ARE YOUR EYES
(TOUCH SENSITIVITY)
Any Age

This game will teach your child to feel objects carefully with relaxed flexible hands and fingers. It's fun and can be played anywhere, even if your child is sick in bed. Your child will be amazed at how much he can learn through his sense of touch.

Make a "touch-box" by cutting out one side of a covered shoebox. Place inside it some objects of various textures, shapes, and temperatures. Ask your child to close his eyes and feel the objects to identify them by touch only. He can take them out of the box and feel them with his hands so long as he keeps his eyes closed.

You can make him more aware of touch by asking questions. Suppose you've placed in the box a sheet of coarse sandpaper, an emery-board file, a scrap of vinyl, of velvet, of terrycloth; a soup spoon and a demitasse spoon; a piece of lump sugar and a rubber eraser of similar shape. Your child feels in the box and says, "I feel some rough things." You ask, "Which is the roughest?" He takes out the emery board, the lump sugar, the sandpaper, and discovers that the sugar and sandpaper have the coarsest texture. You ask him, "What about the shape?" He feels the sandpaper and says, "It's very rough on one side, it's flat, and on the other side it feels like paper." At this point he'll probably be able to tell you what it is. Can he use the sugar lump for sanding? No. Why not, if it's as rough as the sandpaper? Because when he rubs the surface of the sugar, the grains separate. What about the emery board? Do the grains separate? No, but it's not very rough and it has an unusual shape—long and narrow and curved at the ends. If your child can't figure it out, tell him that the shape fits the contour of your hands and fingernails—it's fine sandpaper for filing fingernails.

Another question about shape: Is there any other object in the box that is small and square like the sugar lump? Yes, the eraser, but it's smooth in texture. What happens if your child rubs the eraser? Like the sugar, the eraser separates into grains, but they're very, very soft. Why? To sand out bits of pencil without ruining the paper underneath.

Is there any other rough texture in the box? Yes, the terrycloth is bumpy, but the bumps band together. What could it be used for? Gentle rubbing that does not change the shape of the rubbed surface, as do the sandpaper and the emery board (and the eraser, if your child is accurate). What is the velvet like? *Very* soft. Ask your child what it could be used for. Rubbing? Never. He may answer, "It just feels nice," or "I bet it looks pretty." You might mention that in addition to its beauty as a fabric, velvet is used to line containers for fine silver or jewelry, because it is soft and clinging, which prevents movement and scratches.

What about touch qualities of relative shape, weight, and temperature? The two spoons are the same shape, but one is larger and heavier. Ask your child what the "little bowl" on the spoons is for. He'll answer (in his own words): to hold the liquid. Why is the soup spoon so much larger? Because you use it to carry the soup to your mouth. The demitasse spoon is used mostly to stir the coffee and to give you one, perhaps two sips of the liquid to check taste, temperature, and amount of sugar.

The spoons and the vinyl feel colder than the other objects. If your child asks why, you can check into the scientific reason, which has to do with how rapidly the substance conducts the heat away from a finger, thus creating a cool sensation. Metal and plastic are better heat and electricity conductors than fabric and rubber. That is why an electric cord is wound with rubber or elastic fiber, never with metal or plastic.

These are just a few of the facts your child can learn from touch while he is improving his tactile ability.

YOUR FINGERS SOLVE A PUZZLE
(FINE TOUCH DISCRIMINATION)
Ages: 6–12

This game will increase your child's ability at fine touch discrimination, an important part of any activity involving manual dexterity, from dressing to drawing.

Take a simple wooden puzzle of eleven or twelve large pieces, the kind that are on the market for very young children. Ask your child to work the puzzle with eyes closed. This is quite a challenge, but if your child enjoys it, you can try timing him. How quickly can he complete the puzzle with eyes closed?

Use a more difficult puzzle with cardboard pieces. It will be a larger puzzle and it is harder to discriminate among the pieces of cardboard than among the wooden ones.

Most difficult of all are the three-dimensional puzzles of plastic and wood. Be sure to tell your child that many adults can't do these puzzles even with eyes open. But you might also mention that some sightless people have developed such fine touch ability that they can sew and weave beautifully and even repair clocks, watches, and other intricate machinery.

FROM SHAPES IN SPACE TO SHAPES ON
PAPER
(FLEXIBILITY)
Any Age

This game is based on a drawing lesson in Adelaide Sproul's wonderful book, *With a Free Hand.* Many children develop tight, stiff fingers from the effort of learning to write, or the need to write rapidly as in timed achievement tests, or simply because they fall into a touch pattern that is not efficient and they don't know it. Stiff, tense fingers will affect your child's manual ability, and therefore the way he feels about himself. He needs flexibility for control in art and crafts, and useful skills such as legible handwriting, cooking, and carpentry, and in such daily activities as brushing teeth.

You can change your child's approach to using his hands (including his handwriting), but you have to start with his whole body.

Ask your child to stand up in a relaxed position and circle his arms, one at a time and then both together. He can go clockwise, counterclockwise, and also do figure eights.

Next, darken a room by pulling down the shades. Give your child a flashlight, and have him repeat the circles in front of him holding the flashlight first in one hand, then in the other. Tell him to look at the light on the wall, and to vary the rhythm—from slow to fast, slow and steady, a series of stops and starts. Be sure he does this with each arm.

If your child is a mover he'll have lots of ideas on how to move. If he is a hearing child, you can put on some music and he can follow the rhythm he hears, or he can make up a chant and move to it. If he is visual, the design on the wall will stimulate him to move in different ways. Whether he is moving, listening, or chanting, be sure to call his attention to the circles his arm and flashlight are making on the wall Otherwise, he'll lose the focus of this game.

When your child has spent a few minutes observing the light-circles, he can experiment with creating other light-shapes with the help of the flashlight. What he does will depend on his age and skill. An older child can form letters, numbers, and other designs. A younger child can make all sorts of curved and straight lines, perhaps squares and triangles. Make sure that your child continues to move freely, no matter what pattern he wants to create. He should also remember to form the design first with one hand, then with the other.

Now tape a roll of shelf paper on a wall or a piece of large painting paper on an easel. Give your child a black (washable) crayon, and ask him to repeat the wall patterns on the paper. Tell him the crayon is his flashlight. Be sure he holds it as loosely as possible and doesn't clutch it just because he's supposed to be writing. Urge him to continue to work with both hands, and tell him that each hand should feel equally relaxed even though not equally accurate.

Place a large piece of paper on a table or desk and help your child find the most relaxed and comfortable body position he can for working on this surface. This involves the relationship between the height of the writing surface and your child's torso and arms. The ideal situation is a desk at about waist level, with the writing surface at a 20 degree tilt. If his feet don't reach the ground, put a book under them. Even if it takes quite a while for him to get comfortable, don't rush because it's very important.

Now have your child use his hand and fingers on the horizontal plane as freely as he did before on the vertical plane. If he is of school age and wants to write letters and numbers, make sure he feels that he is making shapes on the paper just as he made shapes in space. If he forgets, he can get up and circle his arms for a minute to remind himself of the sensation.

WATCH HOW HANDS WORK
(FLEXIBILITY, ACCURACY, TIMING)
Ages: 6–12

See if you can find an artist or skilled craftsman for your
child to observe at work close up. This might be a musician,
Indian dancer, weaver, leather worker, architectural drafts-
man, laboratory technician, jeweler, dressmaker, tailor, or
chef.

Almost as good as the real thing in this case are close-up
camera shots on television. Point out to your child what
indicates a master artist or craftsman: the fine sure touch
that needs no adjustment, the speed of the movement, the
relaxation of the body, hands, and fingers, the lack of strain
but just enough pressure applied and released with perfect
timing to achieve the desired result.

MAKE YOUR HANDS DANCE AND PLAY
(FLEXIBILITY, ACCURACY, TIMING)
Ages: 6–12

Your child may be intrigued and amused by the following
games, which are fun and also encourage flexibility, good
timing of pressure and release, and accuracy in the way he
uses his hands. This will improve your child's self-confidence as he improves his skill in arts, crafts, and in daily
activities.

Finger puppets. Have your child draw on his fingertips
with washable colored felt-tip pencils and make a puppet
show. He can put his hands on top of a table and pretend
that it is the stage.

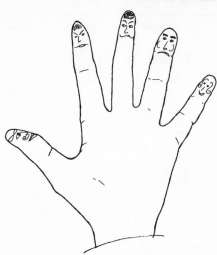

It is difficult to use both hands at once, but he ought to try each hand for practice. A variation of this is the horizontal face:

He may want to combine one horizontal face with five or less finger puppets to use both hands.

Hand Dancers. If you are waiting with your child at a restaurant or airline terminal and there is music in the background, ask your child if he would like to pass the time by dancing with his fingers. He can use his index finger and his middle finger to create dances: modern, ethnic, acrobatic, or ballet.

Charlie Chaplin Hand-Dance. If you or your child have seen the film, *The Gold Rush,* you'll remember the famous dance Chaplin performed with two rolls stuck onto forks. See if your child would like to choreograph his own dance with such objects, perhaps to the accompaniment of a record.

"Marble Hockey" or "Marble Pool." If you own a serving tray with a narrow rim, your child can practice flicking marbles into a "goal" or a "corner pocket." The two of you can play together if you like. Cover the bottom of the tray with some felt-surface adhesive-backed paper or glue in a few squares of indoor-outdoor carpet, cut to the inside dimensions of the tray.

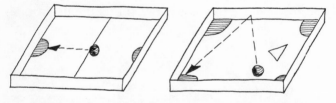

For *Marble Hockey,* draw a horizontal center line in chalk and two chalk goal posts. Line marbles up on center line, and take turns flicking them toward the opposite goal, using finger against thumb as a hockey stick. The marble will bounce out of the goal area after it hits the edge of the tray, but you can score a point each time it crosses the goal line. If no goal is made, marble remains in play wherever it lands until an agreed-on number of goals is reached. For more practice, hit with different fingers, and also the thumb (use another finger for leverage). The little finger is very hard to control, but you and your child will find that you need to shoot carefully with any finger to get where you want.

Marble Pool involves more control, since the player must

calculate the force of the rebound. Use the same playing field as before. Rub out the chalk goals and center line, and make four corner pockets and a small triangle for a starting area (see diagram). The players use a finger or thumb as before and take turns hitting marbles into the corner pocket, either in a straight line or with a shot which rebounds from the side of the tray into a pocket. The winner is the player who has scored the least number of strokes to make a pocket. Repeat for longer game.

Indian Hand Pantomime. The most challenging art form for the hands is the Hindu dance. The classic hand pictures, called *mudras,* contain thousands of intricate hand poses.

Your child can try some of the poses pictured below. A good way to practice is by making a shadow picture on the wall with a lamp. Each pose can be performed in a variety of ways, such as pliant, fluttering, undulating, firm, and still. Your child can practice these movements with either hand in the one-hand poses and should also try some of the two-handed shapes. He can make up his own originals as well. Here are some easy poses:

Lotus in bloom

Bird in flight

Budding lotus

More easy poses:

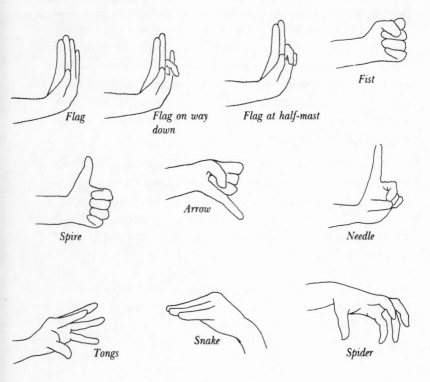

Flag

Flag on way down

Flag at half-mast

Fist

Spire

Arrow

Needle

Tongs

Snake

Spider

Some more difficult poses:

Deer

Bee, landing on his nose

Sleeping Deer

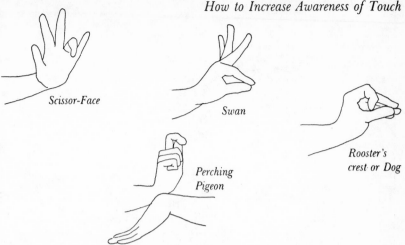

Scissor-Face

Swan

Rooster's crest or Dog

Perching Pigeon

Two different hand positions of the same pose:

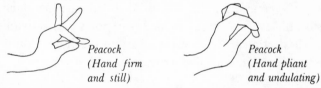

Peacock (Hand firm and still)

Peacock (Hand pliant and undulating)

A younger child may invent a story to act out in hand pantomime. He can watch it as he performs if he uses a lamp to form shadow pictures. For example:

> Here is a proud peacock. He walks like this (move hand up and and down in jerky motion). Sometimes he leans way down to eat something (bend wrist forward slowly). He hears a noise (back up, quickly). It's a tiger! He flies away (move hand back and forth in wavy motion, as if flying). He gets tired (slowly relax fingers and continue wavy motion). He falls to the ground (move hand down slowly). He lies on his back (turn over wrist). The tiger finds him and eats him (make shadow disappear).

And here is an original pose courtesy of my daughter:

Gorilla

THE EYE LEADS THE HAND
(HAND-EYE COORDINATION AT A
DISTANCE)
Ages: 6–12

This game will help your child coordinate his touch sense with his eyes, a necessary skill for sports and activities such as driving a car, sewing on a sewing machine, ironing, and fine touch activities like writing, hand sewing, carpentering, preparing food.

Tell your child that you're going to set up a bowling game. Mark a chalk line in a long hallway in your home and ask your child to practice rolling a rubber ball or a tennis ball along the line. You can use masking tape if you prefer. If your child has trouble, you might mention that success depends on his body position, the angle of his arm and hand, his timing, the force of his throw.

For an older child you might add makeshift pins (paper cups or plastic containers are good.) This will give your child practice in aiming at different points at a distance.

A more difficult variation is pool. For this, you need a small closed room which has an empty floor. Your child can practice angling the ball off the sides into the corner he's aiming for. Incidentally, this is a marvelous practical illustration of the principles of trigonometry, as is *Marble Pool*, pages 172 and 173.

THE HAND LEADS THE EYE
(HAND-EYE COORDINATION CLOSE UP)
Ages: 6–12

This game will help your child to develop the skill required for fine touch activities such as sewing by hand or on a sewing machine, ironing, carpentering, preparing food, writing by hand or typewriter. *Preparation:* Encourage your child to play all or part of the game for flexibility on page 000.

Now, ask your child to sit down easily and watch him as he makes figures on the paper. Success depends on his body position, the angle of his arm and hand, his timing, the flexibility of his fingers, the fluidity of his stroke when he is not lifting the pencil intentionally.

Let him experiment with graphic design as if his pencil were dancing across the page. Suggest that he try the following exercises.

1. Various shapes—circle, square, random:

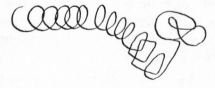

2. Various pressures and releases (accents)—heavy, less heavy, heavy light, light light; increasing pressure, decreasing pressure:

3. Combining the repetition of pressure accents into a rhythm:

If your child is a mover and has trouble sitting still as he works with his hand, tell him to think of the following: "You're using your whole body as you write. Part of your energy goes to keep your body quiet in a good position; the rest of your energy goes to your arm and hand so that they can move as you choose."

Although the design on the paper will show up any difficulties in touch, tell your child to feel first, then look. That way the touch will improve and so will the appearance. Otherwise, it's as if your child were trying to learn to dance while looking in the mirror. The effort to see inhibits the movement.

4. Penmanship. To finish the exercise, ask your child to experiment with shape, pressure accents, and rhythm with words on lined paper. If he's very skilled, you might buy him a lettering pen, some India ink and drawing paper. Here are some examples:

If your child is interested, see if you can find pictures of handwriting styles, such as Italic, old-style Roman, Gothic.

You might also show him an illuminated medieval manu-
script (either a print or an original in a museum).

WATCH YOUR CHILD'S HANDS:
MANUAL DEXTERITY OBSERVATION
GAME FOR PARENTS

Here is a check list for you to use as you watch your child
use his hands:

Overall position	Pressure
Flexibility	Timing and speed
Accuracy	Fine touch discrimination when necessary

Naturally you don't want to nag your child or interfere with
his spontaneous play, but there are some situations where
your child might welcome some help. For instance: Your
three-year-old son really wants to learn how to lace his
shoes. He's been trying to lace one for several minutes and
can't manage. You notice that he's holding the end of the
lace in an awkward way. His hands are stiff, which gives him
no control. You help him change and relax his grip until he's
able to thread the lace into the eyes of the shoe accurately.

The same approach will help a twelve-year-old who wants
to manicure her nails. The last time she did it by herself and
mangled her cuticles. You can show her how to sit down
calmly, take her time, and hold the orange stick gently but
firmly as she does the job.

Watch your child as he learns to take care of himself. Does
he really know how to brush his teeth efficiently? The dentist
probably showed him the pattern—up to down, down to up,
but what about his *overall position*—the way he stands in front

of the washbasin, and the way he holds his hand? Does he have a *flexible* grip on the toothbrush so that he can control it *accurately*? Does he apply *pressure* on the stroke, or does he grasp the brush as if it were about to fly away? Is he brushing *too fast* to do the job well?

You wouldn't want to correct all these difficulties in one session, but you could casually mention something like, "Your arm doesn't really need to work so hard. Just hold the brush easy." Or, "Your teeth will get more out of it if you slow down."

In other grooming activities such as hairbrushing and even simple washing, encourage your child not to *rush*, but to enjoy the feeling of slight *pressure* as he moves the brush across his scalp or the washcloth over his skin, and keeps his fingers as *flexible* as he can. This is not only more efficient, it feels better too.

Even dressing can be a pleasant activity for the hands, especially with today's zippers, snaps, and "Velcro" (burr-like fastening). And some buttons are such a challenge they need *fine touch discrimination*. Incidentally, your child might be interested in pictures of old-fashioned clothes with their buttons and button-hooks, hooks and eyes, and laces.

When your child is learning to feed himself, he'll experiment with the feel of a piece of bread, a bit of muffin from the toaster, a narrow strip of sliced bologna, or a carrot stick between his fingers. Later, as he learns to eat with more formality, he can continue to enjoy the touch sensations of eating: the coolness on his fingertips of a glass full of milk or chilled juice; the sensation of spreading butter on warm toast; the feel of the fork as it spears a piece of juicy steak. If he *takes time* as he eats, *sits comfortably*, keeps his hands *flexible*, and applies *pressure* on the eating utensils only when he needs it, he'll really get the most pleasure out of the food, the meal, and the company.

Watch your child as he does chores around the house. In the kitchen, there's peeling, scraping, cutting, slicing, and chopping. When you watch a young child work, think what these words mean. "Peeling" is to cut lightly, so that just the skin comes off. A young child usually cuts an apple instead of peeling it. You should correct him specifically in terms of the way he's holding the knife and applying the *pressure.* Say, "Johnny, don't push the knife so hard when you move it, or you'll cut into the apple instead of just the peel." Show him the difference between slicing and chopping: one long stroke cuts a larger slice than lots of little chops, which make smaller pieces. Show him that it all depends on what he wants to do. Incidentally, a boy can become a terrific cook if he has half a chance.

Repairs on small appliances such as toasters and radios require little strength, and girls can be as good at this as boys —sometimes better if they excel in fine touch. If you have a daughter, show her how to handle pliers and a screwdriver and how to scrape insulation off an electric wire. Just explain what you're doing, why, and how. Correct her *overall position,* the way she's holding the tool and applying the *pressure,* her *speed* and *accuracy,* her *hand-eye coordination* just as if she were in the kitchen. If she's working with her father, he may be amazed at her aptitude.

Watch your child as he does written homework. Check his *body position,* support for his feet if they don't reach the floor, the *flexibility* of his fingers, the *pressure* on pen or pencil, his *speed* of work. You might prefer to play the game on page 177 rather than make a suggestion.

Watch your child as he plays. With jacks, marbles, stick-knife (mumblety-peg), pick-up sticks, jackstraws, slotted building cards ("Eames cards"), doll house, model trains and cars, construction toys, blocks (both plain and interlocking), Erector sets, Tinker Toys, pegs and board, puzzles. How is his *overall position* when he plays? Is it one from which he can use his hands easily? Are his shoulders relaxed? Tension can travel from his shoulders right down to his hands. Are his fingers relaxed and *flexible?* Is he using a *fine touch* where he needs it? He'll never get the model car on the track if his hand is like a paw. Is he *rushing* too much to be accurate? He'll always lose at pick-up sticks, and the doll house will be a shambles. Is his *hand-eye coordination* all right? Does he have the right touch and accuracy when he builds a house of cards, but fail to place the card to balance the overall structure? If so, he probably needs practice and some encouragement to discover what works.

If you find that your child really can't manage the toy or game because it's beyond his aptitude, take it away. It will just make him angry and won't teach him anything.

Watch your child as he creates with his hands. *In Art activities* such as painting, finger painting, clay, collages of different texture, mobiles, and sculptures of wood and soap. Crafts, such as weaving, knitting, sewing, jewelry making, mosaics, assembling model cars, boats, or planes. Puppets: finger, hand, and marionettes (very difficult to handle).

In Science projects such as collecting and mounting shells, ferns, or butterflies; a dissecting kit, with specimens. Also, experiments in physics, chemistry, and working with electricity or objects such as a buzzer or a clock.

When he plays a musical instrument. Most children create spontaneously in many areas, but before a parent comments on the method, he should find out what the child is after. Unlike a game or toy, the purpose or orientation of creative expression is not always apparent, and you need to know what it is or you may just stop your child short. For instance, your daughter is knitting a scarf, and you notice that she's holding the wool so tightly that the needle will not go through. Ask her what she is trying to make. She may answer, "A scarf like your red one." If "your red one" is woven, and she is using bulky yarn, correcting the way she is using her hands will not solve the problem. You have to explain to her that a weave looks tighter than a knit, and bulky wool and needles make looser garments. Then you can show her that holding the yarn so tightly will not create the scarf she has in mind and makes it harder for her to handle her material.

If your son is painting a picture with large black splotches, made by poking sharply with his brush, ask him what it is before you correct the way he's working. It may be "Black Rain" or "Angry Bees," and his unusual technique may be intentional. (If you look at art by Jackson Pollock, you will see that he's in good company.)

In science, you also need to make sure of your child's approach. Your daughter may not want to reassemble the clock. She would rather experiment with the interlocking wheels. In music, when your daughter plays a piano scale in a rhythm like a waltz—"*wash*-ing-ton, *wash*-ing-ton . . ."— and you think it should be evenly spaced, ask her what she's trying to do. If she is experimenting with rhythm, her teacher will probably be delighted. So determine your child's intention in his creative activity. Then, you can go through your check list (body position, hand flexibility, accuracy and pressure, speed and fine touch discrimination) and give pointers if you wish.

PANTOMIMES
(COMMUNICATION BY TOUCH)
Any Age

This game is for child and parent who have a rapport in wordless communication and would like to try some experiments in mime.

Begin by taking turns with your child in expressing emotion through silent touch and gesture. See if the audience can guess the performer's intention. As you play, be aware of the physical puns you can create—a play on movements that look alike but have very different meanings.

Examples: Your child folds his arms tightly and shakes his body, with mouth open and eyes staring. You guess: "You mean, 'I'm scared.'" You repeat the same pattern with mouth closed and eyes in normal focus. He guesses, "You mean, 'I'm cold.'"

Your child puts his hand over his heart and weaves back and forth. Meaning: "I'm dying." You repeat the pattern but hold your body still and focus your eyes intently. Meaning: "I love you."

More examples for two people: A jab with the finger on the other person's body and a pointing: "Hey! Look at that."

Stroking the arm gently: "You poor thing."

Stroking the arm repeatedly, in the same rhythm: "You poor thing" *(sarcastic).*

Jab with the elbow, followed by a broad smile: "Ha ha! That's a good one!"

Jab with the elbow followed by a warning look: "Watch your step."

Grabbing the arm suddenly: "I'm scared."

Grabbing the arm unsteadily: "I'm weak. Help me."

You and your child will notice that these emotions are

broad to the point of caricature. If you experiment with more subtle feelings, you will find that you need a dramatic situation that also includes words. For instance: At seven-year-old Laura's birthday party, her sister Jane becomes very jealous but doesn't show it openly. During a game of Musical Chairs, Jane "accidentally on purpose" bumps Laura, then quickly says, "I'm sorry." If Jane had bumped Laura with no verbal apology, her mother or father might have restrained her, or sent her out of the room, but the words create an ambiguous situation.

An older child will understand a more sophisticated scene of communication by touch. For example, after a formal dinner party during which everyone has conversed politely, a man and a woman pass each other in the hall. They are secretly in love and their hands touch briefly before they continue on in opposite directions.

Your older child will find this blending of words and touch in many films. In the example above, the director might underline the sequence by camera shots of the meal in progress, then a close-up of the man gazing at someone, then the woman's face, his point of focus, then another general shot of the dinner. In many cases, the eyes supplement the sense of touch in wordless communication. Later there is a detailed shot of the two hands touching for a moment.

If your child seems to have a flair for communication by touch, he would probably flourish in a children's acting class that makes use of improvisational techniques.

FINGER DRAWINGS
(AWARENESS OF SKIN SENSITIVITY)
Ages: 6–10

This game can be played by two children or an adult and a child at home or while waiting at a restaurant, for a bus, or during a car ride over a smooth highway. The purpose is to recognize "finger drawings" on the skin, which helps your child to become aware of skin sensitivity, and that no two people "feel" alike.

Suppose your two children are in the back seat of the car and the road is smooth. One child holds out his hand, palm down, closes his eyes, and the other child traces a figure lightly with his finger on the back of the hand. It can be a letter, a number, a simple shape like a triangle, or a drawing, such as a stick figure. The other child tries to guess what it is, and then takes his turn to draw.

If it is summer and the children are lightly dressed (and are not ticklish), they can try this game on a car trip on one another's back, knee, arm, and palm. Which parts of the body are more sensitive? What is the least amount of pressure needed to make a recognizable figure? At what point does the pressure approach pain? If your children notice a difference in skin sensitivity, tell them that this is an individual physical characteristic, like curly hair or blue eyes.

HOW'S THE WEATHER?
(CLIMATE AWARENESS)
Any Age

This game encourages you and your child to talk about the weather, and to acquire a better understanding of one another's responses to climate. It can be played indoors, out-to play it for the first time on a day when the weather is extreme. The game simply consists of taking turns to describe to one another the effects of the weather on your skin.

For instance, it's a hot summer day and you and your child are outdoors. Ask him questions about how he feels, such as "Where do you feel the heat? Does your head seem to glow? Is there wetness in the hollows under your eyes? Under your arms? Dripping down your back?" Tell him what you're feeling. Suppose the wind rises slightly. Where do you feel the breeze? In your hair? At the back of your neck? Pulling at your clammy clothing? And if it starts to rain, how do the drops feel to you both? Warm on the head and back? Squishy in the shoes? Who is the first one to feel chilly, even though a moment ago the thought of coolness seemed so far away?

When you have played this game a few times in different climates you can begin to experiment with imaginary weather. Suppose you and your child are waiting in the dentist's office, and the air-conditioning is broken. You're both terribly hot. Pretend that you're sitting in a snow bank, and carry on a conversation: "Are your toes cold? You'd better wiggle them." "I can feel the snow under my rear end. I can feel it on my back." "Look—it's on my hands. See it? Here, melt a piece on your tongue." You may notice that an additional benefit to be gained from this game is that it can help you and your child sail through some rather uncomfortable experiences.

13 How to Increase Awareness of Movement

Is movement really one of our senses? Yes. Moving, or kinesthetic perception, is a kind of internalized touch sensation. It's what we feel as our muscles, tendons, and joints work. Actually, movement is different enough from touch so that you could classify it as a separate sense.

If you are aware of how you and your child move, you will already know that all of us communicate by movement. No matter what shape you are in, your child relates to the quality of your movement to read your mood. Are you angry? Nervous? Loving? Tender? Your child can tell without any words from you, just as he can recognize the meaning of your tone of voice. Also, your child often copies your posture unconsciously. You can adjust this process if you are aware of movement and posture.

Your child's concern for his own physical appearance is an important aspect of his growing up. He knows that his body is the part of him that the world sees. It is nice for him to realize that he has quite a lot of control over how he looks and what he chooses to do with himself. You will be a more complete parent if you have some knowledge of movement and movement patterns. You will also be able to help your child more effectively if he is struggling to learn carpentry, how to make a bed, cook, garden, tinker with a car, and any other work activity.

All of us move constantly as long as we are alive. If you have never looked at life this way before, you will have fun exploring a new approach.

YOUR OWN AWARENESS OF MOVEMENT

The best way to become more aware of movement is to look at yourself and notice how you move. This can be interesting, no matter how you feel about your figure. You can look at yourself objectively as a body machine and determine how you work. First, you have to discover what is individual about your particular model. How are your body segments stacked up (literally, not facetiously)? In other words, what is your posture?

Your Posture (Alignment). If you think of yourself as made of blocks, you will be able to get an idea of your alignment or posture. This is important because it affects

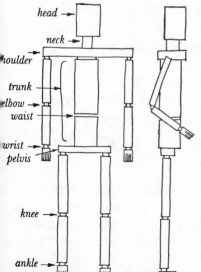

your movement, just as the wheel alignment affects the motion of a car.

What we call good posture is the correct upright balance of the body segments in relation to the pull of gravity. Perfect balance is individual, since no two people are alike, but there is an actual vertical positioning of the body that is ideal for each of us. Any variation from it creates a pull which is then counteracted by the other segments of the body.

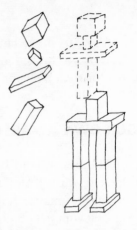

This picture shows unbalanced segments pulled straight out to the side, but since our body can also bend and twist—in other words, we are three-dimensional—there are hundreds of possible misalignments. Thus you could never really maintain perfect posture unless you are a robot who never moves. And the minute a robot moves, even he is temporarily out of balance.

Our own way of standing gives us individuality. With this positive thought in mind, look at yourself in the mirror, stripped if possible. How does your *balance* deviate from perfect alignment? Do you have a raised shoulder? Does your spine curve and make your stomach stick out? I'm not talking about fat, but about the position of your bones. Turn sideways and look at your *articulation*—the jointed parts of your skeleton. Is your neck curved forward? Your pelvis tilted back? If so, it means that the muscles have become accustomed to functioning in a way that is out of balance, either through weakness or through a movement pattern. That is, you might have weak muscles in the back of your shoulders, so your neck droops forward. Or you might be an accountant who works bent over a desk all day, so your muscles gradually accommodated to this position. It is possible to keep good alignment on a job if you can get up and move around periodically. But unfortunately, few of us can do this at work.

A reasonable goal might be an awareness of how our ideal posture feels, so that we can achieve it momentarily when we think of it. This would also keep our muscles in better shape. If you want to, you can find your ideal, or "zero point," in the mirror. Or have someone else look at you and straighten you physically. Don't be surprised if it feels wrong at first. Or you might examine a full-length photograph of yourself to identify your postural quirks.

If you can be objective, try to examine the alignment of your face. Our facial muscles also fall into habits of tension and laxness, but because our face reveals so much about us, sometimes it's hard to examine it. The muscles of a serene face are in better tone and alignment than that of someone who is feeling miserable. A well-balanced adult has a balanced face. This is the practical meaning behind the saying, "A beautiful young face is a work of nature, a beautiful old face is a work of art." No one can deny that it is an art to find such a philosophical and physical adjustment.

The major tension areas occur around the mouth, the forehead, and between the eyes. Look at your eyes for a moment. Are they wide open, or do you let the lids droop? Do the eye muscles hurt when you turn sideways and look at yourself? Many of us have stopped using the muscles of our eyes as fully as we did when we were children. Try rolling them around, up and down, side to side. If they ache, slightly, they are less active than they can be.

Your Movement Pattern. How does your body move? Now that you have an idea of your alignment, examine your movement pattern. Try to visualize your body as if it belonged to someone else. If you have a movie camera or access to videotape, you can actually see yourself in motion. But if you haven't, imagine yourself at some activity that is continuous or frequent: reading, or writing a report, typing at a desk, standing in front of a blackboard, or doing some active job at home such as carpentry, vacuuming, waxing a floor. Try to analyze the way your body functions. Has it adjusted in some way? Shoulders forward, back curled, standing with weight on one leg? Where does your body hurt when you get tired—feet, back, neck?

This will give you an idea of how you work, and where your body is strong and weak. You can double-check this by remembering activities that are extremely difficult for your body; they hurt or they take you a long time. For example, if you habitually curve your shoulders forward because you work at a desk, you will have trouble wearing a knapsack, which requires strong, straight shoulders to balance the weight on your back. If you have a weak back, changing the sheets on a bed can be quite a project. If you are lopsided because you stand with your weight on one foot, you will have trouble ice-skating for any length of time.

When you have a mental image of how your body functions, check it as you work. Be aware of how you feel as you walk, sit, move. What is your body position? Does it help or hinder your performance? Are you flexible? Do you work efficiently, without wasting *effort*? What is your *tempo,* or speed? Rapid, but not careless? Slow and deliberate? Does your work have a good *rhythm*? Not rhythm imposed from the outside, as on an assembly line, but from inside, according to your own motor. Everyone has an individual rhythm, and a good worker finds a relationship between his own body rhythm and the job to be done. Of course this relationship will be a different one for each of us. And someone can be physically ideal for a job, even though his body type is far from average. During World War II, midgets were employed to rivet wings on aircraft. Their size gave them access to areas too small for the other workers.

Compared to your size, a child is a midget. He is smaller and less strong, but also probably more flexible and agile. When you teach your daughter how to make her bed, you should try to find an individual work pattern that takes advantage of her characteristics. This will change the rhythm of the whole activity from the one you are used to; she will display a different balance and body articulation, new tempo, and new application of force, or effort. For example, she may not be strong or tall enough to lift the mattress as you do in order to tuck the blanket in at the side. But she is on the right level to slide the blanket in under the mattress, first on one side, and then on the other, after pulling it taut. In order for you to slide it you would have to bend over uncomfortably low, and you would probably prefer not to run around the bed. So be aware of the way in which you function, what your movement pattern is, and how you differ from your child in these areas.

Incidentally, this same theory can be applied to adults of different sexes. Men and women of comparable strength can perform the same job so long as the work pattern is adjusted to the basic difference in the body type. The brilliant man who first stated this was not a proponent of women's lib but Rudolf Laban, a German choreographer. Laban was the originator of movement analysis and a precursor of our contemporary efficiency experts. Because of the shortage of male labor during World War II, Laban was hired to make time and motion studies of work sites in England.

The aim of the investigation was to determine operations suitable for women. In the whole concern of rural industry connected with agriculture and forestry only a dozen jobs had been estimated as being suitable for women. The investigation showed that 180 operations can be easily done and done better by women. . . . In the early stages of our experimental investigation we visited a factory where motor-car tires were subjected to certain manufacturing processes. . . . One of the activities involving a certain weight effort, was to hang the tires on pegs at above shoulder height. Our investigations proved that the prescribed limits for handling weights are based on prejudice. The action of hanging the tires on the pegs contained, if well performed, almost no lifting effort, so that the women could easily handle tires of almost double the weight of those quoted in the official scales. It was, of course, necessary to instruct the operators not to lift but to give the tire a swing, by which it is carried by its own momentum to the desired height. *(From* Effort *by Rudolf Laban and F.C. Lawrence.)*

Your Physical Relationship to Space. Once you have become aware of your own work patterns, you can complete your movement profile by analyzing how you relate to space. This depends on your own physical makeup and movement characteristics. Look at the traffic pattern in your home. Does your living room have a lot of furniture, or is it open in plan, so that you can move freely through it? Are there nooks and corners in your house with chairs and pillows? Some people like to nest in enclosed places. Open doors and high ceilings make them feel exposed. A psychiatrist can find many interesting reasons for this, but you can also look at it uncritically, just from the viewpoint of movement. Some of us vary from day to day. You may hate to be crowded on a Monday, but on a Tuesday you enjoy having a lot of people around you. Neither way is good or bad, if it's not extreme. But you should try to be aware of how you feel in general and on any particular day, even if you don't know why.

I once went to a supermarket that remained open during extensive renovations. The carpenters and electricians, who were seated on scaffolds above the shoppers, kept up a steady stream of abuse and angry yells to each other, at the customers below, and at the staff of the store. The situation was so extreme that it became comical. The customers fell over each other to get out of the way. The clerks, who were putting supplies on shelves, gave up, so that many staples were missing. The manager began to scream at the checkers, because long lines of complaining customers were slowing them down. One assistant manager quit on the spot. It was chaos worthy of Charlie Chaplin. I was describing this scene to a friend who is a contractor. I couldn't quite figure out what had triggered it. "It's the workers," my friend told me. "They can't stand to work with people underneath them. It crowds them. They have to be so careful, it upsets their whole routine and makes them furious." It is important to know that crowding can cause a sudden rush of anger in a workman, a parent, or a child.

YOUR CHILD'S MOVEMENT PATTERN

Once you have become aware of your own body and movement patterns, it is not hard to apply the same approach to your child's movement (or to any one elses's).

What is individual about your child's posture? Check from head to toe, front, and sides. Notice the separate parts of the body—head, shoulder, pelvis. See how they are connected by twistable joints—neck, waist, wrist, etc.,—and by joints that have limited movement—elbow, knee, etc. You now know the *articulation* of your child and how he holds himself.

How would you describe the overall quality of your child's movement? Is it fluid? Bouncy? Jerky? What is his customary *tempo* or *speed?* It can range from very slow up to very rapid. What is the *effort* or *energy* involved? Slow speed with little energy is lazy, like a floating feather. Slow speed with great energy is menacing, like an approaching locomotive or a bull beginning to charge.

What is the *rhythm* of your child's movement when he plays or works? For example, if your child is learning how to pump on a swing, he must time his change in body weight so that it falls at the end of the swing back, in order to make the swing go higher when it moves forward again. This is a matter of timing that is based on physical laws. However, no two children shift their body in exactly the same way. The result is fixed, but the manner in which your child manages to get there is his own individual rhythm. (If he doesn't get there at all, his rhythm is not yet adjusted to what he intends to do—like a beginning horseback rider.)

How does your child's average movement relate to space? Think of his feet as a brush and the earth as the paper. Is the picture free or restrained? What is the design? Now add the vertical dimension and decide what you think is the overall shape of the movement.

QUESTIONS AND ANSWERS ON THE WAY YOUR CHILD MOVES

Before I describe the movement games to play with your child, let me answer a few questions that parents frequently ask me.

Will I inhibit my child if I comment on the way he moves? Not if you use common sense. If your child is playing happily in the playground, you would not be likely to call out, "Jackie, stick in your stomach," any more than you would comment at such a time on his hairdo or ask him to tuck in his shirt. Any of these remarks might interfere with his enjoyment.

But suppose you see your daughter and a friend playing outside. Her friend does a "skin the cat" (an aerial somersault, where you land facing in the opposite direction from which you started) while hanging from a tree branch. Your daughter tries and tries, but she is not using her weight correctly so she keeps flopping back to the ground. After her friend leaves, you might show her how to shift her weight in the air so it turns her over. This is just helping her to learn something that is important to her, and is no different from showing her how to clean her fingernails to look nice for a birthday party.

Or suppose that your twelve-year-old son has been invited into the living room to meet your dinner guests and after shaking hands politely, he plops down on the sofa and sprawls out his legs. His body position is rude, and later you should tell him so. You might mention that politeness toward guests includes shaking hands (which he did) and sitting in a way that says, "Here I am. I'd like to listen to your conversation and maybe add to it," instead of using body language to say, "I'm here. What are you going to do about it?" A child may be physically impolite without knowing it because he feels awkward and just happens to do the wrong thing. Or he may be physically rude on purpose. In either case, you owe it to him to point out in a pleasant way that you and others can read what his body is saying and that physical or verbal rudeness are equally bad.

You can also help your child by discussing how he moves when he is learning to perform a new work activity. Many parents do this naturally. If eight-year-old Lucy is sweeping the kitchen so energetically that she is raising more dust than she can collect, you will spontaneously tell her to take it easy. You may need to go one step further and guide her arms on the broom in a more gentle motion. Then you can follow through on her average movement pattern in other situations—if, for example, she bangs the door shut, or leaves a rumpled bed which she's "made." Tell her that the situation is like the sweeping, and that she needs a more gentle way of moving for these activities. What you are doing is being aware of your child's physical individuality, just as you would be aware of his intellectual individuality in choosing a school for him. Your child's way of moving is as much himself as the way his mind operates.

You will also want to comment on your child's physical activities when his safety is at stake. Any parent would interfere with a child's activity if it's obviously dangerous. If you are aware of how your child moves, you may be more perceptive about potential danger. Is your four-year-old son about to go down the slide on his tummy for the first time? If you know he operates at peak energy, you had better get ready to catch him. A less forceful child won't throw his body onto the slide so violently that he can't stop himself at the bottom. Does your nine-year-old daughter have rather weak arms and shoulders? If her new friend Susie is a tree-climbing tomboy, you should let your child know that she won't be able to hang from a branch as long as Susie can. You can be matter-of-fact about it and tell her Susie's had more practice. If she wants to practice too, you can show her some exercises. (A fine sourcebook of exercises is *Fitness from Six to Twelve*, by Bonnie Prudden.)

My children don't stand and move well, and I know it's not good for their appearance and health. But my son takes basketball at school and my daughter studies ballet. Won't this straighten everything out? Not necessarily. Unfortunately, sports or dance class may not strengthen a body weakness because they do not specifically counteract the difficulty. For example, basketball will not help your son straighten rounded shoulders. The emphasis will be on footwork and accuracy with the ball. He may become a good player, and gain some speed and stamina, but he'll probably keep the rounded shoulders and accommodate the rest of his body accordingly. A ballet class may not help your daughter's tummy if the teacher is concentrating on turn-out. But unlike sports, a dancer can't accommodate to an unbalanced muscle structure and be successful. Esthetically, she needs perfect balance for graceful movement and a clean line. But your daughter may benefit from ballet if she loses some weight, gains stamina, and becomes more interested in the line of her body, which would open the door to more specific improvement.

My child doesn't stand and move well, and it bothers me, but he really doesn't seem interested in changing. Should I comment on it? Not if commenting would annoy him. There is no way for your child to improve unless he is motivated. He'll just consider your comments as nagging. But you can keep your eye out for situations that may make him want to change his posture and movement. Here are some examples.

If your daughter says something like, "I hope when I grow up I won't have a hump on my back like that old lady," you can tell her that muscles are pulled out of shape by a bad body position. First the muscles get weak, then the ligaments (connecting tissues) which hold organs and bones become strained. The final result is a warped bone-structure like a widow's hump, a curved spine, or a bent torso.

If your son says, "I'm fat" (but he really isn't overweight), you can tell him that good posture can help a fat appearance. If your muscles are well-balanced, the muscle tissue stays firm and fat tissue does not develop. Those little bulges of fat on the tummy and the hips may not be extra weight but a visual reminder of bad alignment. Sometimes the only answer is specific exercise, but occasionally, a child can lose this fat just by changing the way he stands, and carrying this new alignment over into his movement. The change in muscle balance makes a kind of continuous spot reducing.

Sometimes a child thinks he's fat when he's actually out of proportion. His chest, his thighs, and his calves may look too small for the rest of him. And his normal-sized hips or waist appear too big in comparison. Good muscular balance builds up weak parts of the body by increasing the muscle tissue. Your son can develop his physique and your daughter can improve her shape by an awareness of body alignment. A good muscular balance keeps muscle tissue strong, so that the body doesn't appear caved-in or skin and bones. The weak muscles may need special attention. Or, as in spot reducing through better posture and movement, your child may manage spot building-up.

If your child says, "I don't like the way my clothes look on me," you can tell him that clothes hang on his body's bone structure. Even a perfect figure won't make a dress look good if the form underneath is out of line. That's why fashion models, in addition to dieting, study dance. But even a less than perfect figure can be attractive if the structure underneath is well aligned. This can also make a short person look taller. Choreographer-dancer Martha Graham held her short body with such regal energy that on stage she always looked extremely tall.

How clothing fits can give your child a clue to his posture. For example, if your daughter buys a long-sleeved blouse which she tried on standing up in the store, but miraculously it becomes too small when she wears it to school, she probably slumps her shoulders when she sits. This will make the sleeves pull up and feel too tight at the cuff.

Suppose your child says, "I'd love to exercise to get rid of my tummy, but it takes too long." Tell him that because he's young, he only needs to work at it a few minutes a day. If he waits until he's older, it will take much more time per day.

Your child's motivation toward movement and alignment may improve because of a new interest in certain sports, a new desire for health and stamina, or sudden desire to get back to nature and his inner self.

Sports for balance include bicycle-riding, riding a scooter or skateboard, roller-skating, ice-skating, skiing, and surfing. If your child wants to do well in any of these, he will need to have a good body alignment.

Many pre-teen-agers become very conscious of health and stamina and natural living because of their concern with the environment and themselves as part of it. You may be able to increase your daughter's desire for good posture by saying (truthfully) that it promotes good health, it's more natural, and it's the way her body is supposed to be. You can tell her that her internal organs don't function as well if the bone structure around them is poorly balanced. Bad alignment squeezes them all out of shape. You can also show her pictures of the beautiful carriage of African and Jamaican women who carry baskets on their heads. If she wants to try it herself, she'll discover that she needs perfect alignment or the basket will fall. If she expresses an interest in yoga, encourage her. Regardless of her muscle development or coordination, there is nothing better for body alignment than the yoga exercises (except for the headstand, which is an advanced pose in yoga).

A different type of child may like the idea that his stamina and endurance will improve from good body alignment, because this means less wasted effort. If he has a feel for applied science, you can tell him that there is a parallel between a straight body and a vertical tower: they need less support than a crooked body or a leaning tower. If he's keen on body conditioning, he'll like the idea that he's building up the strength of his body by using the muscles correctly. Here's an impressive statement for him, about the relationship between muscles and strength: his magnitude of force is proportional to the number and size of muscle fibers contracting.

Should I try to interest my child in the way other people move even if he doesn't want to change himself? Of course. Just as your child can learn to love music without playing an instrument, we can learn to enjoy observing patterns of physical movement. Movement is such a big part of life that it is a shame for a child not to be aware of it, no matter how he feels about his own body. A strong interest in how others move might lead a child toward a field such as movement therapy or choreography, which do not require an exceptional body but rather an unusual sensitivity to movement. And probably some day he will begin to relate to his own patterns.

MOVEMENT GAMES

The first three games here are movement observation games that should interest almost any child. The others are for the child who wants to practice and improve his own way of moving. Unlike the other senses, movement requires a real effort and motivation on the part of your child. If he complains that the latter games are more like work, he is probably not motivated enough to give the movement practice games a try. In any case, play some movement observation games first. They will give your child a fuller approach to his own movement. The last game in this chapter is a movement observation game for parents (page 222) that will help you to evaluate your child's movement pattern in daily activities.

WATCH THE WORLD MOVE
Any Age

This game is like the General Hearing Game on page 112, but you'll be noticing movement, not listening for sounds. The game is fun, and will make your child more aware of the world around him as it helps you to discover how your child responds to movement. Pick a time when you and your child are together in a large space, hold your ears if you want to, and look for movement.

If you and your child are waiting at a bus stop in the city, you will see cars moving in the street; and on the sidewalk, people walking, dogs trotting, baby carriages and bicycles rolling. There are traffic lights and red brake-lights flickering, and up above perhaps an airplane, a pigeon, or scraps of paper flying through the air.

If you look up at the buildings above you, you can sometimes see someone opening or shutting a window, shaking out a rug, or pulling a shade down or up. Sometimes there are house painters working near the window. And if you are in the business district, you see business going on at the street level and above: men cleaning sidewalks and windows, making deliveries, shopkeepers working or waiting on customers.

It's rarely so still that the wind doesn't create movement in clothing or flags or leaves on the trees. Rain moves through the air, running down window panes, and along the gutters. Sunlight gives us many visual impressions of movement, as it is blocked out by a cloud or by a building and then reappears through a slight shift in our position.

As you play this game with your child, you may discover that one of you focuses on light, color, and forms positioned in space much more than on the movement of objects. It is easier to consider movement patterns in this chapter and visual characteristics of a still image in the next one on seeing. Of course both experiences are visual. But if you concentrate on movement while your child sees primarily forms, and you are both in the same place, you will need some games in both areas in order to understand and communicate with one another. A spider making his web provides a beautiful bridge between the two approaches. You see the spider move, and the pattern of his movement remains as a still design in space.

When you have both become aware of what is moving around you, try to compare the *quality* of the movement. Cars, perambulators, and bicycles roll. People walk in a variety of ways: bouncily, lightly, rapidly, carefully, slowly, painfully. A bird may glide, paper floats. Lights flicker from on to off to on. Wind makes clothing and flags billow, leaves shake and vibrate. Rain glides, sunlight shimmers. It is not necessary to go into why these movements occur, unless your child is interested in mechanics. But it is nice to become aware of all the different types of movement in our surroundings.

You can also find random movement in the country: wind on trees, bushes, grass, flowers, bird, animal, and insect movements in the air, on land, underground, in the underbrush; reptiles, fishes, and aquatic plants in the water. The movement of a brook over stones. Outdoor workers in fields and gardens. And sunlight flickering to shade in a forest.

You and your child can also find some random movement in an enclosed space if it is a very big one, such as a stadium. The large number of people and activities creates a moving panorama. But a small enclosure imposes limitations on movement, so that it becomes movement in a place.

WATCH WHAT MOVES IN A PLACE
Any Age

This game, like the previous one, is fun, helps your child to become more aware of the world around him, and helps you to discover how your child responds to movement. However, in this game your child explores what movement he sees in an enclosed space.

The next time you're at the doctor's for a check-up with your primary-school-aged child, ask the child to notice the movement activity in the waiting room. The children all wait in different ways. One little boy crawls on the floor intently shoving and arranging the blocks. Another sits on a little chair, slowly turning pages of a book. A little girl kicks her feet, screaming in fear and rage. The nurse may be filling out records, or talking on the phone, or giving out a lollipop, but usually her movements are smooth and gentle. A nurse with jerky movements and a jumpy manner just cannot last at a pediatrician's office.

During a walk or a family outing, stop to look at the scene of a strenuous work activity, such as a building construction site. Watch the way an experienced workman lifts a concrete block. He counterbalances the weight with his pelvis and back. He carries it in a slow steady rhythm, and lowers it to the ground with a sudden but sustained motion. This uses minimum effort for the job, and is best for his body. He will be able to continue working effectively for many hours at a stretch. You and your child may be able to spot a new worker by his less efficient, hasty movements and poor judgment of space, weight, and balance, as he approaches the block; as he lifts the block, and as he tries to counteract the weight with his body. This worker wears himself out. He needs constant work-breaks because his body is working so hard, even though he may not be accomplishing very much.

Incidentally, although this sounds like a "father-son" game, it is not. I have noticed that most of the men who watch construction sites comment on the progress of the work, not on the movement of the workers. So both parents can learn to observe movement along with their children.

Soon you and your child will be able to recognize patterns in work activities. These vary, depending on the purpose, the material, and the worker. When men spread concrete on a sidewalk, they must work swiftly, before it hardens, and evenly, in order not to break the surface. They kneel on a board placed over the frame, which is slightly above the level of the freshly poured concrete. This position is best because it makes it easier to control the hard pressure on the trowel and to smooth the concrete. The operation requires tremendous strength in the back, because unlike the job of waxing a floor, there is nothing to lean on as you work. If you watch two good workers of different body types, one tall and husky and one short and wiry, you will see how each has adapted the required movement to his own frame.

There are many heavy work activities on a farm, if it is not mechanized: carrying grain and fertilizer, raking stones, pitching hay. When you and your child watch a farmer pitch hay into a wagon, you will see him give a sharp thrust with the pitchfork to pick up the hay, then a large heave to lift it. This movement is slow because the load is heavy, and it's steady, so that the hay won't separate and fall. When the hay is at the right height, the farmer shifts weight to one side and uses the pitchfork as a lever to throw the hay over his head into the wagon. This last movement is quick because it's easier for him and because he wants to dislodge the hay from the fork. So the job effort is in three parts: one, a quick sharp thrust; two, a slow steady lift; and three, a fast sweeping throw. Each of the three movements has a fairly even beat or stress, so the rhythm of the movement pattern would be like the first three syllables of the word *Mediterranean.*

Me   di   ter   (anean)
ONE   TWO   THREE

If the farmer has to chop some wood, the ax goes up quickly and comes down heavily into the log. The rhythm of this movement pattern would be like the word *canoe.* The beat, stress, or accent, is on the second syllable:

ca   NOE
one   TWO

If you encourage your child to keep his eyes open at home, too, he'll see many heavy work activities in different rhythms: carrying groceries, scrubbing a floor, rubbing in furniture polish, installing storm windows, repairing gutters. This may help him to understand objectively how much hard work is needed to run a home as well as to become more aware of movement.

WHAT TYPE OF PERSON MOVES LIKE
THAT?
(DETECTIVE GAME)
Ages: 5–12

This game will help you to explore what your child sees in other people's way of moving. Most children have a wonderful ability to mimic movement characteristics. Perhaps you tried not to laugh the day your son walked "just like Uncle Ed"—with shuffling feet and a trembling arm. Or the day your daughter imitated the loose, sexy walk of her favorite rock hero. Did your child ever scare you to death by limping just for fun? One of mine did. I thought she'd really hurt herself.

You and your child are influenced by the way people move as well as by their speech. When he calls someone "a timid mouse," or a "pushy kid," chances are he's responding to some extent to a movement pattern. Perhaps the mouse curls his body in on himself like a snail, while the other uses his hands and shoulders to get where he wants to be, no matter who's in the way. Recently, anthropologists and psychologists have begun to study the significance of how people move, ranging from behavior in social groups to the most minute flicker of a facial muscle. Experts can interpret this body language to discover the dynamics of a group or the hidden fears of an emotionally disturbed individual. Incidentally, a friend of mine once discovered that a tilt to her head was affecting her work opportunities. She was an attractive actress in her thirties, and the mother of a large family, but she was consistently hired as an ingénue, not for roles in her own emotional or chronological age. In a mime class she became aware of how she held her head and was able to correct it. I noticed how this changed her image:

from a soft girl to a positive woman. (She actually was awarded a leading lady role in a Broadway play shortly afterward.)

This game will help you and your child to become more aware of how people move, and how this affects you, without going too deeply into the psychological causes. As in the hearing-speaking game on page 115, your child's response may be sharper, but you have the benefit of greater experience.

The next time you and your child are waiting on a busy street, or sitting in a restaurant with a street view, watch the people go by. The French mime, Etienne Decroux, once said that people walk as if they were children making faces in the dark: they think that nobody can see them. Try to find a single-minded man with an attaché case, tunneling through the crowd because he's late. Or a self-centered woman ambling along as she window-shops, without being aware of the people trying to get past her. Notice the variety of body articulation: one man tilts his head up, pushes his stomach out, and waddles slightly even though he's not fat. Another may push his pelvis forward as he walks, like a fashion model, which gives him an effeminate appearance. An elderly lady may appear as a coy young thing because she holds her hands out from her body and carefully places one foot in front of the other, as though she were walking on eggs. It may mean that she is ignoring her age, or it may mean that her feet hurt—you can probably tell which by her clothing and her expression.

Here are two more imaginative methods to observe the way people move, adapted from Viola Spolin's splendid book, *Improvisation for the Theatre.* The first is based on *animal images.* Try to think of an animal that moves like the person you are watching. Suppose you and your child are at the library, and the librarian is very solemn, blinks her eyes slowly, and moves her body in a tight block. Does she remind you of an owl? How about your neighbor's son, who can leap over your front gate like a cat? And the heavy lady at the dry cleaner's, who lumbers around like a friendly elephant?

The second approach is a little more difficult. It might be named *What Does He Do for a Living?* The idea is to become aware of how a person's physical background or occupation affects his movement. A construction worker who uses large muscles in a relatively open space may have trouble managing tiny sandwiches at a crowded wedding reception. On the other hand, city children who walk on level sidewalks in a regular layout can't move freely on rough country terrain. They trip, they don't know how to deal with the underbrush or the overhanging branches, they hesitate to leap a small brook. You can find people who move as if they sit a lot: businessmen, secretaries, some elevator operators. Others seem more adapted to walking, as if they were letter carriers, waitresses, delivery boys. Try to guess if that man running for the bus is a tennis player. It doesn't matter if he plays tennis or not, but if you and your child both decide that he does, you have probably noticed certain qualities of speed, fluid motion, and coordination that characterize a good athlete. That is, this game increases your child's awareness of motion, whether or not the accompanying conclusions are true.

SIX PRACTICE GAMES FOR
MOVEMENT

HOW DO THE PARTS OF YOUR BODY FIT
TOGETHER?
(ARTICULATION)
Ages: 6–12

This game will help your child become aware of the movable parts of his body. Your child needs this body awareness in order to find his own natural balance.

Tell your child he has an individual balance that is different from anyone else's, and that this game will help him feel what it is.

Preparation (Relaxation).   Ask your child to lie down on his back, close his eyes, and pretend to fall asleep. Tell him to imagine a black velvet curtain descending over his eyes, or that his closed eyes are seeing green or blue, or that he hears gentle music, or that his body is floating on water—any image that relaxes him. (Incidentally, this actually is a good way to fall asleep.)

When he is lying still, tell him to listen to you but to keep his eyes closed. Try to talk in a calm but natural tone of voice. Tell him that every human being has his own rhythm which begins before he is born and continues day and night. He can become aware of his rhythm by breathing easily, the way he does when he's asleep. Tell him you'll wait a few minutes as he tries to feel his rhythm of natural breathing.

If he's trying, he'll be quite relaxed by now and you can go on to the next step. If he's jumpy or giggly, he's not in the mood and you'd better stop for the day.

Articulation of the Body (Lying Down).   Tell your child that he is going to move each part of his body one at a time in his own rhythm, beginning at the bottom. He should keep his eyes closed and feel his body move. Ask him to breathe in gently as he raises his left foot a few inches off the floor, circle the foot on the ankle joint from left to right and from right to left, and let it drift back to the floor as he breathes out. When he's ready, he does the same with the right foot. After this he should wiggle all ten toes.

Now tell him to lift his left leg from the hip joint a few inches off the ground, twist the hip joint slightly, bend the knee back and forth, lower it gently as he breathes out. If he has trouble finding his hip joint (or any other articulation) tell him not to open his eyes and help him gently—in this case, rotate his leg with your hands until he feels the movement of the joint. Repeat the instructions for the right leg. Remember to speak and move calmly and try to blend the rhythm of your speech with your child's breathing and rhythm.

Next, help him to become aware of the relationship of his hips to the rest of his body. Ask your child to press down with his elbows and raise his hips off the floor an inch or so, wiggle them a little, and lower them as gently as possible. (You may need to help him by lifting him up once.) He should keep his legs as still as possible.

Now comes the chest. Ask the child to slide the back of his head a few inches toward his feet, which will simultaneously raise his chest off the ground (the weight is on the back of his head). Ask him to wiggle his shoulders and to feel his waist moving before he slides back down.

Now he moves his left arm, starting from the shoulder joint. Ask him to lift it a few inches from the floor, circle the shoulder joint, bend the elbow joint, circle the wrist joint in both directions, and wiggle the fingers. Then, tell him to do the same with the right hand.

Last come the head and neck (eyes should still be closed). Have him lift his head up a few inches, drop it gently back down, roll it from side to side.

Your child may have speeded up or slowed down, but if he has managed to complete the whole series of movements, congratulate him. He has moved each part of his body in more or less his own rhythm.

FIND YOUR BEST BALANCE STANDING UP
(ALIGNMENT)
Ages: 6-12

Tell your child that his balance is different from anyone else's, and help him find his natural body position standing up by juggling the weight of the different parts of his body until they are in good balance. If he does not quite understand what this means, you can show him the diagram on page 189, or illustrate with your own body, or use a jointed model—the kind used by artists for sketching, which is available at art supply stores. If you and your child are visual you might make some clay figures of various human body types.

Ask your child to stand in front of a full-length mirror, front and side view, and help him line up his body segments. If he is quite out of line, such as from a sway back or the opposite curve, his natural balance will feel wrong at first because he's not used to it. However, he'll probably be able to see that it looks better, even though in side view he'll be twisting his head out of line in order to look. This twisting motion is good for his eyes, though. You might take the opportunity to tell him to roll his eyes around, up and down, from side to side, diagonally lower left to upper right and vice versa. Also, have him wiggle his face—forehead, nose, cheeks, mouth, tongue, jaw, and ears if he can. Tell him that his eyes and face sometimes need some practice in alignment as well.

A novel way to show your child his alignment in profile is by silhouettes, (the way Alfred Hitchcock's shadow appears in his television program). At night, take a lamp and cast his shadow on the wall, with as little distortion as possible. Then, he can try out some unusual shapes. Have him end up with the way he looks best. Tell him that this is his own zero point, his natural balance, and that if he learns to feel comfortable in this position, he'll get less tired, be able to move more freely and look better, no matter what he's doing.

FIND YOUR BEST BALANCE IN YOGA
POSES
(BENDING AND STRETCHING IN GOOD
ALIGNMENT)
Ages: 6–12

This game will help your child become aware of how his body can bend and stretch in good alignment. The series of movements will give him flexiblility and strength, both of which are necessary for easy movement in sports and in daily activities.

Tell your child that his muscles move like pulleys: as one stretches, the other relaxes. If one of his muscle pulleys is less strong than its partner, the body is pulled out of line— just as a car with a flat tire pulls toward the side where the tire has weakened.

The following positions are based on yoga poses that relax and stretch in turn all the most important muscles of the body. Since the poses are geometrical, it is easy for a parent to tell when the child's body is on the right track. Look at the poses on the next page and show them to your child. A few simple instructions are given on page 216.

How to Increase Awareness of Movement
Bending-Stretching Based on Yoga Poses

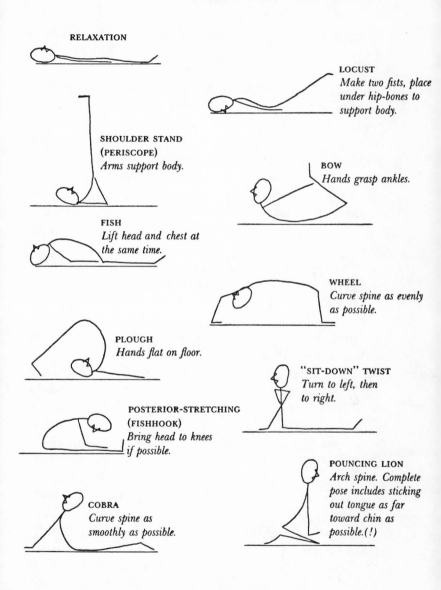

RELAXATION

LOCUST
Make two fists, place under hip-bones to support body.

SHOULDER STAND (PERISCOPE)
Arms support body.

BOW
Hands grasp ankles.

FISH
Lift head and chest at the same time.

WHEEL
Curve spine as evenly as possible.

PLOUGH
Hands flat on floor.

"SIT-DOWN" TWIST
Turn to left, then to right.

POSTERIOR-STRETCHING (FISHHOOK)
Bring head to knees if possible.

POUNCING LION
Arch spine. Complete pose includes sticking out tongue as far toward chin as possible.(!)

COBRA
Curve spine as smoothly as possible.

If your child wants to try these poses, here is how to help him.

1. Tell him he should feel the pose, not try to see it. If he doesn't mind, he should close his eyes as he works. Tell him that you'll let him know if he's way off.

2. The poses will be easier for him in the afternoon and at night than in the morning when his body is stiff from lying still.

3. A good way for him to start is with the relaxation on page 211. This takes out any kinks he may have from the day's activities, such as slumping over a desk or lounging in a chair.

4. It's not good for him to work on a full stomach. The best time is roughly two hours after his last meal.

5. Tell him to look at each picture and then to do the poses in order. Each position counteracts the one before it. Once he knows the positions you can call out the names for him so that he won't have to get up or open his eyes.

6. He should go into each pose slowly in his natural breathing rhythm (see page 211). He should come back to the relaxation position the same way, and rest a minute before he goes on. He can ease any strain from the pose (neck, hips, legs, etc.) by moving gently before he continues.

7. By checking with the picture, you will be able to encourage him if he is on his way to being correct. He should go as far as he can in the pose until he feels a good stretch. Then he can stop, hold for a few seconds, and come down to rest.

8. Try to talk together as little as possible. This, plus the closed eyes, will make it easier for your child to concentrate on the feel of the movement. Whenever possible, correct him gently with your hands instead of your voice.

9. If a pose is easy for him to do correctly, he should try

to hold it without moving for a minute or so. This has an isometric effect on the muscles and strengthens them. (A child who gets the feel of a pose correctly can practice on his own if he wants to.)

10. If a pose is really difficult for your child, omit it (the Wheel and the Locust require a fair amount of strength). Your child should be able to achieve the others, with practice. If he has trouble, you might try to pin down the specific areas of difficulty. For example, your daughter can't reach beyond her calves on the Fishhook (posterior stretching). Which muscles won't give? The ones in the back of her legs or the ones in her back? Or your son makes a wobbly periscope on the shoulder stand. Is the wobble in his pelvis because his stomach muscles are weak, or are his shoulders muscle-bound from baseball so that he cannot push up far enough?

Even if you don't know much about how the body works, you can usually see what is out of line and ask your child to move that part of his body as a check.

These positions will eventually correct such difficulties, but for more rapid improvement of a weak muscle, the best thing is a *spot exercise* for that part of the body. If you and your child are "movers," you can make up your own exercise. If not, there are a number of excellent paperback books that give simple exercises for specific parts of the body. For a more complete approach, you might invest in a copy of Bonnie Prudden's *Fitness from Six to Twelve,* mentioned earlier.

CHANGE THE WEATHER AS YOU MOVE
(MOVEMENT EFFORT AND MOVEMENT
QUALITY)
Ages: 6–12

This game will give your child an awareness of the energy behind his movement in various activities and how this affects the quality of the movement. This is important for skill in sports and effectiveness in any physical activities, from making a bed to climbing a tree.

The next time your child complains about picking up in his room, ask him to pretend he's doing the same job somewhere else. Maybe he's on a planet where the air is full of feathers, or the air is like honey or molasses. Or he's underwater or on the moon, where there's less gravity and everything floats. This gives his movement a totally different quality. Heavy changes to light, fast becomes slow and sustained, strong effort or energy becomes easy and floating. It also makes the job more fun and shows him a different way of working.

Perhaps your daughter is in a big hurry but has to set the table first. She bangs the silver down so roughly that she has to stop and rearrange each piece a second time. Some day when she is calmer, suggest that she set the table as if she were on the moon. She'll discover that less effort and a more sustained movement will get the job done more quickly.

You might also suggest pretending to function in an unusual environment of weather and temperature, such as getting dressed in an imaginary cloudburst (it really speeds things up) or brushing the hair in a hot windstorm (this makes your child brush harder and more slowly—very good for the scalp).

In addition to air, wind, and water, your child can imagine

a change in the surface on which he's moving. Suppose you and your child are both walking home tired from a shopping trip. What if the pavement were a field full of little flowers? You'll walk more gently and easily. A cotton sidewalk is soothing, and sponge rubber would be bouncy, or what about little wooden slats, exactly one foot apart? (Watch out or you'll fall in.)

Even if you feel a little silly about this game, the imaginary conditions make your child stop and become aware of how he's moving, and specifically, the amount of effort he puts behind certain movement patterns. Since he develops these patterns in relation to certain constant conditions—that is, gravity always pulls with the same force, air resistance doesn't change much unless it's windy, and it's not windy or rainy indoors—change the conditions and you change the pattern. If gravity suddenly pulls your child with a different force, even in your child's imagination, he'll need to readjust all his movements. He may end up with a movement pattern which works much better for that activity than his usual way.

MOVE LIKE SOMEONE ELSE
(MOVEMENT TEMPO AND MOVEMENT RHYTHM)
Ages: 6–12

This game will give your child an awareness of the speed and rhythm of his movement and how he can alter them if he wishes. This is important for skill in sports and effectiveness in any physical activities.

The game involves pretending to move like someone else. Suppose your son is grumbling because he has to straighten out the tools in the garage. Ask him to pretend he's a robot who has a constant speed of movement, which gives every action the same rhythm. This makes your child aware of his own normal rhythm for that activity, whether it's fast and sprinting, slow and methodical, slower and slower like a clock running down, or an erratic rhythm, now fast, now slow.

Ask your child to be an old person. For instance, your daughter may want to try moving like her grandmother. What's hard for her to accomplish? How does she handle the job in view of the difficulty? If her shoulders are stiff and painful, how does she manage to put on a sweater? She will have to subordinate the natural rhythm of the movement to her body and what it can do. It may give her a new understanding of what it is like to have aches and pains.

Some children love to move like dancers, especially girls, who pretend to be ballerinas. It helps to make them conscious of a smooth flowing rhythm. You might also suggest that your child imitate animal movement. Have him practice the crouching, springy walk of a lion or tiger, the preening, jerky steps of a rooster, and then an elephant, strong, slow, and steady. You should mention to your child that animals move as they do for physical reasons related to their survival, but that because he is a human being, he has the choice of moving whichever way seems best for what he is trying to do.

If he has a long, heavy job, such as putting books up on bookshelves, he'd be better off moving like a slow and steady elephant than a jumpy deer. Otherwise, he'll be worn out before he finishes.

The opposite movement patterns apply to a baseball batter. He needs to bat like a tiger springing, and run as hard and fast as he can like a cheetah. Otherwise, there's no point in playing.

Your child can learn to collect himself before he starts on anything, the way a diver stops still on the diving board before he jumps. Once he's decided *how* he'll move, he can throw himself into the activity in a way that's both right and beautiful.

TRACE A PATTERN AS YOU MOVE
(MOVEMENT IN RELATION TO SPACE)
Ages: 4–12

This game will help your child become aware of himself moving in relation to space. Besides being fun, it makes your child more aware of the world around him and is important for an understanding of architecture, dance, natural science, and physics.

If your child is age four to six he can practice this in a jungle gym at the playground. Tell him to pick a figure to walk through within the bars of the jungle gym, as if it were a maze. He can trace a geometrical shape such as a square, two diagonals, or a checkered pattern, if he walks straight ahead on the paths between the bars. Once he gets the idea, he can start making movement designs in the open. The next time he accidentally knocks over a chair at home, suggest that he slowly walk through all the designs that work in that room. There should be several, unless it is very tiny.

For an older child, a more sophisticated version of this game is the giant chessboard. In a large area, your child can pretend that he is moving as chess figures do, in diagonals, straight lines, *L*'s, and one-steps.

If your child is interested, here are some additional spatial designs for him to study: football plays, country folk-dances, ballets. If you wish, you can make a floor plan of the movement patterns in your home. If you know an architect, he can show your child how a good building encloses space and how this design creates an interior space pattern for people to follow.

Spatial designs for machinery include traffic patterns and controls in a large city; navigation lanes for boats in a harbor; the work of an airport controllor as he plots airplane landings, takeoffs, and holding patterns. And some of nature's movement patterns through space are: ritual dances of animals, birds, fish, for courting, mating, staking out territory; and migratory habits of animals, birds, and fish on land, in the air, under water.

WATCH YOUR CHILD AS HE MOVES: MOVEMENT OBSERVATION GAME FOR PARENTS

You can help your child become more skillful in controlling his body, a process that will give him pleasure and self-confidence.

What is Special About Your Child's Way of Moving?   Your child has his own way of moving which reflects his temperament, body type, and conditioning. You probably know very well how your child moves, but you think of it mostly in terms of personality and appearance not in terms of the characteristic movement as such. If you take a moment to find out what's special about your child's overall movement pattern, you can help him when he needs it.

What you are looking for is: *alignment* and *balance*—how he holds his body when he stands, sits, or moves—and movement characteristics such as, "Is my child slow and calm? Does he work too hard so that he wears out? Is he very energetic and constantly moving? Does he tend to break things because he's so rambunctious?"

More specifically, movement characteristics are a combination of: *effort*—your child's degree of oomph; *speed* (tempo)—fast, medium, slow, and in between; and *rhythm*—how your child's body combines effort and rate of speed in a repetitive movement. For example, Ann and Sally are bicycling up the same hill. Ann sits slightly forward and pushes smoothly with her legs. Sally stands up on the pedals periodically and uses her whole body weight to turn the bicycle wheel. Ann's effort is less than Sally's, her speed is probably the same, and her rhythm is steady and even: push, push, push. Sally's effort is energetic—more so than necessary (unless her legs are weak and she is using her body weight to compensate). Her speed is the same, but her rhythm is full of strong body accents: rise, PUSH DOWN, sit, rise, PUSH DOWN, sit.

This example also illustrates *use of space*. Ann's measured bicycling covers less body area in space than Sally's energetic "rise, PUSH DOWN, sit."

If you are a parent of these girls, you can learn to predict how each child will tackle a movement situation. Ann will do a nice job of making her bed or paddling a canoe; Sally will do better at nailing up a shelf or running a short-distance race. Of course each child should learn to do what the other does best. Sally needs to learn how to make a bed even if she's better at running races. Furthermore, movement-expert Rudolf Laban states that it is better for everyone to have a wide movement vocabulary because a repeated movement pattern becomes exaggerated and loses effectiveness, even if it started off well. Laban found that too much strong motion becomes cramped and too much light motion becomes sloppy. Too much direct motion (like the flight of an arrow) becomes obstinate and inflexible, whereas too much flexibility turns into fussiness. Slow steady motion

Your Child's Sensory World

becomes lazy and without direction while too-quick motion becomes hasty.

These findings had a practical application for Laban in finding adult workers' abilities for certain activities. But you can give your child a similar bonus. Make sure that he has a wide range of physical activities and that he is using his body as well as he can, even if the activity does not come easily to him because his overall movement pattern is one suited to other tasks.

Does Your Child Have a Wide Movement Vocabulary at Work and at Play? Watch your child while he is at work and at play. If he is direct and forceful in his movement, he would be good at pushing a hand lawn-mower, moving heavy furniture, opening a jammed door. He could play football, lift weights, carry a heavy back-pack on a camping trip. All these activities involve *good alignment* of the body so he or she doesn't strain a muscle under the weight. (Yes, girls too. I know several who can lift very heavy weights.) These activities also require a *steady, strong rhythm* with a *pushing or pulling movement quality*.

Activities that are more difficult for such a child are raking leaves or sweeping, which need *light effort* or he'll chew up the lawn or scatter the dust. He will also have difficulty clipping a hedge, which needs *short slashing movements* and *jerky rhythm* in order to cut through the branches, and a *constant shift in space* to get an even hedge. Some other activities of similar pattern include making a bed, folding sheets and towels, and dusting funiture, all of which require *flexible motion and rhythm* because of the *enclosed space* and the *light weight* involved. A compromise might be vacuuming a heavy carpet. Your child needs *pushing energy*, but within the *spatial limit* of walls and furntiure.

Some sports that make use of *flexible* movement qualities in an *enclosed space* are basketball, tennis, squash, and fencing. Other movement characteristics of these sports, and others, such as soccer, field and ice hockey, are *speed,* variety of *rhythm,* and a *body alignment* which is more *balanced* than *forceful.*

Even if your child is not athletic and really doesn't like to move, you can still vary his activities and increase his movement vocabulary. For instance, your twelve-year-old daughter hates sports and heavy work but loves to knit, which is a *light, flicking, repetitive* motion. See if she would like to iron, which is also light and repetitive but *glides smoothly* instead of flicking sharply and has a *varied rhythm.*

Another job that involves a repetitive gliding motion, but with a *stronger effort* is sanding furniture. Your child will need to be aware of her body alignment as she applies the pressure or she'll get a stiff arm or pains in the back and neck. This job also involves much more *movement through space* than knitting. Your daughter will be working much harder than she realizes.

Here are some other activities that should intrigue your child, even if he is not a mover: For *steady, sustained* movement with *light effort* and *good body alignment* and *rhythm*: painting a wall or other large surface; sweeping; polishing furniture. If by any chance you have access to a large loom, weaving a wall-hanging gives the same physical benefits with a creative result. Play activities of similar movement pattern include pumping on a swing, bouncing a ball, jumping rope. A ball, rope, or swing are all governed by the laws of physics, so there is a natural rhythm to any such games.

For *steady sustained rhythmical* movement of *greater effort*: hiking in hills or mountains, sledding (climbing back up the hill), climbing trees, skiing, skating, shoveling snow. (The last is so tiring because of the heavy sustained lift. If you could use momentum to lift the shovel, it would be easier, but all the snow would fly away.) Similar movement activities in the house include mopping floors and carrying groceries or laundry.

Some activities require *jerky sharp movement* with *good rhythm* and varying amounts of *effort* and *use of space*: these include playing the drums or xylophone, cooking and baking, scrubbing floors and cupboards, nailing and hammering, gardening, and swimming. Whereas the expert horseback rider knows how to ride smoothly, the expert competitive swimmer has learned to do just the opposite; the smooth strokes become choppy in order to cut through the water and gain speed.

How to Help Your Child Move Better If He Wants To.
Sometimes a child becomes very upset because he can't do something his friend can do, such as turn a somersault on a tree branch or run a fast relay race. His mother or father may feel the same way about their golf game, or bowling. They can go to a professional for lessons, ask someone else for pointers, or at least read a book about the sport. Your child can't do any of these things, so if his game is important to him, he'll appreciate some help from you. The approach is the same with an adult or child for any movement activity, whether a game or work.

Pinpoint the result you want. What is the purpose of the game or activity: For instance, getting the ball in the hole or the basket, running as fast as possible, jumping from a high place without losing balance and spring, climbing up and down a tree safely, smoothing a sheet gently on a bed so it will feel comfortable against the skin, lifting a load of books or groceries and carrying them without dropping anything and with no strain.

Look at your child's movement and discover at what point it is not working. The areas to check are alignment, balance, effort, speed, rhythm, movement quality, use of space. For instance: Your five-year-old daughter can't pump on a swing because her balance and rhythm are off. She moves her body forward before the swing has completed the backward arc.

Your nine-year-old son can't stand on his head because his alignment throws his balance off so he tips over. His pelvis is tilted back too far, a habit he also has when he is standing and walking. When he runs, it slows him down enough so that he is always picked last for the team at school.

Your twelve-year-old daughter has decided to assemble her own bookshelf out of a ready-made furniture kit. She can't screw in the hardware because she keeps getting a cramp in her arm. She needs to change her alignment, balance, and work pattern so that her body is in a good position to apply pressure on the screwdriver. Also, the push of using a screwdriver has a rhythm; press only when the screw is turning, not when you're readjusting your hand on the handle. Otherwise, the arm tires very quickly.

Correct the difficulty on the spot with a specific suggestion.

To your swinging daughter: "Let me tell you when to move. Not yet . . . NOW!" (I once heard a tennis instructor give his adult pupil the same instructions for timing a tennis stroke.)

To your son: "You're not straight. Let me show you what's out of line." (Correct him with your hands while he is upside down, then right-side up, then get him to walk and run with the same alignment.)

To the twelve-year-old carpenter: the best way is to show her by example and explain the difference. "Kneel like this, so you can push better. Use a pushing and twisting motion, as if you were screwing on a bottle cap, and relax your hand between turns."

If your child still has trouble, you can play a movement practice game to make him aware of the movement characteristic he should be using, or substitute another game or activity that's easier for him to manage. If you do this, you might mention that not everyone's body is equally suited to every activity, and give some examples of movement specialists in sports or dance. You might even make a comparison: "Joe Namath can't dance; Nureyev can't play football." Be sure to tell your child what movement pattern he is especially good at: "You're fast and light when you move, that's why you run so well," or "You can pull, push, and lift heavy weights—you're really very strong for your age."

14 How to Increase Visual Awareness

The average adult is an experienced "see-er" because so much of our information about the world comes to us through our eyes. Seeing is different from your other senses in that you can block out a large amount of your seeing awareness and still function. But you are losing out on a great deal of visual pleasure and you are also losing out on a big part of your child's experiences: answers to questions like what his favorite colors are, how well he sees form in three dimensions, how he visualizes himself in relation to his surroundings, and much more—up to 80 per cent of his life experience.

What you see can be divided into four categories: (1) form, (2) color, (3) light and shade, (4) spatial relationships. Although your sense of hearing or of smelling is involuntary, you can control what registers with you visually, first by turning your head, second by focusing your eyes. Two people in the same place can have a totally different visual experience because each one focuses on different items. Imagine a botanist and a geologist standing side by side on a forest path. One focuses on the plant life, the other on the soil and rock formations. Later if each man were to describe to you what he saw, you might not even know that the two had been standing in the same geographic spot.

You and your child also have different seeing patterns based on what is most pleasurable or distasteful or most important or interesting to each of you. Also, don't forget that your child's eyes are looking from a point several feet below yours because he is smaller. The best way to increase your seeing sensitivity is to become aware of what you choose to focus on most frequently—thus you will become aware of your personal seeing pattern.

YOUR OWN SEEING PATTERN

What do you notice first when you walk into someone's living room for the first time? Do you look at the *floor plan* —how the furniture is placed within the four walls of the room? Perhaps you notice *shape and form.* Artists, sculptors, and other sensitive see-ers distinguish a wealth of planes and curves, perspectives, cones, spheres, and other solid forms wherever they are. In a room, this view is a floor plan or bird's-eye view, plus the vertical dimension in space, known as the elevation. Some of us notice the *color* scheme first. A room full of browns and dull purple and black may depress you. You prefer white and bright orange, red, or azure blue. Two of my nearsighted friends have a marvelous color sense. They don't see forms accurately but colors are very important to them.

Now consider your response to *light.* Do you adore sunlight? Does a dark room (or a rainy day) depress you? What type of artificial lighting do you prefer: well-spaced floor and table lamps, overhead light fixtures, spotlights, diffused light, indirect light, or fluorescent lights? A friend of mine who is an artist won't shop in any store that has fluorescent lighting. She says it makes the people look sick, their complexions turn bluish, their veins and blemishes stand out, and she can't take it.

What in your own home gives you visual pleasure? The overall layout or spatial relationship? Does the arrangement of walls and furniture enclose you in a comfortable way, or are they free-flowing because you need open space? What kind of pictures are on your wall, and why did you select them—the composition or design, the shapes, the colors, the light and shade? You may have been attracted to the treatment of depth—the placing of one object in front of another, or to the illusion of perspective receding into the distance. What about knick-knacks or favorite treasures? Do you like the texture, the proportions of shapes, the color, the way an object reflects light? A friend who is an architect has had a running argument with his wife for years on the subject of plants. She enjoys leafy plants of all types and he complains that they clutter up the room. She looks at each plant individually, leaf by leaf, and he sees the scattered shapes of the leaves in relation to the overall plan of walls and furniture.

What colors are the furniture, the rugs, the draperies, the throw pillows in you home? What colors are your bedspread and bathroom? Do you have patterned wallpaper or do you prefer flat colors? What is your lighting scheme—direct, diffused, area, or general lighting?

Now focus on what you like least at home. If someone gave you money to improve your apartment or house, what would you change? The overall space, or area? The amount of light? The layout of the rooms? Would you remodel for more natural light? space? color? Would you repaint? Would you change the furniture, draperies, floor-coverings? What shapes, colors, textures? Would you want a new lighting design? What kind? More light? less light? different in some other way?

Here are some other indicators of your seeing patterns.

Your wardrobe: Are you more concerned with color or with drape and fit? Will you buy a plain brown dress if it's flattering to your shape, or a smashing print that hangs loosely? What are your favorite colors for clothes? Bright? pastel? muted?

Your concept of physical beauty in a person: Do you admire bone structure? Beautiful body proportions (structure plus form)? skin? hair coloring?

How do you watch movies and television? Are you aware of creative photography? Light and shade? Sunlight? Shapes within the framework of the picture? Movement within the film, both moving objects and the visual rhythm of the film in terms of editing?

By now you should have an increased awareness of what you see and what your eyes pass by. If you find that you are ignoring something you would like to hang onto, either for yourself or for your child's sake, you can. How? By changing and improving your visual (and mental) focus.

DOES YOUR CHILD HAVE A FUNCTIONAL SEEING PROBLEM?

If your child has anything wrong with his eyes, you will want to consult an ophthalmologist, an M.D. who specializes in diseases and abnormalities of the eye and who can also diagnose a defect in vision and correct it with lenses or other means. Most ophthalmologists recommend yearly eye checkups to establish that the eyes are healthy.

You should also have your child's visual function checked to make sure that the visual mechanics that your child uses to explore and orient himself in his environment are effective. The specialist for this is an accredited optometrist; he has had a minimum of five years of college training and has been graduated from a school or college of optometry accredited by the American Optometric Association, plus licensing examinations conducted by state boards of examiners. His practice is legally limited to the function of the eye; he is not permitted to use medication, and he must refer any evidence of disease to an ophthalmologist.

The doctor of optometry will check your child's ocular motility (eye movement), teaming, (use of both eyes together), eye-hand coordination, visual form perception, and his refractive status (including nearsightedness, farsightedness, crossed eyes). He may prescribe corrective lenses or a series of training procedures or visual learning activities to be done in the office and practice at home. This often clears up puzzling problems in other areas. For example, a teen-aged girl who had always excelled in mathematics gradually began to make more and more careless errors. It turned out that her two eyes had stopped fusing (or teaming) properly and she was seeing double. The strain interfered with her concentration and affected her performance. Visual training corrected this problem.

One of the pioneers in the study of visual function in children was Arnold Gesell, and the Gesell Institute included work on vision in its massive behavioral study of normal children. The physician and optometrists who participated found that it is normal for a young child to use his eyes in a variety of ways—sometimes nearsighted, sometimes farsighted. At certain periods in his development a child is more adept at focusing his eyes than at others. Gesell, in his book, *Vision, Its Development in Infant and Child,* says of a normal six-year-old:

> In building a tower with small blocks, he works with less speed and accuracy than he did at five years of age. Eye and hand function in looser coordination. . . . He tends to approach with too much abandon or too much deliberation. Often there is more activity than accomplishment. At five, ocular fixation is superior to ocular pursuit. At six, pursuit tends to be superior. (*From Arnold Gesell, et al,* Vision, Its Development in Infant and Child, *New York: Harper & Row, 1949, p. 123.*)

Scientific concern with the development and optimum function of the senses is still in its infancy, but most of the studies have been in the field of vision.

All eye-doctors agree on the importance of good posture for reading, writing, and other close work. Optometrists also stress the visual distortion that occurs when a child tilts his head too far to the side, or sits below comfortable eye-level; an "o" becomes an "◯", like a blimp. Some adults keep this tilted world-view, like the electrician with a stoop who installed new switch plates for me once. They were all slightly off horizontal, just like his posture and eyes.

Here are some tips from the American Optometric Association. Move your baby's crib around, so that he will exercise his eyes in different ways. Keep general light on in the room for close work. This prevents eyestrain because your eye can wander now and then, without being drawn to the lighted area by the severe contrast in illumination. Avoid doing close work which incorporates sharp color contrast in the visual field, such as a white paper or page of a book placed on a dark brown desk. This makes your eye jump back and forth from the white page to the point of color contrast, a process which is visually fatiguing. Unfortunately, most schools cannot avoid this type of visual problem, but you can provide a good visual environment for your child at home.

SEEING GAMES

The first three games are seeing observation games that most children should enjoy. The fourth and fifth help your child to relate visual symbols for letters and numbers to his senses of hearing, touch, and moving. (Some children prefer to play the practice game for flat shapes on pages 248–250 first.)

The six games on pages 248 to 272 will give your child practice in seeing shapes, forms, light and shade, color, and spatial relationships through optical illusions, charting, measuring, and estimating distance. You might be interested to know that according to Piaget and other psychologists, the ability to judge distances varies with age, but an older child is, oddly enough, not always more accurate than a younger child. However, the *effort* to see accurately is of value at any age, regardless of results. The spatial relationships games encourage such an effort.

OPEN YOUR EYES TO FORMS, COLORS, LIGHT AND SHADE
Any Age

This game will explore what your child sees, especially form, color, light and shade. Besides being fun, it will help your child become more aware of the world around him, and will help you to discover what your child likes to look at.

Find a familiar place that is relatively empty of people and activities, such as a room in your house, a nearby meadow, a mountainside in the country, or a deserted beach at the seashore. Stand or sit quietly with your child and move only your eyes—around, up and down, across. Now pick a category: form, color, light or shade. Ask some leading questions such as, "How many circles can you see? How many squares?" (If your child is very young and doesn't relate to a concept like circle or square, you'll have to begin by helping him understand what you mean. If he has trouble, perhaps you should wait until he is older. Slowly, begin to add questions of size and depth such as "Which square is larger? Which is thicker? How do you know?" Once your child gets the idea of the game you can move around if you want to.

Example: Your child is indoors with a cold. You can start off by finding all the circles in the living room: lampshade, top and bottom. Coffee cup, top and bottom. Round table, caster under furniture, saucer under coffee cup. What's the smallest circle you can see? The largest? Is there a "solid" circle, or sphere? Yes, the doorknob. How can you tell it's not flat? By the shading of the light that gives it depth. What about cylinders, such as a pen or a piece of chalk? How do they differ from a straw? You can use the same approach with ovals and ellipses, like scatter rugs, Princess telephones, and some drawer handles that may be shaped like the handle of an egg-beater. Look for squares, cubes, rectangles, triangles, both flat and solid. If your child is able to understand more complex shapes, you can seek out trapezoids, pentagons, cones, etc. You'll both be surprised how many forms you're not seeing.

Take a new look at colors. Suppose you and your daughter are walking in the country. What colors around her does she like best? The deep blue of the sky? Purple-blue asters, or yellow black-eyed Susans? Does she like greens? Pale for new leaves through to dark blue-green for pines? Reds? Are there any red birds about? Is there a rock that is rusty-red because it contains iron? You will begin to be aware of the different hues of the same color: bright cardinal red and clay red, rich earth brown or the dull brown of a dead branch. You can look at an intermediate color such as orange or green and decide if it contains more red than yellow, or more yellow than blue.

When you explore light and shade, you can pick all the brightest spots. At the beach, begin with the sunlight, then the reflections that bounce off the water. Perhaps someone way out in a boat is wearing a silver barrette that reflects the light like a mirror. You can find the bright colors that reflect light most strongly: white, bright yellows, oranges, reds. What are the darkest colors? Is there a cool shaded spot? A deep murky pool among the rocks? Can you tell shallow and deep water by the light reflection that changes the color? Is there something in the water that changes the light refraction, such as seaweed or a school of fishes? If you look out over the water, can you see that the color seems to fade as it approaches the horizon? Do the waves have white caps as the water mixes with wind?

At this point, a child will be more than ready to take over the game. All you have to do is follow his lead.

OPEN YOUR EYES TO SPATIAL RELATIONSHIPS
Any Age

This game, like the previous one, will explore what your child sees, especially spatial relations.

Stand still with your child in front of a window or outdoors where you can see both stationary and moving objects. Ask your child which ones are closest to him. How can he tell? If you are at an apartment window looking at a cityscape, you will see *overlapping* buildings—the ones in front partially block the ones farther away. If your child is very young, say three to five, ask him what he thinks the invisible part of the building looks like. Let him draw his image of it if he wants to. He'll probably draw a continuation of what he sees— windows, fire escapes, and so on. If he is very imaginative, he may invent a surprise such as a dog or a funny face at a hidden window. Incidentally, his ability to retain the idea of the part of the building which is out of sight is one of the first steps in child logic, according to Jean Piaget.

At street level, look at a man waiting at a bus stop some distance from the two of you. Ask your child, "Is he a tiny man?" No, he *looks small because he's farther away.* A tiny man would look even smaller.

If you have a photograph or painting at home that shows perspective, you can show your child that even in two dimensions we interpret smaller objects as being farther away.

You can give your child another spatial clue: on a street or road, point out to your child that the cars closest to him are *clearer* than the ones a distance from him. If he is a car buff, ask him to identify cars at different distances. Close up, he can tell brand names. Farther away, car types (convertible, station wagon, compact). Still farther away, beyond a hundred yards, he sees only that they are cars. Farthest away, he'll just see something moving on the road, which he assumes is a car.

You might also point out to him that the cars in the distance seem *higher in space* than the ones directly in front of him. This is because he gauges distance in relation to the horizon, and as the car moves away from him it appears to be climbing upward into the sky.

Now ask your child which cars are going faster. Depending on his age and aptitude, he'll answer, "The ones near me," or he will try to adjust the ratio of speed to distance because he knows *things that are closer to him seem to move more quickly.*

Before you finish playing this game, ask your child to look at an object, such as a tree, that is about thirty feet away and make it jump from side to side by closing first one eye and then the other. Have him do the same with a finger held twelve inches from his nose. Explain to him that each eye sees from a slightly different place because they are inches apart in his face. This makes it much easier for him to judge distance in space. He may want to try distance judging with just one eye. Be sure that he looks at new objects, not the ones he has already seen with normal vision. Otherwise, his memory of the first distance judgment will influence what he believes he's seeing with only one eye.

If your child is very mobile and has trouble standing still, show him how his eyes need to examine distant objects in relation to his own body in space. If he moves around a lot, his eyes can't keep up with him.

WHAT DO YOUR EYES REMEMBER?
(VISUAL MEMORY GAME)
Ages: 6–12

This game will improve your child's visual memory. Good visual memory is important for many activities, from following directions on how to get somewhere to school subjects such as mathematics and social studies.

This is a simple but effective game that is used for visual training by Dr. Richard Kavner of the New York Optometric Center. Ask your child to picture the visual characteristics of a particular place with as much detail as possible. The best time to do this is en route to a familiar spot. Suppose you and your child are walking to his music lesson. See if he can remember the entrance to the building. He may describe the arched entryway with a doorbell on the left and an interesting dark wooden bench on the right. When you arrive, he can check his observations. Perhaps the bench has a high back and curled armrests that he did not recall, or the bell is higher on the wall than he remembered. Try to encourage him to picture the area visually, in terms of form, color, light and shade, and spatial relationships. Otherwise he may just relate obvious features without using his visual sense. But once he learns how to imagine what is not in front of him, he should be able to improve rapidly. Be aware, though, that this game is difficult for a young child; he should be praised for recalling even a few details.

MATCH THE LETTER PATTERN
Ages: 3–7

This game will help your child to develop a sensory approach to the written word. He will become aware that the words he sees on a page can be parallel to sounds he speaks, to touch patterns he feels with his hand, and to movement patterns he makes with his body.

MATCH THE LETTER PATTERN WITH THE SOUND PATTERN

Show your child that a pattern on the page can become a pattern in his speech. Encourage him to look at a verse like "Mary, Mary, quite contrary." Show him how the rhyme and syllable "ary" makes a pattern for his ear and eye:

MA**R**Y
MA**R**Y   QUITE
CONT**R**A**R**Y

Other examples are tongue twisters such as "Peter Piper."
(See also the tongue twister on page 133.)

PETER
PIPER
PICKED A
PECK OF
PICKLED
PEPPERS

Mirror words, like OTTO, MOM, and ANNA may be
used:

OO	AA	M
OTTO	ANNA	MOM
OTTO	ANNA	M
OO	AA	

Have your child find both horizontal and vertical versions of
the word.

Here is a sentence that works from left to right and from
right to left: ABLE WAS I ERE I SAW ELBA.

Once your child gets the hang of this, he should be able
to pick out the visual pattern of his words even when the
printed form is more conventional. Here is an excerpt from
a poem by T.S. Eliot, *The Hippopotamus,* for him to speak and
look at:

The broad-backed hippopotamus
Rests on his belly in the mud;
Although he seems so firm to us
He is merely flesh and blood.

Your child should be able to find the repeated *b* in *broad, backed, belly,* the *p*'s in the word *hippopotamus,* the *d*'s in *mud* and *blood,* and at least some of the *m*'s in . . . *mus, mud, firm, merely.*

Incidentally, new techniques in speed-reading try to increase the student's ability to visualize rather than hear the words.

MATCH THE LETTER PATTERN WITH
THE TOUCH PATTERN.

Show your child that a seeing pattern on the page can become a pattern in touching. First, take a piece of 8 1/2-by-11-inch paper and write a pattern of words using the capital letters B, C, D, E, H, I, K, M, O, W, X. Show this letter pattern to your child. Take a second piece of paper, and use a pin to form the identical letters in pinprints (see the example on page 142). Have your child feel the tactile letters with closed eyes, and then have him open his eyes and move his finger along the letters of the first sheet of paper. Point out that except for the texture, the movement of his hand is the same on this paper as on the paper with the pinprick letters. He is looking at a visual pattern that he can also touch. You might tell him that this is how blind people read the Braille symbols.

MATCH THE LETTER PATTERN WITH THE MOVEMENT PATTERN

Show your child that a seeing pattern on the page can be parallel to his way of moving. Pick a singing and moving game he knows, such as "Here we go loop de loo" or "Wind, wind, wind your bobbin/Wind, wind, wind your bobbin/Clap—clap—turn a-round." Write the verse down in big letters, clap the rhythm as he moves, then chant the words as he moves. Encourage him to move and chant the words at the same time. It doesn't matter if he sings the melody or not. The main thing is for him to get a physical feeling for moving and speaking at the same time.

Show him that his body repeats certain movements just as the song repeats certain phrases. Point out on the page where this happens. If you want to you can reverse the process and ask him to point to a section of the song on the page while you show him the matching movements.

You may also be able to point out certain words that look and sound like the movement: "clap" is short and sharp; "wind" is longer and smoother; "loop" sounds like a scooping or skipping movement.

MATCH THE NUMBER PATTERN
Ages: 4–7

This game will help a child who can count to become aware that the numerals he sees on a page can form a seeing pattern, and that the numerals can also be parallel to touch patterns he feels with his hand, movement patterns he makes with his body, and sound patterns he speaks with his voice. This is important for mathematics.

Preparation: Arrange the number pattern to make a seeing pattern. Ask your child to look at a series of simple problems that contain repeated numbers, such as

$$1 + 3 = 4$$
$$4 - 3 = 1$$
$$4 - 1 = 3$$
$$3 + 1 = 4$$

See if he can look at the numbers as if they were a design. Help him invent a code of new symbols, such as

$$1 = \triangle$$
$$3 = \bigcirc$$
$$4 = \square$$

If he writes out the number sentences in his code, he'll get

$$\triangle + \bigcirc = \square$$
$$\square - \bigcirc = \triangle$$
$$\square - \triangle = \bigcirc$$
$$\bigcirc + \triangle = \square$$

He can rearrange this to form a better "picture:"

$$\triangle + \quad \bigcirc = \square$$
$$\triangle = - \bigcirc + \square$$
$$\square - \triangle = \quad \bigcirc$$
$$\square = \triangle + \quad \bigcirc$$

He might like to look at the following algebraic symbols as
if they were a design:

$$x = \frac{-b \pm \sqrt{b^2 - 4ac}}{2a}$$

MATCH THE NUMBER PATTERN
(OR NUMERICAL OPERATIONS)
WITH THE TOUCH PATTERN

Show your child that a seeing pattern on the page can
become a pattern of touching. For example, your daughter
has been told that it's all right to add and subtract by counting on her fingers. Ask her to count $4 + 2 = 6$ on her
fingers:

> Beat, beat, beat, beat,
> *and* Beat, beat
> *are* Beat, beat, beat, beat, beat, beat

Show her that you can make a mark on the paper every time
she presses a finger down, and that this looks like:

ı ı ı ı   and   ı ı   are   ı ı ı ı ı ı

Then tell her that the regular numerals are just a different
(and easier) picture of the same operation:

ı ı ı ı	is	4
ı ı	is	2
ı ı ı ı ı ı	is	6

This will give her another approach to touching and seeing numbers.

MATCH THE NUMBER PATTERN
(OR NUMERICAL OPERATION)
WITH THE MOVEMENT PATTERN

Show your child that a seeing pattern on the page can become a pattern in moving. Get a basketful of apples and help your child "act out" a written number operation like

$$4 \ + \ 5 \ = \ 9$$

He can place four apples in the basket one after the other —he repeats the same movement four times. Make a mark on the paper every time he moves. Have him lift the basket to feel the weight, and then have him add the other five apples. Tell him to lift up the basket again—he'll feel that it's heavier because of the larger number of apples. Show him that you have on the paper

1 1 1 1 (*lift basket*) and 1 1 1 1 1 (*lift heavier basket*) = 1 1 1 1 1 1 1 1 1

Show him that the pattern his body feels when he moves is expressed in a seeing pattern on the page, and that in this case, the "plus" is another way of expressing the greater effort required to lift a heavier basket of apples. To finish, remind him that the conventional numerals are a shorter way of writing the marks you make on the page.

MATCH THE NUMBER PATTERN WITH
THE SOUND PATTERN

Show your child that a pattern of numbers can become a parallel pattern of sounds. Give him equations like:

$$2 + 3 = 5$$
$$2 + 4 = 6$$
$$2 + 3 = 5$$

and have him repeat the words in a rhythm as if it were an advertising jingle:

> *Two* and *three* are FIVE.
> *Two* and *four* are SIX.
> *Two* and *three* are FIVE.

Write out his arithmetic song with numerical symbols, using relative sizes: small for the words "and" and "are," larger for the words "two," "three," "four," and largest for the words "five" and "six," which are the most important because they represent the point of the sentence.

$$2 + 3 = 5$$
$$2 + 4 = 6$$
$$2 + 3 = 5$$

Show him that the words he stresses more with his voice are the bigger numbers on the page. That the symbol for the word "two" is repeated on the page, just as his ears hear it repeated by his voice. Then ask him to write down a "number jingle" as you speak it. Tell him to space it on the page as your voice spaces it in time. If he needs to relate the sound of the numbers to a numerical concept, he'll have to learn to move as he speaks or chants (see page 246). The rhythm and effort of his body will show in the sounds of his voice. He'll be making a sound picture of a physical operation using numbers; in this case, the number and weight of apples in a basket.

PRACTICE GAMES FOR SEEING

LOOK AT FLAT SHAPES
Ages: 5–9

This game will help your child become more aware of shapes, which is important for reading, writing, mathematics.

From points to lines to shapes. Ask your child to make a series of evenly spaced dots with a pencil on a piece of paper. The dots can be about one-half inch apart on 8 1/2-by-11-inch paper. Now ask the child to connect the dots with lines to form shapes. The simplest shapes he can make are a line, a square, a triangle and a rectangle. If he hasn't found these shapes, show him. Have him cut out all the shapes and put them aside.

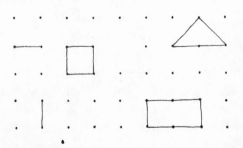

From points to curves to shapes. Now have your child take another piece of paper and place dots in a circular pattern, using the same scale as before; help him do this if he has trouble. Have him connect the points with curved lines. He can form many interesting shapes, but the simplest are the circle, the half-circle, and the quarter-circle. If he has not found these shapes, show them to him and have him cut them out.

Shapes to make letters and numerals. Print the alphabet in block letters, using a separate piece of 8 1/2-by-11-inch paper for each letter. Do the same with the arabic numerals between o and 9. If your child wants to, he can help you draw, so long as the results are pretty accurate. Last, have your child match his basic shapes with our symbols for letters and numerals.

Example: An A is a small triangle plus two sides of a larger triangle. B is two half-circles. D is one half-circle. H implies a square shape. The numeral 2 is a half-circle plus a line; the numeral 3 is two half-circles.

If you are a very visual person, this game may seem a little foolish to you, but many less visual adults fail to see the basic shapes in letters and numerals, and it is a great way to help your child organize his visual thinking.

LOOK AT LETTER SHAPES AS A DESIGN (GRAPHICS)
Ages: 5–10

This game will help your child become aware that the letters and numbers he writes on a page create a graphic design. This will provide him with a visual approach to hand-writing and writing numbers.

If your child is visual, he will enjoy making the shapes that are letters. He will see that the cursive writing taught in most schools is a variation of the line and circle shapes of printed type. If he hates to practice his writing, or if it's messy and he doesn't know why, ask him to make a design out of a letter. He can turn it anyway he wants to, repeat it or not, place it on the paper in any position.

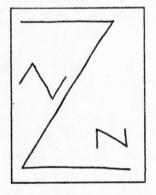 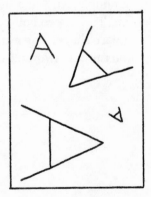

Together, look for examples of good graphic art and creative use of type and spacing in magazine and newspaper advertisements. Then, encourage your child to look at his handwriting as if he were drawing a picture. Explain to him that it is easier for others to understand what he means if the lines are straight, the circles round, if the writing moves from left to right in a straight line, and if the spacing on the page is generous. The same is true of numbers and written number problems.

Now, create some examples for each other of ambiguously drawn letters and numbers.

$$4 + 2 = 12 \qquad Cat$$

21 + 3 = R?   cat?   cot?   cut?
4 + 2 = 12?   lat?   lot?   lut?
4 + 8 = 12?

See if he can fool you by writing unclearly or with poor spacing on purpose. Then have him correct what he did. Tell him to make the best letter or number picture that he can, using generous spacing and clearly drawn symbols. Look at the page together at arm's length and see the overall pattern as if it were a magazine advertisement. Does it make a nice design? Now look more closely to see if the letters are clear. If they are, they will make an attractive pattern as well.

Incidentally, you can also improve your child's spelling if he learns to look at the picture of the word on the page.

LOOK AT FORMS
Ages: 5–12

This game will help your child become more aware of forms, which is important for mathematics (measuring volume, and later on geometry) as well as physics, engineering, architecture, and art (especially sculpture).

From flat shapes to solid forms. You and your child can draw and cut out enlargements of the following flat shapes, one to a page. If you fold them and tape them, they become solid forms.

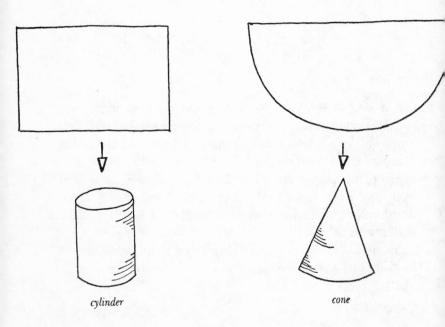

cylinder   cone

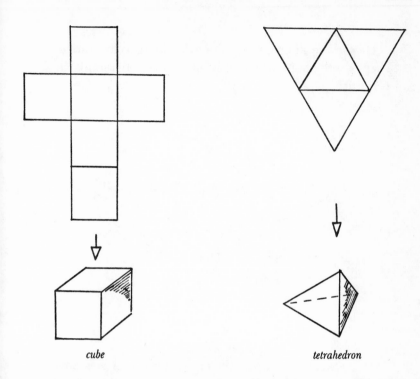

cube   tetrahedron

Solid forms out of clay.   Your child can look at flat shapes
and make them three-dimensional. Use clay to form balls
(spheres) from circles, eggs (ellipsoids), snakes (cylinders)
from lines. Now he can mould these basic forms into familiar
animals and people. Add toothpicks if necessary.

He can use a popsicle stick or a dull knife to form solid clay shapes with flat planes. Build some houses, pyramids, boats, furniture.

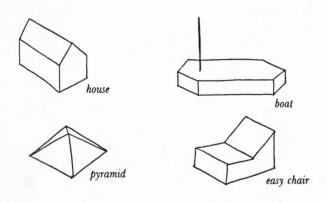

house

boat

pyramid

easy chair

How do solid forms change in appearance as you move?
Before your child puts aside his clay creations, have him look at them from different angles. Ask him to check a bird's-eye view (from directly above) and a frog's-eye view (from directly underneath). For a real look from "down under," put the clay model on a glass table, on a pane of glass, or on a piece of plastic wrap that you hold above your child.

Ask your child to imagine how a bird sees a cube. (Like a square.) How does a frog see it from directly underneath? (The same way.) Then ask your child if he can really see the whole cube at once from any angle. No, but he knows it's there. Check a sphere. Does a bird or frog see a circle? No, because the light molds the form so that it looks round. How about a cylinder? It's a circle from above and below, a cylinder from the side because the light molds the curve, and your child can see the outline of the top. You might make him aware that the top circle actually looks crooked from the side angle, but because he knows it's round, he sees it as round. Any one view includes his knowledge of the object from other views. Mention that the light molds the round objects but bounces off the flat ones and changes the way they look from certain angles. (For more work on light and form, see the next game.)

LOOK AT LIGHT AND SHADE
Ages: 7–12

This game will help your child become more aware of light and shade, which increases your child's understanding of the world around him. It also gives your child insight into the basic elements of photographic, film, and video technique.

Have your child use the clay figures described in the previous game. After he's checked the figures with normal light (either daylight or electric light) he can take a flashlight and check the lighting from below in a dark room at night or in a closet. He'll notice some strange visual effects. We're so accustomed to light from above that a light from below confuses and even frightens us. If your child is allowed to watch scary movies on television, he'll see many people and forms lit from below for "shock effect."

See if your child can spot any lighting mistakes on television or in the movies. Sometimes when an actor turns on a lamp, the whole room lights up in a disproportionate way. Or the sound microphone or another actor casts a shadow on the set which doesn't make visual sense in the scene.

Have your child look at a photograph album of black and white pictures to see the importance of light and shade. He can probably find some snapshots where the lighting distorts the person so that he looks fatter, thinner, more or less attractive, smaller, or taller. The next time the child is outdoors, remind him to notice the effect of direct sunlight or diffused light (light through clouds). How does this affect what he sees?

Your child may be interested in photography. Some young children are suprisingly good at it, and end up with many fine candid shots. One of my daughters at five had a gallery of pictures of her relatives with the oddest expressions, because they all thought her camera wasn't real when she took their pictures.

If your child is interested in art, he can draw forms in charcoal or soft pencil and try to duplicate the way light models solid forms.

He might also be interested in the treatment of light and shade by such masters as Dürer, Rembrandt, Vermeer, and Michelangelo.

Here is an interesting optical illusion caused by light and shade contrast. Can your child see the dark spots where the white bars cross? He should look straight at the page, not from an angle. Explain to him that his eyes are tricked by the pattern of black and white into seeing spots that are not really there.

LOOK AT COLOR
Ages: 8–12

This game will help your child become more aware of how color gives pleasure and information about the world.

Color in art. Give your child some poster paints in red, blue, and yellow. Let him experiment with splotches of unmixed primary colors. Ask him which colors seem warm and which colors seem cold. The reds and oranges usually appear warmer than the blues and greens. Also, if he makes a painting of bright red-and-blue squares, the reds will appear to be closer to him than the blues. When he starts to mix the colors he can experiment with various degrees of brightness. The brighter the hue, the closer to him the color will appear to be. Other art supplies you might want to provide for work in color mixing are craypas (a type of pastel crayon that does not smudge) and the regular chalk type of pastels, which are good for more delicate tints. Have him discover which looks nearer and warmer in a series of colors ranging from orange-red to purple, or pale yellow-green to dark blue-green.

If your child has occasion to look closely at work by Impressionist painters like Seurat and Monet, he will notice the individual dots or strokes of different colors, which the eye combines into a uniform color. He might want to try this technique of creating a color blend in the eye instead of a color mix on the paper.

Another interesting color experiment is painting people of different races—brown, yellow, red, white. My art-teacher friend Alice tells me that most children distort skin color in their art work. Brown children painting from a white model will usually exaggerate pink tones. White children painting from a brown model will darken the skin tone. One way to help a white child to shift focus from color to form is to ask him to paint people on brown paper without changing the "skin" color of the paper.

Alice also believes that children from different backgrounds use color in very characteristic ways. Puerto Rican children have a bright palette: red, blue, orange, green, yellow, reflecting the sunny colors of their country. Children from middle-class homes tend to use varied colors, and black to outline shapes. Most lifetime ghetto children of all races have a dark dreary palette: black, grays, washed-out blues, dirty pinks. It is sad to think of any child seeing the world made up of such dull colors.

Color in science. Perhaps your child would be interested in the perception of relative colors—how a color seems to change in relation to its surroundings. Supposing your daughter takes a shiny red apple and puts it on a white piece of paper. She then takes another equally red apple and puts it on a wooden cutting board. The apple on the paper will appear to be a brighter red than the apple on the wood. She can check this by changing the apples around. Here's another experiment using "wrong" colors. If your child paints a ripe pear blue, how does it affect his desire to eat it? How does he feel about a familiar yellow cereal box painted red? You can show your child an example of the illusion of color some time when you are out after dark. Ask him to pick a familiar colored object, such as the red family car, and tell you the color. He will probably answer, "Red, of course." It is surprising to learn that our eyes see only shades of gray at night, but our memory changes what we actually see into the color we know exists in light.

You can also suggest two other simple experiments: give your child some yellow, red, or blue cellophane candy wrappers so that he can look at the world through a different color. Ask him what stays the same and what changes the most. Or show your child the rainbow colors of a prism.

There are many color changes that occur every day in your child's surroundings. You can point out that red meat turns brown when it is cooked. Green vegetables become very dull when they are overcooked. You might also show him what bacteria can do to the color of meat, such as when a piece of spoiled ham has turned bluish. You probably have in your home at least one garment or furnishing that has been bleached into a lighter shade of color by the sun. Also, you might point out that a dirty room reflects light in a different way from a clean one. The dirt particles dull the colors.

If your child is really interested in science, he may want to follow up color as an indication of chemical and physical change: the different colors of flame in a fireplace for instance, and how they relate to the temperature and to the chemistry of the substance being burned. He can study spectral lines and how scientists use analysis of brightness and color to find out about unknown substances, including distant stars. He might also find another fascinating area for color study in natural camouflages. See how the stripes of a zebra, the bright red of a coral snake, the brilliant feathers of a mallard duck disappear in the natural environment.

LOOK AT SPATIAL RELATIONSHIPS

OPTICAL ILLUSIONS
Ages: 8–12

This game will help your child become more aware of his spatial surroundings. This is especially important for geometry, physics, engineering, and navigation. Optical illusions will intrigue your child as they teach him something about how his eye sees objects in space.

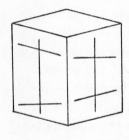

Illusion of linear perspective and relative size. If your child measures the three posts with a ruler, he will be amazed to find that they are all the same size. If the two larger-looking posts were really receding in the distance, they would appear to him to decrease in size as do the other objects in the picture. Since they are the opposite of what his eye expects, he judges them to be much larger.

A more subtle illusion also based on perspective. Ask your child to check all the angles of the two crossed figures. He can use a compass if he knows how, or just the corner of a book. He'll discover to his surprise that there are two intersecting right angles (lower left and upper right side of figure). This is because his eye is fooled by the perspective of the cube, so all the crosses seem crooked.

Op Art Illusion of movement. Show your child the picture on page 261 by Bridget Riley. As his eyes follow the wavy lines, he'll have the sensation that the picture is moving.

More illusions of movement. Your child can make his own illusion of movement; this one operates on the same principle as a movie. Tell him to take a roll of paper (such as adding-machine or cash-register tape) and draw some stick figures in a series of formations, like a cartoon. If he takes a shoebox, cuts out both ends and makes a frame by cutting a rectangle in the top, he will see a movie by pulling the

paper rapidly from one side of the box to the other. His eye
fills in the spaces between the figures so that they appear to
move.

Your child can notice the same effect with the lights of a
blinking neon sign. The fast sequence of individual lights
creates an effect of motion.

You can point out a different illusion of motion when
driving in a car. The trees and houses by the side of the road
seem to be moving, not the passengers. Your child will also

notice that he can focus clearly in only one area, either near or far. If he is looking into the distance, the windshield and dashboard blur, and vice versa.

(Based on a drawing by Ernst Mach.)

One-eyed vision. Although this looks like an optical illusion, it's what a man with a moustache might see if he lies down, closes one eye, and draws whatever he can see with the other. Your child can try this experiment as well. Now tell him to close the other eye and compare the two pictures. Explain to him that his normal two-eyed vision blends the images from each of his eyes, so that he's not aware of this strange one-eyed view.

Angle of Vision. If your child likes to draw, he will enjoy this record of what he sees. Ask him to make a simple sketch of a room or object while standing still. Then have him climb on a chair and draw the same thing, as if he had just grown two feet. He can also create the opposite effect by sitting on the floor and sketching. If he is very imaginative and skillful he can even draw the furniture as if he were as small as an ant. Or have him put his head between his legs, look at the room upside down, and then draw.

Your child's normal view of the world may surprise you. Here is how one short six-year-old sketched his very tall father:

It is a good idea for adults to stoop down to the child's level now and then.

CHARTING MOVEMENT
THROUGH SPACE
Ages: 6–12

This game will help your child learn to orient himself in space. It is also valuable for geography.

Movement Prints. You and your child can get a dynamic feeling for movement paths in space by looking for prints of all kinds. What does the web show about the path of the spider? Can you see where the cars were by tire tracks in the rain? How about shoe prints in soft earth and footprints on wet sand? Was it a long step or a short one? Did the person leave a deep print? Was it a child's small foot? Does he have a big arch? Animal tracks in the snow make beautiful prints and so do the curves of sled-runners on a hill. You can also look for ripples in a pond from a pebble, fish, or water insect.

If your child is interested in seeing waves of motion, a physics textbook would probably have a picture of sound waves taken by a machine called an oscilloscope.

A tree is also a movement print, but over a long long time.

Where did the wind hit and make the tree bend away from it? How did this affect the growth of the tree? Did ice storms break off any branches? How about the leaves on the side of the tree that gets the most sun? Do they grow better than on the other side? A different movement or growth print in a tree is formed by the rings of the cross-section.

Incidentally, this dynamic approach to space makes for wonderful art work if your child likes to draw and paint. If he becomes sensitive to the dynamic force of a series of lines, he will learn to balance his picture so that it forms a good visual composition.

You might also suggest that your child look at his own room some day when it is very messy. See if he can trace his own movement patterns. How was he standing when the coat dropped to the floor? Which way did he move when the toys ended up in that corner? This just might give him a new attitude toward straightening up.

Floor Plans and Maps.   Sometimes when a child is old enought to go to school alone or to run short errends, he seems reluctant to be on his own. This is not always a lack of self-confidence. It may be because the child is not a good see-er and feels lost because he doesn't know where he is in relation to key points.

You can teach your child to look for landmarks—for example, "Start to get off the bus when you pass the big shoe store." But what if someone is blocking his view from the window? What if the buzzer is broken or he can't reach it and he passes his stop? Which way should he walk? This is the kind of situation that can make a child really anxious. He needs an overall sense of his home, his school, and the route between, or the path to and from any other place he is going to be traveling to by himself.

A good way to teach your child this spatial awareness is with a map. If he doesn't relate to the concept of a map, begin with a floor plan. You can help him to draw the furniture in his room and where the paths are between the furniture. If your child has a doll house, a car, a train-track set, or a miniature garden, he can draw a floor plan of it. Point out that that the floor plan can be any size he wants, regardless of the actual size of the area, provided his spacing is consistent. Mention that the plan is a miniature bird's-eye view of his room or toy layout.

Next show your child a regular street map and tell him that you will help him draw a "giant's-eye" view of his own route to school, the corner drug store, or some other important place in his life. Put in a great many landmarks: your house, the house up the street, the bus stop at which he gets on, the shoe store, the bus stop where he gets off, and the supermarket at the stop *after* he should be off. This will give him a total picture of the route and help him to know what to do even if something unexpected happens.

Always encourage your child to orient himself in space when the two of you are out together. Ask him, "Which way is home?" or "Now where do we walk to reach the store?" Be sure to make a game of it so that he does not feel worried about not knowing where to go.

You can gradually enlarge your child's map sense by showing him maps of larger areas: the whole city, the state, the nation, the world. He should be able to estimate where his house would be on a globe. When he is older, he can even learn to point toward Alaska or toward Chicago from his living room.

MEASURING SPACE
Any Age

This game will show your child that space can be measured and will help him to visualize area and volume.

In two dimensions. Ask your child to watch you mark off a room in your house by paces. Then ask him to do the same. (If the total amounts to more than he can count, tell him you will make a mark on a piece of paper for every step or for every ten steps.) Let him discover that you can walk around the room with fewer steps because each of your steps is longer (estimate to nearest whole step).

If your child is very young, he may insist that the room has changed size, but the game is of value to him anyway because it makes him aware of measuring space. For an older child who is interested, you can extend this game to give him an idea of area. Take a piece of graph paper and mark it off to illustrate the room you just paced. Show him that he can add up all the squares it would take to cover the floor. A mathematics-oriented child can continue this approach to include measurement of triangles and other flat shapes.

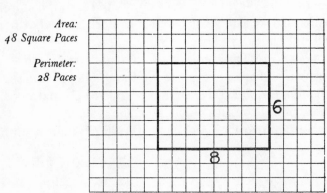

Area:
48 Square Paces

Perimeter:
28 Paces

See if your child is interested in the relative size of other objects—toys, plates, long food such as carrots and bananas. Measure with fingerwidths or handwidths. When your child learns about inches, feet, and yards he can change his unit of measure to the conventional one.

Even if your child is already familiar with linear measurement, it is good for him to know that mathematical concepts have a meaning outside of the classroom.

In three dimensions. You can give your child an awareness of volume by means of simple experiments. For instance, at the dinner table give him two empty glasses, one tall and thin, the other short and fat. Take a pitcher of his favorite drink (not carbonated) and ask him which of his glasses you should fill up. If he is around five, he will probably say the tall one because it looks as if it holds more. Show him that he can pour the drink back and forth between the two glasses and that the amount looks different in each even though it does not change. The intellectual grasp of this type of experiment figures importantly in Piaget's description of the growth of logic in children. He calls it the theory of conservation of quantity, and found it in most children by the time they were seven years old.

As you play this game, you will find that there are two different ways of seeing. Your child may like the idea of magic: "They look so different, but they contain the same amount." He is intrigued by the appearance of the two containers, although he acknowledges the constant amount of the liquid. Or, he may focus on the sameness of the liquid inside, and disregard the containers (the approach usually described in textbooks). Either way will bring your child to an understanding of the theory when he's ready.

You can also play this game with fine solids such as sugar

or flour. When you are baking, fill a measuring cup and pour the contents into a small bowl, then a tall glass, to give your child an awareness of volume. Another place where you can do something similar is at a sandy beach with two different-sized pails and a cup.

Here is a different experiment in relative volume. Buy a box of lump sugar and have your child count the number of lumps that fit into the original container. Then he can guess and verify how many lumps would fit into boxes of other dimensions.

If your child is older, you can play this game with cans and bottles at the supermarket: Ask him to estimate the contents of two different-shaped containers, then check the label to see if he is right. This is a good habit for your child to develop anyway, for practical reasons.

Another practical application of these space-measuring games is in helping your child learn how to look for lost objects. Many young ones who misplace mittens, socks, scarves at home and at school do not know how to scan space to hunt for the missing object. They fix their eyes on one area where they think they will find the object, and then if it's not there, they say, "I can't find it," instead of looking further. You can encourage your child to sweep his eyes systematically over the surfaces of a drawer or cubby or shelf —sides, back, bottom, and top, as if he were painting with his eyes. Artist Paul Klee uses the term "graze." He says that the eye grazes over a surface. Sometimes the annoyance of losing something makes one too tense to see; therefore, you might tell your child that his eye should graze (touch lightly in passing) and graze (as if it were a cow moving through a field of grass). This should put him in a more relaxed frame of mind as he looks.

ESTIMATING DISTANCE
Any Age

This game orients your child in relation to the world around him and has practical value for innumerable activites from packing a suitcase to driving a car.

Estimating distance close up. When your child plays with puzzles and construction toys such as blocks and slotted playing cards, he is learning to estimate space with his eye. He figures out what size of puzzle piece might fit into a particular shape, or how many blocks he can stack one on top of the other before they topple over. If he is very ingenious, he may even discover how to cantilever blocks out from the construction by placing extra weight at one point. Your child's hand coordinates with his eye to give him the spatial sense he will need for activities like arranging a shelf or packing a suitcase. If your child is especially interested in this type of spatial relations, take him to see some mobiles by Alexander Calder. The delicate and ingenious balancing will delight him.

If you think your child needs some practice at estimating space close up and if he doesn't like to play with puzzles and blocks, give him some grown-up activities that involve the same skill.

Pack a small suitcase for neatness. Start with a few articles, then see if he is able to pack a larger number of articles neatly in the same space.

Wrap a gift in paper. A square gift is the easiest, but any neat wrapping involves many spatial judgments as your child enfolds a three-dimensional object with the two-dimensional paper.

Arrange silverware in a drawer or towels, washcloths, bedding in the linen closet, books on a shelf, or tools and hardware in the workroom.

Arrange cut flowers attractively in a vase; fresh fruit in a bowl; a raw vegetable plate of carrots, celery, radishes; a platter of assorted cookies.

Estimating distance far away. Children need to be able to judge space at a distance as well as close up. Unfortunately, our culture develops this skill more fully in boys than in girls. That's why so many women have trouble parking a car—lack of practice in gauging distance and large angles. There are many activities that will give your boy or girl this skill.

For eye-hand coordination, throw a ball back and forth between you. Use a large ball for a small child or child who really has difficulty with catching, throwing, and seeing. Use a smaller ball for the more experienced child. Suppose your daughter really has trouble catching the ball. Tell her to look at your hand before you throw and then follow the curve of the ball with her eyes as it comes toward her. At the end of the arc in space, she puts out her hand and catches the ball. When she throws it to you, she should imagine your hand at the other end of the curve and then try to put the ball in space so it will follow this arc. Once she knows what she's trying to do, any child can learn this. Incidentally, not looking at the ball is a problem that plagues many adults in sports like tennis.

For eye-hand coordination, tell your child to practice throwing a ball up in the air in a hallway or garage so that it just misses the ceiling. (This is much more difficult than the first game because he's looking from below.)

Sports such as basketball, baseball, football, volleyball, soccer, and field hockey all call for the ability to judge space. If your child is interested in any of these sports, make sure he knows that he has to practice with his eyes as well as with his body.

When you and your child are out for a walk, ask some questions about distances: "How far away do you think that house is?" If he is not familiar with feet and yards, he can use another measure such as "half a block" or "about the length of our back yard." A child under nine will tend to underestimate the distance, but you can play the game anyway. If you keep it fun, the game has value for him. Teach your child some cues to distance if he is not using them: nearer objects overlap those farther away and texture smooths out as it recedes; for instance a lawn or indentations in the sidewalk start to melt into a smooth surface in the distance. Here again, don't expect as much from a younger child.

You might also ask your child to judge the relative speed of cars. If he's in the middle of the block and two cars are approching from opposite sides, where will they pass? When you're out driving, make him aware of relative speeds as you slow down or speed up to overtake another car. Ask him to try to judge the distance of an approaching car from the time he first sees it, as it gets larger and larger, to the moment when it passes him.

If you are out together where there is a long-distance view such as from a high building, up on a hillside, or at the beach, ask your child questions like, "How far away is that car [or house, or boat]?" "How long do you think it would take us to walk over to that large tree?" Even though you don't know the answer yourself, you will have an opinion based on your experience and what you see. With practice your child will learn to see and judge distances intelligently also.

15 How to Increase Awareness of the Sense of Smell

Is your nose sensitive to smell? Scientists claim that the average person is aware of 2,000 different odors and that this amount can be doubled with training. Some of the best smellers in the world are Arabians. They enjoy body smells, unlike deodorant-conscious Americans. Many Arabic matchmakers believe they can actually tell by odor whether a prospective bride is sweet-tempered. An angry person has a characteristic odor because anger is a strong emotion which affects the body chemistry and changes the body odor. Anthropologist Leonard Hall describes an American psychiatrist who also could smell anger in his patients; he had a very successful career.

How convenient it would be for a parent to be able to smell how his child feels! In prehistoric times our ancestors did use smell in this way—as a very direct communication system with the outside world for carrying messages conveying danger, food, pleasure, anger, fear. Later the eye became more important for survival than the nose, and smell became less sensitive. Yet it is still a powerful catalyst to emotions and is connected with vivid memory impressions.

Unfortunately there is no real technique for improving your sense of smell because scientists don't really know how smell works and have no effective means of measuring smell sensitivity. Smell is a chemical sense that seems to operate through an electrophysical reaction between the substance and the nose, but how can you standardize a sniff? How do you isolate an odor when no room except a vacuum is truly odor-free? Even if you achieve such a climate, the second odor you smell is affected by the preceding and following odors. That is, if the order is changed, so is the response. Everyone's sensitivity to a smell decreases after a period of time. For instance, someone may enter your home and comment on a food odor which you no longer smell. Temperature is another factor in smell response. On the positive side, there are general types of odors that most of us recognize.

YOUR OWN SENSE OF SMELL

Of the following scents, which smell good or bad to you?

Floral odors such as rose, lily of the valley, narcissus, jasmine. Are any of these too sweet or too heavy for your taste (or nose)? What about gardenia? Honeysuckle? Sweet alyssum?

Fruit odors such as lemon, lime, or orange please most of us. In the past these citrus scents have been associated chiefly with men and after-shave lotions, but now the stores are full of lemon fragrance for women.

Spicy smells such as clove, cinnamon, nutmeg. Do you like them, or do they become cloying, as in some household deodorants?

Herbs and woodsy odors. Do you enjoy lavender and thyme? Pine, as from a Christmas tree? Newly cut grass after a rainfall?

Pungent odors such as leather and fur are unpleasant to some, enjoyable to others.

Putrid odors such as toilet smells or the odor of rotten eggs displease just about everyone, but the response can vary in degree from discomfort to severe nausea.

After you have become aware of certain smells, relate them to your experience. Close your eyes and try to conjure up an odor—a newly opened can of coffee, a new leather handbag, frying bacon or onions. You may remember some long-forgotten incidents—the bitter smell of seaweed, which recalls a summer trip; the smell of newly sharpened pencils, which you noticed in first grade at school; an old aunt's living room, which is brought to mind by the smell of lemon-oil polish on the wood furniture.

Your child has his own vocabulary of smells also, and you can discover it by playing the following sensory games.

FRAGRANCES AND ODORS GAME

This game will make you more aware of your child's vocabulary of smells and will help you examine your child's behavior from a different point of view. Because smells are so elusive, you'll have to play this game in various locations over a period of time. (It can be played with children of any age.)

FOOD SMELLS

A meal is a good place to start. Ask your child, "What smells good? Is it smell or taste? Hold your nose and check as you eat." Some common breakfast favorites are bacon, coffee, toast, warm muffins. Ask your child if any smells from the kitchen made his mouth water before he saw the food.

peanuts, char-broiled steak, frying chops, corn on the cob, cucumbers, apples, pears, peaches, oranges, warm fruit pies, chocolate, cookies.

Take a sniff of your spice shelf with your child. How about the smell of cloves, cinnamon, nutmeg, allspice, ginger? The woodsy herbs such as basil, oregano, thyme, sage, mint? Citrus extracts of orange, lemon, lime? The strong smell of vanilla and almond flavoring?

Check and see if your child dislikes the smell of broccoli, cabbage, cauliflower, frying pork (except bacon), fish, organ meats such as liver or kidneys, strong cheese, and milk. If your child hates milk, ask him to smell some ice cream. The odor is almost the same but the ice cream is so cold that it does not smell as strongly (also it tastes so good). Two pungent-smelling foods which your child probably likes are cola drinks and honey.

FLORAL FRAGRANCES

Look for favorite scents among flowers with your child. You can go to a florist shop, walk in a flower garden, or smell a series of floral perfumes or colognes. Incidentally, there is a garden of fragrant flowers for the blind at the New York Botanical Society in New York City. Some of the most heady floral scents are jasmine, gardenia, magnolia, lily of the valley, narcissus, and fragrant roses. Honeysuckle and sweet alyssum may please your child or he may find them too sickly-sweet. In fact, I know one child who thinks alyssum smells like urine.

WOODSY ODORS

Besides the woodsy odors on your spice shelf, you can track down lavender, new-mown hay or cut grass, pine, fresh-cut lumber or sawdust, the smell of leaves and grass after a summer rain. If you can't find these odors in nature, you'll discover them in sachets, colognes and perfumes, room deodorizers, soaps, and sometimes even impregnated into facial or toilet tissue.

When you notice a smell, ask your child if he likes it, what it reminds him of, does it smell like anything else he likes. You'll find that certain odors are connected in his mind with happy or unhappy memories. Some favorite smells that are difficult to classify are: clay, phonograph records, glossy magazines.

LEAST-FAVORITE SMELLS

As mentioned earlier, some odors are distasteful to just about everyone: toilet smells, rotten eggs, decayed meat or vegetable matter. But if you and your child explore some of the *pungent* aromas you may be surprised at the difference between you. Besides the smell of milk and burnt toast, check on vinegar, leather, horsy smells, manure, fur, frying onions, burning leaves, hot chestnuts, hot tar, gasoline, and burning tobacco—pipe, cigar, and cigarette.

How your child reacts to certain body odors is also important. Besides sweat and breath, everyone carries characteristic food smells such as garlic and curry, clinging tobacco odors, occupational smells of medicine, paint, plaster, as well as colognes, perfumes, deodorants, hair sprays and shampoos, soap; these may repel or attract your child and thus may actually affect his relationship to the person.

WHAT CAN WE LEARN FROM ODORS?

You can help your child become aware of odors and how they can affect his life. They are relevant to chemistry, biology, physics, ecology, social sciences. Often a nonacademic child is intrigued by the novelty of this information.

CHEMISTRY FROM SMELLS

You can point out to your child many common cleaning-aids around the house that have a distinctive odor because of their chemistry. (Since all of these are dangerous, you should mention that the nose can give a warning of danger.) Among these are products like: drain cleaners, in which the characteristic odor is caused by potassium; oven cleaners, with sodium hydroxide; cleaning ammonia, with ammonia gas in solution; bleach, with chlorine gas in solution; the odor of dry-cleaning fluids such as chlorothene; floor waxes, with petroleum distillate. Naturally you'll want to inform your child in a way that won't be hazardous. For instance, if you're waxing the floor, you could comment on the odor and tell him it's toxic—that's why you need to keep the windows open.

You should also tell your child about the bad smell that is artificially added to our odorless cooking gas in order to warn us in case any begins to escape.

Some chemical changes in food smell bad to us. Show your child how he can use his sense of smell to detect that food is unfit to eat: rotten eggs, sour milk, tainted meat, and mildewed bread are some examples you might have occasion to notice. Your child might be interested in knowing that nature makes the odor of bad food unpleasant to us as a means of protection. That is, the meat doesn't smell bad for its own sake. We interact with it through smell because it's not good for us. If you have a dog or cat at home, you can show your child how the animal's nose checks everything he eats.

BIOLOGY FROM SMELLS

Some animals such as the skunk emit odor as protection. You might want to study with your child how smell functions in rats and insects. This is a rich subject that includes communication of food sources, messages of sex and mating, warning of danger. For example, a rat can smell what event happened in a given area, such as a fight evoking emotions and odors of fear and anger. Bees have 12,000 scent organs on their antennae and can recognize friend or enemy immediately by smell. They can even be trained to associate a sweet syrup with certain smells.

PHYSICS FROM SMELLS

Certain physical changes in nature have a characteristic odor. Go outdoors with your child sometime after a thunderstorm. You'll smell the ozone that is formed when the electric charge in the atmosphere interacts with the oxygen in the air. Important indoor odors to teach your child to recognize are that of overheated electrical wiring, the hot-metal odor of a saucepan that has boiled dry, the smell of an open light-bulb in contact with a curtain or parchment lampshade, smoldering ashes on a rug or under a sofa cushion. Another odorous physical change is mold on clothing, shoes, or books. In some of these cases, the nose tells us what our eyes and ears can't.

ECOLOGY FROM SMELLS

If your child is interested in preserving the environment, he will be aware of air pollution and how what we breathe affects our body. Most children are sensitive to the bad odors of smog and industrial haze, as well as to the stale odor of poorly ventilated rooms. Here is an unusual ecological fact about odor. Dr. Luther Terry, chairman of the advisory council of the Monell Chemical Senses Center in Pennsylvania warns that man is changing the odor of his environment, thus affecting the lower organisms that depend on smell for survival. They can't recognize the scents of predators, food, or sex, and die out. This in turn affects the food supply of higher organisms and sets off a chain reaction that will sooner or later reach us.

HISTORY FROM SMELLS

Your child can do a kind of historical study of "man's nose through the ages." A zany, fact-filled book he might enjoy is *The Common Scents of Smell*, by Russel C. Erb. An interesting book for parents is *The Hidden Dimension*, by Edward Hall. Your child can read about early man, who used smell as a means of communication. From there, he can use several approaches. For instance, how smell affected more civilized man; for example, in regard to sanitation. Why were the

Roman sewers such a remarkable achievement? How did they prevent disease and improve the quality of life? The child might be intrigued to know that during the Middle Ages, sanitation affected architecture; the rooms of the house were carefully arranged to minimize the unpleasant odors caused by lack of plumbing. Your child probably knows about outhouses and the importance of modern plumbing. If he is up-to-date, he will be aware of the latest problem in sanitation—pollution of water and putrid odors that can ruin a whole community.

Another approach to the area of smells is via the history of perfume. Perfumery was used by the ancient Egyptians and "precious ointments" are mentioned in the Bible. The Romans used many scents, but the medieval church prohibited perfume as an instrument of the devil. Perfume reappeared during the Renaissance, when English, French, and Italian nobles were highly perfumed (and poorly washed). Americans today are well-washed and perfumed and deodorized. Even our meeting rooms, theaters, and restaurants are chemically treated against odors.

What about the use of incense? Does it have a mystical significance? Not according to Erb in *The Common Scents of Smell.* Incense was first burned for a very practical reason—to mask the smell at early human and animal sacrifices. Later on, it served a similar function in churches, because deceased church members were buried in the basement.

If you have played the general game of fragrances and odors with your child, you will know that perfume is important to modern merchandising. The next time you are at the market with your child, compare the smell of some laundry and bath soaps. You will notice that the perfumed soaps are more expensive, but in fact the chemical composition is often identical. Even nylons and facial and toilet tissue are sometimes scented. And see if your child can track down some odorous advertising in a newspaper or flyer. Odor-carrying ink sometimes whets the appetite in food ads. One insurance company actually used ink with a charred smell to advertise fire insurance!

SMELLS AND CULTURAL CHARACTERISTICS

Certain climates and ways of life produce characteristic odors. If you and your children vacation in a subtropical climate, you will notice many unusual odors: floral scents, heavy vegetation, and sometimes mold and decay. Men and women in these climates use very sweet perfumes. This can cause a negative reaction in a foreigner: dislike or confusion, as in the case of a heavily perfumed male.

If your family goes to a small town where there are few cars, you will be amazed at the number of smells: people, animals, food, flowers. The exhaust fumes of cars drown out all these odors.

Eating habits affect personal odor. To a foreigner, many Indians smell of curry and spices; a Japanese may smell of fish; a native of southern Italy may carry the odor of garlic. These smells cling to the breath and clothing of the person and also to their homes. Incidentally, to an Oriental, an American smells of butter.

If you and your child live in a large city, you can smell characteristic food odors on a walk through ethnic neighborhoods: meat frying in hot oil in Spanish and Haitian districts; bagels, and maybe soup, in a Jewish neighborhood; garlic in a South Italian district; fish at a Japanese restaurant; sweet and sour sauce in Chinatown; ham hocks and chick-peas in a Black American neighborhood.

OCCUPATIONAL ODORS

Your child may enjoy spotting odors characteristic of an activity. For example:

Doctor and dentist: medical smell
Veterinarian or horseman: animal smell
Bakery worker: bread or sweet pastry
Car mechanic: grease
Worker in hand laundry: ironed clothing
Painter: paint, turpentine
Plasterer: plaster
Crane operator: Diesel fuel
Road builder: asphalt, diesel fuel or earth, depending on what he does.
Passenger in airplane: odor of cabin pressurizing system

Each of these odors will be mixed with the body odors of perspiration, staple food, emotional state, deodorants, and perfumes. A detective with a good nose wouldn't need to ask many questions.

SUGGESTED ACTIVITIES

If your child has an unusually keen sense of smell, he might especially enjoy gourmet cooking and gourmet eating, working with flowers in the garden or arranging cut flowers indoors, and studying perfumes and perfume manufacture. Since smells are intimately connected with memories and past emotions, your child may wish to express this sensitivity through creative projects in writing or drama.

16 How to Increase Awareness of the Sense of Taste

What you taste indirectly affects what your child tastes. If you enjoy many different taste sensations, mealtimes will be varied, pleasant, unhurried—you won't be likely to serve and eat too much food. If a food problem comes up with your child, such as dawdling at the table or being unreasonable fussy, your basic appreciation of food will help your child understand the situation. It's hard for him to make an effort to eat if he senses that food doesn't mean much to you. But if you delight in your sense of taste, you child will develop his own. And if you regret that taste has never seemed important to you, it is easy for both of you to increase your taste sensitivity.

YOUR AWARENESS OF TASTE

Collect some representative tastes: *Sweet:* refined sugar, apple, honey; *salt:* table salt, fish, ham; *sour:* lemon, yogurt; *bitter:* almond, quinine water. If possible, taste them with your eyes closed. Be aware of the differences between refined sugar and honey, and other examples within the same category. You will find that taste buds on different parts of your tongue respond to the four basic tastes. In general, sweet is on the tip of the tongue, salt on the tip and sides, sour and bitter on the sides and on the palate. You'll discover that solid food needs slow chewing for maximum taste, and liquids need sipping, not gulping. Also, that taste diminishes after the first few bites or swallows. If you are really curious, you can swallow a small piece of something without chewing it, or chew while you hold your nose to check the loss in sensation. (As mentioned before, odor and taste mingle—hence the decrease in taste when a cold stops up your nose.) Also, some foods taste better after, before, or with others, just as some sequences of musical notes and certain chords are more satisfying to our ear than others.

The mechanics of taste and smell are chemical, not physical like our other senses, and scientists are not really sure how the chemical senses work. This makes it difficult to catergorize types and blends of tastes, and no norms have been established for taste, as they have been with seeing and hearing, for example. But in your experiments, you will notice that certain sensations hit you right away and others are more subtle. A true gourmet can recognize and identify the most delicate combinations of tastes: For example, "This paté contains a base of liver and pork, seasoned with garlic, onion, bay, and thyme. The paté is firm in appearance and very fresh, but the onions were not chopped finely enough, which affects the smoothness of the texture and creates particles of isolated onion taste, instead of an overall taste blend. There is also too much thyme—the taste stands out individually instead of harmonizing. Finally, the paté was not properly chilled. It was served almost at room temperature." You will realize that this gentleman is using his tongue plus his eyes (appearance of food), his nose (odor of food), and his sense of touch (texture and temperature of food in his mouth). With crisp food such as lettuce and carrots, he would use his ears too.

If this expertise motivates you to further practice in taste, play the following sensory games with your child.

TASTING GAMES

These games will help your child become aware of his sense of taste. Besides being fun, this helps your child socially, because a fine "taster" enjoys eating, and eating is often a social activity. (They can be played with children of any age.)

SWEET, SALT, SOUR, BITTER

Ask your child to close his eyes during a meal and move different bits of food around on his tongue. Suppose that for dinner you are having fish with lemon, creamed spinach, french-fried potatoes, and salad with oil and vinegar—and for dessert, fresh apples and chocolate-chip cookies. See if your child can separate the taste sensations and place them. For instance, he will taste the salt of the fish and the french fries on the tip and sides of his tongue, the sour of the lemon on the sides of his tongue and also on his palate. He may trace the bitter taste of the spinach to more or less the same area: the sides of his tongue and his palate. The sauce in the creamed spinach may blend so well with the bitter taste that it is hard to separate the two. You should mention to your child that this blending of tastes is what makes a good meal. He can prove this himself by taking a small portion of salad and experimenting with the blend of oil and vinegar. Too much oil is greasy and bland, too much vinegar is so sour he will choke. The right amount brings out the taste of the salad greens and doesn't impose an additional taste of its own.

Sweet-taste buds are on the tip of the tongue. See if your child can taste the different degrees of sweetness in a fresh apple, a piece of the cookie, and a chocolate chip. He'll have the most luck if he tastes them in that order, starting with the least sweet. If he wants to start over, he'll need to wipe his taste palate clean first by eating a piece of bread or cracker or a bit of cheese.

Once your child gets the hang of this, he may want to try some fancier taste experiments, such as tasting with his eyes closed. See if he can identify a pretzel, a potato chip, a salted nut; a piece of lettuce, parsley, green pepper; a slice of apple, orange, peach. If he can do this easily, you might check him on some other, more similar, tastes. With eyes closed, can he tell the difference between: lemon and lime? nectarine and peach? Concord grape and green grape (you will have to remove the seeds beforehand)? How about iceberg lettuce and Boston lettuce? Semisweet and bittersweet chocolate?

Another variation of this game is to serve your child a dish of blended ingredients and ask him what tastes he can recognize. (He can open his eyes for this.) You can use a home-made food or read the label on a store-bought mixture. For instance, if he's very sharp, he will be able to taste the caraway in a box of Seasoned Ry Krisp as well as the salt and rye flour. If you bake some sugar cookies that contain (among other ingredients) vanilla, chopped walnuts, and grated lemon rind, see what your child can taste besides the sugar and flour. (He probably won't mention the shortening unless he cooks himself.) Vanilla is a strong taste and so are the nutmeats, but which nuts are they? And the lemon rind may fool him unless it is not finely grated.

Ask your child what unusual taste blends he enjoys. Some are: almond cookie—bitter and sweet; Chinese sauce—sour and sweet; Lemon drop—sour and sweet; peanut butter—salty and sweet; fresh orange—sweet and sour; cheese cake —sweet and sour and salty.

If your child's sense of taste is very sophisticated and he doesn't hate milk or cheese, ask him to compare the tastes of bleu cheese, sour cream, and yogurt, and contrast these with the taste of sour milk. What makes the first three palatable and the last one disagreeable? He might also sample various types of cheese and compare tastes. Tell him that gourmets often have cheese- and wine-tasting parties. Your child may have already noticed that odor and texture affect his taste. So does the temperature of the food, its looks, and even the sound as he chews it.

DO YOU SMELL WHAT YOU EAT?

Ask your child if his mouth waters at the smell of certain food. Tell him that this is a chemical change in his body that prepares it for eating. It also changes the taste sensation.

Food odor hits a second time when your child chews: his teeth cut open the food and the odor is released into the mouth-nose cavity. Sipping a liquid, as an alternative to gulping it, also gives smell a chance.

If your child does not believe you and has not had a cold recently, he can hold his nose as he eats fried onions, pizza, broccoli, bacon, or sharp condiments like pickles, kechup, and mustard. He will notice a loss in sensation that is smell, not taste. Although he cannot swallow with his nose held, he may be able to smell the difference between a sip and a gulp of a milk shake.

For more experiments with food odors, see pages 275–276.

TEXTURE, TEMPERATURE, AND TASTE

Show your child how texture in food affects the blending of taste. If you're baking cookies and creaming butter and sugar together in a mixing bowl, or stirring lumps out of a gravy, he can taste the difference before and after. It's not just the feel of the food or liquid on his tongue that changes. It's also a flavor shock in the before caused by a concentration of one ingredient—a lump of butter or flour.

Other foods—like Jell-O, some hot cereals, very sticky peanut butter, and of course, raw oysters—may taste all right but feel awful to your child's lips, tongue, mouth, and throat. These are not really taste, but touch sensations. So is the temperature of the food—hot, cold, in between. But temperature also affects taste in a chemical way. Odor and taste are stronger at certain temperatures—perhaps you are familiar with the misery of eating a lukewarm pork chop as the tangy odor fades and the fat begins to congeal.

Some of our temperature preferences are conditioned. In England, Scotch whisky is served without ice. Beer is not always chilled. And many European countries serve raw fruit and vegetables and fresh butter at room temperature. Ask your child to be aware of temperature and texture during a meal. For instance,

soup: hot and liquid
rolls: warm and chewy
butter: cool and smooth
meat: hot and very chewy
sauce: hot and smooth
salad: cool and crisp
ice cream: very cold and smooth

SEEING AND HEARING FOOD

Tell your child that the way food looks affects his taste chemistry. In fact, if it looks really terrible, he may gag and not be able to swallow at all. I read of one banquet where an imaginative chef had created a seascape out of broiled whole fish swimming in blue-dyed whipped potatoes. Nobody could eat the food. Another revolting food-color scheme (this one from a college dining room) was that of an all-white lunch, consisting of white fish, white sauce, and white cauliflower.

Ask your child to imagine some other bad food-color ideas, such as green milk or blue carrots and tomatoes. Then have him help you arrange some visually tempting meals. Some suggestions:

Raw vegetable plate with celery and carrot sticks,
parsley, and black olives.
Lamb on a platter decorated with fresh mint.
Carrots with fresh dill.
Frothy chocolate milk shake.

Your child will notice that most crunchy foods that look good will also sound right. Wilted carrots and celery look sad and won't sound crisp when he chews them. Neither will old parsley or lettuce, or tired potato chips. An exception is old crackers, such as saltines, which look normal—but what a shock to bite into that noiseless soggy texture!

WHAT CAN WE LEARN FROM TASTE?

You can help an older child become aware that taste is an important sense that he shares with every human being past, present, and future. This is relevant to social studies, history, science. As with a smell, a nonacademic child may be intrigued by the novelty of this information. (Ages 8–12.)

WHAT TASTES GOOD TO DIFFERENT NATIONALITIES AND WHERE DID THE FOOD CUSTOM BEGIN?

If your child follows through on national tastes and how they grew, he will learn a lot about people and history.

Italy—pasta

According to the Spaghetti Historical Museum in Pontedasio, Italy, pasta dates back to 500 B.C., during Etruscan times. Many centuries later Thomas Jefferson ate it in Italy (during a trip when he was ambassador to France) and introduced it to this country. Mussolini, with his flair for public relations, always gave away free spaghetti when a new bridge or road was opened.

Japan—Fish, rice, greens, bean sprouts

These are the most plentiful staples available. Your child might shudder at this little tidbit: prepared dragonflies are considered a special delicacy in Japan.

The United States—Soul food, Thanksgiving dinner

Soul food was originally an ingenious treatment of the inexpensive food given to slaves by their masters. Dishes include pigs' feet, oxtail, barbecued ribs, chitterlings, yams and collard greens.

Most children know the menu and origin of our Thanksgiving Dinner: wild turkey and game, corn that the Pilgrims grew from Indian example, and other indigenous foods such as squash, pumpkin, and cranberry.

Sometimes the taste, food preparation, and social custom blend. The Japanese use a brazier not only for preparing food but also for warmth and family togetherness at meals.

American barbecues taste delicious, but half the fun is in the outdoor socializing.

The French are usually so particular about conditions that outdoor eating is rare. (Most French outdoor cafés serve drinks and snacks, not meals.)

WHAT TASTES BAD TO DIFFERENT PEOPLES AND WHY (RELIGIOUS DIETARY LAWS)

Your child can make a list of religious dietary laws and find out how cultural conditioning has made these foods unsuitable to certain peoples.

Jewish: The Old Testament prohibits pork and the combining of meat and milk.

Moslem: Pork is considered unclean.

Hindu: Beef is sacred and should not be eaten.

Catholic: Until recently, no meat on Friday as a sign of penance.

TASTE, APPETITE, AND HUNGER

If your child is really ambitious, he can make a mammoth study of hunger, appetite, and taste in animals and man. He could include the search for food by primitive one-celled organisms *(hunger)*, then he could study the higher species and their preferred diets—carnivorous, herbivorous, or omnivorous *(appetites)*, and finally study the food habits of man with his more refined preferences *(taste)*.

A reverse study would show your child that lack of food leads man back to the primitive-animal hunger stage. He may learn about wars that were fought because of food shortage; the ratio between population and food supply; today's population explosion; new developments in food for man, such as the use of plankton from the ocean or a nutritious pill.

Your child might want to consider the philosophical question, Should man let part of his species die off when food is scarce, as the animals do—the survival of the fittest—or does every man deserve to eat? If so, how can this be achieved?

WHAT PLANTS ARE FOOD?

Your child can perform some growing experiments that will show him that the vegetables and fruits he eats are actually plants. For example, carrot and pineapple tops will sprout leaves if he puts them in a saucer with pebbles and water; beets, turnips, and potatoes will sprout if planted in soil and watered. So will some seeds of oranges, lemons, grapefruit, or watermelon (depending on their condition.)

Ask your child to make a list of vegetables and to notice what part of the plant he eats:

> Seeds: corn, peanuts
> Roots: carrots, turnips
> Shoots: asparagus and bean sprouts
> Stems and flower buds: broccoli and cauliflower
> Leaves: cabbage and lettuce
> Fruit: tomato, squash, and all sweet fruits

Tell your child that the part of the plant that he ordinarily eats is the most nutritious and the tastiest.

GROWING TASTY PLANTS FOR FOOD — PAST AND PRESENT

This is a wonderful project that can be approached in many ways, such as reading books that describe the history of agriculture from primitive man through the Egyptian, Hebrew, Greek, Roman, and medieval periods to modern times. Your child can find out *what man grew for food;* for instance, a grain fossil indicates that man ate wheat nine thousand years ago. He might then go on to *how man grew food.* You might want to start your child off by taking him to a museum to look at early tools and methods of farming. He may be surprised to learn that way back in antiquity the Egyptians already used a plow. Or you and your child might have a conversation with a farmer and find out about farming today: what machines he uses to prepare the soil, how he compensates for the climate when possible with shading and irrigation; and how he protects the crops from disease and pests. Does he increase yield by fertilizer or rotation of crops? When does he know that the plant is ready for harvesting?

Your child doesn't need to learn this information in chronological order. It will make sense to him if he can relate it to his own sense of taste.

TASTE, NUTRITION, AND ECOLOGY

Your child can perform taste tests from samples in health food stores and food prepared according to the dictates of a natural nutritionist like Adelle Davis in her *Let's Cook It Right.* Health foods are grown with organic fertilizers and contain no chemical preservatives or artificial additives. Your child will notice a distinct taste difference between them and food that is grown and processed commercially. Fruit and vegetables usually have a more robust flavor, which most young ones love, but some products such as unhydrogenated peanut butter may not please him at all.

If your child wants to hear the other point of view about nutrition, he should write to his state conservation department for the names of insecticides considered safe for plant and animal life. Also, the United States Department of Agriculture will send him pamphlets about chemical fertilizers, which detail experiments comparing them with organic fertilizers. The results indicate that the chemical products may be superior in some ways, but when it comes to the relative taste of the products grown by chemical or organic techniques, your child can run his own tests. His results are as valid as anyone else's until scientists discover a way to measure degrees of taste.

TASTE AND FOOD CHEMISTRY

This is a natural follow-up to the preceding game. During a trip to the supermarket, show your child how to judge fresh meat, vegetables, and fruit. Point out the frozen food packages and see if you can discover one that is partially defrosted. Look at the prepared meat products like frankfurters and bologna and notice the preservatives. Also notice the additives to the other products, such as bread, cereal, crackers, cookies.

Your child might want to find out how long meat, produce, and grain products will last with no refrigeration or preservatives. What is the vitamin loss after a period of time? What happens to defrosted products? Then ask him to consider the technical problems of supplying food in a large country like ours. You might discuss questions such as:

Which is better, refrigerated lettuce that has lost taste and vitamins, or first-rate lettuce in season only?

Is it possible to turn the clock back to baking fresh goods without preservatives? How much would this cost? Would the difference in taste and food value be considerable? How much loss would baking companies and food markets incur from spoilage?

Is there any way to check on the temperature history of frozen food? (A recent invention: tape around the package, which changes color permanently when the package thaws.)

WHY DO WE EAT?
(FROM TASTE TO ENERGY)

Your child can study food from his first taste to the final result: energy and wastes. He can find out how the body breaks down the food, what types of food the body uses for differant purposes (bones, teeth, skin, hair, blood, nerves) and what are the chemical elements found in food (iodine, sodium). What does the body do with these chemicals? Where does the body sift out unecessary food elements?

Related topics are:

What is a balanced diet?
What are the effects of malnutrition, especially on children?
What are the effects of drugs and alcohol on the body and its function?

If your child is interested in character traits, he can learn to recognize how people feel about themselves by watching them eat and drink. He'll spot a finicky person who picks at his food; a sloppy individual who slurps and spills; a gourmet who relishes every bite. He may be amazed, as one of my daughters once was, by a fat man in a restaurant who ate for lunch: a salami club sandwich, potato salad, a chocolate soda for beverage, and for dessert, an apple pie à la mode. On his plate he left: lettuce, tomatoes, and a pickle—the only low calorie items in the meal!

When your child develops a feel for eating as a bodily function, he will recognize what's wrong about overeating from a very practical point of view. This may be more effective than any words could be.

SUGGESTED ACTIVITIES

If your child has an unusually good sense of taste, he will enjoy: learning to cook and experimenting with recipes; eating at exceptional restaurants of various nationalities; planning for social get-togethers unusual food such as an all-vegetable meal or a Japanese hibachi dinner (perhaps with chopsticks).

Here are some books that will help your child in his study of foods and nutrition. *What Happens to a Hamburger?* by Paul Showers (Thomas Y. Crowell and Company, 1970) is suitable for a very young child; it has charming illustrations. More ambitious books include *Food Facts for Young People* by Arnold and White (Holiday House, 1968); *Understanding Food —The Chemistry of Nutrition* by Tannenbaum and Stillman (McGraw Hill, 1962); and the most challenging, *From Cell to Test Tube, the Science of Bio-Chemistry,* by Chambers and Payne (Scribners, 1960).

Conclusion

You have helped your child to hear and speak sensitively, to feel with his hands and skin and move with his body; to see, to smell, to taste, and to be conscious of how others respond. Will this sensory awareness be battered down and blunted by the world your child will live in?

Psychological studies on urban violence and drugs point to economic and social factors that diminish sensitivity and natural sensory responses. The isolation and fear of each individual give him no opportunity to sharpen his awareness of how others function and what pleases or angers them. On a cultural and international level, this can lead to massive misunderstandings, sometimes based on the simplest sensory facts. When an Arab engages someone in conversation, he ordinarily stands very close to him, so close that his breath will bathe the other's face, a sign of his good will. If the other gentleman is an Englishman, this proximity will indicate out-of-bounds behavior. The Englishman will step back, and the Arab, who is now insulted, steps back as well.

However, there are positive trends today that hold out some hope for your child's sensory way of life, through solutions to such problems in human relations. Communes, encounter groups, and sensitivity sessions emphasize the need to understand what each person wants, likes, and dislikes, starting from the basic sensory level.

A better environment will please children and all sensitive citizens. Sociologists and scientist are zeroing in on our environment from two different points of view. Th first group is concerned about stress factors that cause social turbulence such as crowding from overpopulation. The second is worried about the survival of man in an unhealthy world. The opposite of stress and sickness is an ordered and organically whole way of life with beautiful surroundings to see, hear, feel, and move through—to smell and taste and share with others. Urban renewal; population control; restraints on noise, air, and water pollution; wholesome food from earth and sea; conservation of trees, birds, animals and other natural resources—all of these areas are now battlegrounds for scientists, sociologists, city planners, industrialists, politicians. If the "good guys" win, so will our senses, and those of our children.

A related problem which will affect our children as they grow up is the poor quality of modern life. Philosophers, religious thinkers, psychiatrists, artists, and even some employers are worried about the rat race and how to make daily life more meaningful. A rat race is an ugly happening that mean and vicious animals endure in order to win. Only, as many young people point out, there is no winning in life. If you do not enjoy the process, "you're nowhere."

What is there to enjoy about the process of living, besides the common ground of basic physical pleasures? Each individual can be happy in at least part of his work activity and in his leisure. To realize this goal, you must know: What do I like, what don't I like, what am I good at, what do I have trouble with? A child who has an awareness of his sensory aptitudes and difficulties will be able to answer these questions. After that, he can ask, How will I find the right job? The women's liberation movement is already tackling this problem, because woman's work was not what many women enjoy or feel most suited for. Many formerly all-male aptitudes were challenged by the ability of women as they became first executives and professionals and then, more recently, commercial airline pilots, cab drivers, jockeys, mechanics, and construction workers. Obviously these are jobs the women doing them enjoy, and part of the pleasure is a sensory one. A woman who puts up a fight to become a jockey or a construction worker enjoys physical movement. An airline pilot must be skilled visually.

It is possible to test sensory aptitude just as one can test IQ. For example, visual tests indicate special skills or deficiencies in spatial judgment, long-distance viewing, close vision. Good spatial sense is essential to airline pilots, cab and truck drivers, engineers, architects. Long-distance viewing is used by all of the above, plus construction workers like a crane operator. Any fine-touch activites, such as sewing or watch-making, require good close vision. Evaluations of physical aptitudes were made by Rudolf Laban during World War II in England. He analyzed body and movement type and prescribed heavy work, light flexible work, or work with changing rhythms. If such procedures become common, it will mean that your child will be able to find work that is tailor-made to his aptitudes, and therefore more enjoyable for him. Another step in this direction is the change in social attitude about creative pursuits and manual labor. An intelligent young person who becomes a forest ranger instead of pursuing the conventional intellectual goals is no longer thought of as odd. If he says, "I like the outdoors and I like to work with my body," that is a plausible and acceptable explanation.

Constructive leisure pastimes also make for a meaningful life, especially since the work week is shrinking. A child who is aware of his sensory aptitude need never become a bored adult. If he knows that he likes to use his eyes and hands, he will find some craft work or scientific projects like building a telescope. A hearer can study music or work with ham radio. A mover can build a cottage or landscape a garden. And if his senses are alive, he can even do "nothing" creatively. According to Alfred North Whitehead in *Science and the Modern World*, "The mere disposal of the human body and the eyesight so as to get a good view of a sunset is a simple form of artistic selection. The habit of art is the habit of enjoying vivid values."

Preventive medicine and education are two other fields which seem to be moving toward a concern with sensory awareness which will benefit your child's senses in the future. Health and well-being now mean more than just not being sick. They mean feeling alive and full of energy and functioning at optimum level. The widespread insterest in good nutrition and health foods, poineered by óld-timers like J. I. Rodale and Adelle Davis, is growing. Medical projections into the future suggest that we may be able to consult a trained specialist who will advise us on: 1. The amount and types of food that are best for our individual body. 2. How to correct tension and pain through relaxation and concentration techinques. 3. Simple exercises that will strengthen sensory weaknesses. In addition to techniques relevant to the body and the eyes, these could include the voice, perhaps even the senses of smell and taste.

More than twenty years ago, Dr. Arnold Gesell, the founder of the Gesell Institute in New Haven, predicted such a future in the area of visual function. His work with children convinced him that the eyes were part of the total action system and that visual function should be periodically checked and corrected if necessary. His testing of first-grade children disclosed that some intelligent pupils were visually immature. This meant that they had trouble with the visual symbols for letters and numbers. In the past, these children were often considered mentally retarded, but today's approach often includes visual training such as the graded symbol-game developed by Dr. Richard A. Kavner, which trains the child to identify visual characteristics of the letters of the alphabet.

If a child with visual difficulty attended a school with an open classroom such as those in the experimental projects in New York City supervised by Lillian Weber, he would have the opportunity to learn through his other senses until his eyes caught up with the rest of him. He might want to practice speech sounds and record his voice and a tape recorder, or carry out some touch experiments with a scale or Cuisenaire rods. These children are encouraged to learn through experience, and a child whose senses are aware is a better experiencer. One outgrowth of this educational approach may well be a type of standardized sensory testing for children—a "sensory awareness quotient." If a child has a learning problem, such a test could determine his best sense, and the teacher would know whether to use a visual, verbal, tactile, or kinesthetic approach to the student. If the child registers low awareness in seeing or in hearing and speaking, for example, the school would provide remedial practice in that sense, since it relates directly to the academic study of mathematics, science, and language.

A teacher who is aware of a pupil's senses is also by example teaching the child sensitivity toward others and the joys of communication. The child learns that people and how they function are part of the world he wants to be aware of.

For all of these reasons, what you have taught your child at home about his sensory world can continue beyond his front door and into his future.

Guide to Sensory Games and Other Creative Activities

TOUCH GAMES

Manual Dexterity Practice Game for Touch Sensitivity. To make your child more aware of his sense of touch. Suitable for any age. Pages 164–166.

Manual Dexterity Practice Games for Flexibility, Accuracy, Well-timed Pressure and Release. For skill in performing daily manual activities and creative work in arts and crafts. Suggested age range (depending on game): 3–12. Pages 167–176.

Manual Dexterity Practice Games for Hand-Eye Coordination. To increase ability in sports, daily activities and fine touch projects such as writing, sewing, carpentry. Suggested age range: 6–12. Pages 176–179.

Manual Dexterity Observation Game for Parents. To help your child become more skillful in using his hands. Appropriate at any age. Pages 179–183.

Communication by Touch Game. To help your child become more aware of touch communication in the world around him. Suitable for any child and parent who have rapport in wordless communication. Pages 184–185.

Over-all Touch Games for Awareness of Skin Sensitivity and Climate Awareness. To encourage your child to realize that no two people "feel" alike. Suggested age range (depending on game): 3–12. Pages 186–187.

More Creative Opportunities Related to Your Child's Sense of Touch. Pages 40–42.

MOVEMENT GAMES

General Movement Observation Games. To make your child more aware of the world around him and to discover how your child responds to movement. Suggested age range (depending on the game): 3–12. Pages 203–210.

Movement Practice Games. For body articulation, relaxation, good posture, bending and stretching in good alignment, energy (effort), movement quality, speed (tempo), rhythm. To make your child more aware of his body and how it moves. Important for ease and efficiency in daily physical activities and in sports, as well as expressive movement such as in dance. Suggested age range: 6–12. Pages 211–221.

Movement Practice Game for Movement in Relation to Space. To make your child more aware of the world around him. Important for understanding of architecture, dance, natural science, and physics. Suggested age range: 4–12. Pages 221–222.

Movement Observation Game for Parents. To help your child become more skillful in using his body. Appropriate at any age. Pages 222–228.

More Creative Opportunities in Movement. Pages 53–54.

SEEING GAMES

General Seeing Games to Explore What Your Child Sees. Especially form, color, light and shade, and spatial relations. To help your child become more aware of the world around him and to discover what he likes to look at. Suitable for any age. Pages 235–239.

General Seeing Game to Improve Your Child's Visual Memory. Important for following directions on how to get somewhere, and for school subjects such as mathematics and social studies. Suggested age range: 6–12. Pages 239–240.

Match the Letter Pattern and the Number Pattern Games. To help your child become aware that the patterns of words and of numerals he sees on a page can be parallel to the sound patterns he speaks, to touch patterns he feels with his hand, and to movement patterns he makes with his body. Suggested age range (depending on game): 3–7. Pages 240–248.

Seeing Flat Shapes Games. For skill in reading, writing, mathematics. Suggested age range: 5–9. Pages 248–250.

Seeing Flat Shapes Game—Graphics. To help your child become aware that the lettters and numbers he writes on a page create a design. Suggested age range: 5–10. Pages 250–251.

Seeing Forms Game. Important for understanding of mathematics (measuring volume), physics, engineering, architecture, art. Suggested age range: 5–12. Pages 252–255.

Seeing Light and Shade Game. Increases your child's understanding of world around him, and also introduces him to basic elements of photographic, film, and video techniques. Suggested age range: 7–12. Pages 255–256.

Seeing Color Game. To increase your child's pleasure in seeing and to help him discover color in the world of art and science. Suggested age range: 8–12. Pages 257–259.

Seeing Games for Spatial Relations.

A. Optical illusions and other visual effects, to make your child more aware of how he sees his surroundings and to give him a feeling for geometry, physics, engineering, navigation. Suggested age range: 8–12. Pages 259–263.

B. Movement prints, floor-plans, and maps. To help your child learn to orient himself physically in space, and to give him a feeling for geography. Suggested age range: 6–12. Pages 263–265.

C. Measuring space in two and three dimensions. To show your child that space can be measured and to give him a feeling for the mathematical study of area and volume. Suitable for a child of any age, depending on the interest of the child. Pages 266–268.

D. Estimating distances close-up and far away. Eye-hand coordination. To help your child relate himself physically to his surroundings. Practical value for innumerable activities, such as packing a suitcase or participation in sports. Suitable for child of any age. Pages 269–272.

More Creative Opportunities in Seeing. Pages 30–32.

GAMES AND ACTIVITIES RELATED TO SENSE OF SMELL

General Games. Food odors, floral fragrances, woodsy odors, least favorite smells. To make you aware of your child's vocabulary of smells. Suitable for child of any age. Pages 275–278.

What Can We Learn from Odors? Relevant to chemistry, biology, physics, ecology, history, sociology. The nonacademic child may be intrigued by the novelty of this information. Suitable for child of any age. Pages 278–283.

More Activities Related to Your Child's Sense of Smell. Page 283.

GAMES AND ACTIVITIES RELATED TO SENSE OF TASTE

General Games. Sweet, salt, sour, and bitter; odor, texture, and temperature; seeing and hearing food. These games help your child become aware of his sense of taste and perhaps will motivate him to get more pleasure out of eating. Suitable for child of any age. Pages 286–291.

Suggested Reading
for Parents

Although few of these books are actually on the subject of sensory awareness, they arrive at this topic from various points of departure. There is at present no scientific study of complete sensory function in children or adults. The range that is considered normal is so broad that it is almost like a driver's test that says, "If you're not totally blind, you pass." However, many scientists have examined various aspects of the senses.

Artists and teachers of the arts have always been concerned with optimum sensory function, but through nobody's fault, this work has remained specialized. For example, one is urged to use one's voice well if one wishes to lecture or act on the stage. But why not also if one wants to teach children? Or just to enjoy speaking, since we do it all the time? Nevertheless, a mingling of the scientific and the artistic approaches has occurred on occasion. Psychologists who made a study of how people perceive visually were amazed to discover the experiential truths known to artists for centuries, such as laws of perspective, distance, and color perception. The Alexander Technique of optimum body movement was championed by George Bernard Shaw and John Dewey as a key to better living. Today, it is taught to laymen and professionals in major cities through the United States. There is a popular interest in yoga and meditation, and brain researchers have discovered that alpha waves can be controlled through yoga techniques that are many centuries old.

SCIENCE, PSYCHOLOGY, EDUCATION

Analysis of Sensations by Ernest Mach. Dover (reprint), 1959. A classic by an Austrian physicist, psychologist, and philosopher who predated Freud by about twenty years.

The Common Scents of Smell by Russell C. Erb. World, 1968. An hilarious and fact-filled book by a professor of organic chemistry which contains background and current information about the sense of smell.

Dibs and *Play Therapy,* two books by Virginia M. Axline. Ballantine (Paperback), 1969. A child psychiatrist writes in a lucid, penetrating manner of her approach to the child through many techniques, including nonverbal (sensory) ones.

Efficiency of Human Movement by Marion Broer. W. B. Saunders, 1960. A nontechnical discussion of body movement in sports and daily life considered from the viewpoint of anatomy and physics.

The Hidden Dimension by Edward T. Hall. Doubleday, 1966. An anthropologist looks at human behavior and cultural conditioning in an entertaining and informative way.

The Mind by John Rowan Wilson, M.D. and Editors of *Life.* Life-Science Library. *Light and Vision* by Conrad C. Mueller, Mae Rudolf, and Editors of *Life.* Life-Science Library. Two clearly written, simple books on very complex subjects involving seeing, perceiving, and learning. Both books have excellent graphics and illustrations.

The Montessori Method by Maria Montessori. Schocken (paperback), 1964. A fascinating description by a brilliant pioneer of former pedagogic methods and how to improve them through the education of the senses. Contains an excellent, up-to-date introduction by psychologist J. McV. Hunt which stresses the importance of the Montessori approach for today.

On the Importance of Infancy by Lawrence K. Frank. Random House, 1967. An unusually readable book about a complicated topic.

The Senses by Wolfgang Von Buddenbrock. U. of Michigan Press, 1968. A simple, interesting description of sensory responses in lower organisms, reptiles, and animals.

The Senses Considered as Perceptual Systems by J. J. Gibson. Houghton-Mifflin, 1960. *Principles of Perceptual Learning and Development* by Eleanor J. Gibson. Appleton, 1969. Two books on the senses and visual perception. These are psychological textbooks and are technical and difficult to read.

Sensory Psychology by Conrad C. Mueller. Prentice Hall, 1965. A short introduction to the senses from the psychological viewpoint by a professor of psychology and neural science.

Six Psychological Studies by Jean Piaget. Vintage (paperback), 1968. Very difficult reading. The correlation between a child's sensory exploration and his cognitive development will interest parents.

Toward a Theory of Instruction by Jerome Bruner. Harvard U. Press, 1966. Another approach to the question of how children learn, with many references to sensory experiences.

Vision—Its Development in Infant and Child by Arnold Gesell, M.D., Frances Ilg, M.D., Glenna E. Bullis (assisted by Vivienne Ilg, O.D., G.N. Getman, O.D.). Hafner, 1967. An early work in this field, readable and interesting.

Visual Thinking by Rudolf Arnheim. U. of California Press, 1969. A fascinating book by an eminent scholar who discusses what we see from a psychological, philosophical, and artistic point of view.

The Voice of Neurosis by Paul C. Moses, M.D. Grune and Stratton, 1954. An exciting description of vocal patterns and what they tell about the personality of the speaker.

A parent who has explored his child's sensory world might enjoy reading or rereading some of the current literature by child-centered educators, such as A.S. Neill, John Holt, Jonathan Kozol, Sylvia Ashton Warner, George Dennison, Herb Snitzer, and Herbert Kohl.

ARTISTS AND OTHER EXPERTS ON CREATIVE SENSORY AWARENESS

An Actor Prepares and *Building a Character* by Constatin Stanislavsky (Hapgood, tr.). Theatre Arts Books, 1949 and 1950, respectively. Two classics that discuss sensory awareness for actors but are useful for anyone who wishes to live fully.

Creative Movement for Children by Jack Wiener and John Lidstone. Van Nostrand Reinhold, 1969. A book for parents and teachers that approaches movement for children as a bridge to awareness of self in time and space. Remarkable photos and text.

Design for Artist and Craftsmen by Louis Wolchonok. Dover, 1953. A step-by-step description, with illustrations, of how to draw and how to see. Useful for anyone interested in creative looking, whether or not you wish to put your views on paper.

Effort by Rudolf Laban and F.C. Lawrence. Macdonald and Evans, London, 1947; and *The Mastery of Movement* by Rudolf Laban, Macdonald and Evans, London, 1960. These two books by Laban contain his remarkable analysis of movement and motion characteristics. The second book is the definitive work, but it is complex and difficult. The first is a good introduction to Laban because of the wealth of specific examples from everyday life.

Fitness from Six to Twelve by Bonnie Prudden. Harper & Row, 1972. A lively informative book with easy-to-follow exercises for body fitness and movement for sports and dance, plus a positive exposition of the importance of movement for a happy, full way of life.

From Two to Five by Kornei Chukovsky (Morton, ed., tr.). U. of California Press (paperback), 1968. A beautifully written explanation of the growth of language and poetry in children, full of delightful examples. The author is a well-known Russian scholar, poet, and writer of children's books.

Improvisation for the Theater by Viola Spolin. Northwestern U. Press, 1963. Theater games for children. This book is for parents and teachers who wish to explore creativity in children. The techniques are original, exciting, and presented in a direct, straightforward manner. The overall message of the book is an approach to children that channels their spontaneous play into an awareness of self, of others, and of the world in which we all live.

Language of Vision by Gyorgy Kepes. Paul Theobald & Co., 1961. A compelling exposition of what we see from the artistic point of view.

A New Look at Movement by B. Gates. Burgess, 1968. A lovely book on movement characteristics in people and in the world around us.

Rhythm, Music and Education by Emil-Jacques Dalcroze. Riverside Press, London, 1967. The pulse of movement and music by the originator of the Dalcroze system of eurhythmics.

The Use of the Self by F. Matthias Alexander. E.P. Dutton, 1932. The originator of the Alexander technique describes his approach to the optimum use of the body, and how he retrained himself and others to inhibit negative habits of responding and to substitute positive habits.

Visual Thinking by Rudolf Arnheim. *See above* under Science.

Wishes, Lies and Dreams—Teaching Children to Write Poetry by Kenneth Koch. Vintage (paperback), 1971. An explanation of his approach by an outstanding poet, with examples by elementary-school children.

With a Free Hand—Painting, Drawing, Graphics, Ceramics, and Sculpture for Children and *Teaching Art* by Adelaide Sproul. Van Nostrand Reinhold, 1966 and 1971 respectively. Two expertly written and enjoyable art books for teachers and parents. Superb photographs.

Index

Some other books published by Penguin
are described on the following pages.

Louise Clarke

CAN'T READ, CAN'T WRITE, CAN'T TALK TOO GOOD EITHER
How to Recognize and Overcome
Dyslexia in Your Child

Developmental dyslexia, or specific language disability, affects between 10 and 20 percent of all children born today, and about three million of these are afflicted to an incapacitating degree. Louise Clarke approaches this problem through the firsthand story of her dyslexic son, Mike. Her dramatic account of Mike's childhood gives parents and teachers many clues for recognizing this disability as she shows how his symptoms could have been diagnosed and treated much sooner than they were. Mrs. Clarke also reviews the situation of dyslexics today and summarizes the various therapies that have proved successful. Her book is uniquely valuable, not only for the parents of dyslexic children but also for everyone who likes to read about success in the face of overwhelming difficulty.

Dick Schnacke

AMERICAN FOLK TOYS
How to Make Them

This entertaining and easy-to-follow handbook shows how anyone can make folk toys at home. Relying on his own research and on the help of folklorists, Dick Schnacke presents instructions, diagrams, drawings, and lists of the materials needed to make numerous classic American toys — from skill and action toys to puzzles, tops, noisemakers, and games. Here are not only conventional items like the apple doll and the cornstalk fiddle but also such exotic amusements as the flipperdinger and the skyhook. Inexpensive and ingenious, all these toys are as delightful to make as they are to play with. Dick Schnacke owns and operates the Mountain Craft Shop, the nation's leading producer of handmade folk toys, in Proctor, West Virginia.